Culture and Customs of Spain

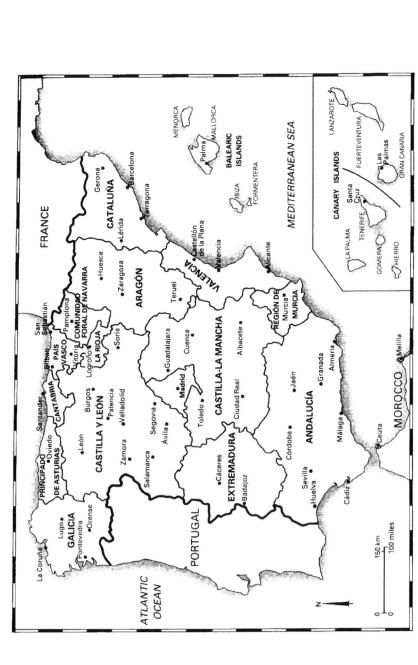

Spain. *Source:* Ian Gibson, *Fire in the Blood: The New Spain.* London: Faber and Faber, 1992.

Culture and Customs of Spain

Edward F. Stanton

Culture and Customs of Europe

GREENWOOD PRESS
Westport, Connecticut • London

Library of Congress Cataloging-in-Publication Data

Stanton, Edward F., date.
    Culture and customs of Spain / by Edward F. Stanton.
      p. cm.—(Culture and customs of Europe)
    Includes bibliographical references and index.
    ISBN 0–313–31463–2 (alk. paper)
    1. Spain—Civilization—20th century.   2. Popular culture—Spain—History—20th century.
I. Title. II. Series.
DP48.S678   2002
946.08—dc21   2001040556

British Library Cataloguing in Publication Data is available.

Library of Congress Catalog Card Number: 2001040556
ISBN 978-0-313-36080-0

First published in 2002

Greenwood Press, 88 Post Road West, Westport, CT 06881
An imprint of Greenwood Publishing Group, Inc.
www.greenwood.com

Printed in the United States of America

The paper used in this book complies with the
Permanent Paper Standard issued by the National
Information Standards Organization (Z39.48–1984).

10 9 8 7 6

Every reasonable effort has been made to trace the owners of copyright materials in this book, but in some instances this has proven impossible. The author and publisher will be glad to receive information leading to more complete acknowledgments in subsequent printings of the book, and in the meantime extend their apologies for any omissions.

To Mom and Dad

Contents

Illustrations		ix
Series Foreword		xi
Preface		xiii
Acknowledgments		xv
Chronology		xvii
1	**Context**	1
2	**Religion**	27
3	**Customs**	47
4	**Media**	91
5	**Cinema**	109
6	**Literature**	125
7	**Performing Arts**	145
8	**Visual Arts**	167
Notes		185
Glossary		195
Index		199

Illustrations

1 Gypsy girls in Maceda, Baños de Holgas (Orense, Galicia), 1986   10

2 Two young girls, Pamplona, July 2000   11

3 Contest among girls for *cruces de mayo* (May crosses),
Badajoz, 1986   36

4 The *Virgen del Rocío* (Virgin of the Dawn), Almonte
(Huelva), 1978   42

5 Penitents, Good Friday, Puente Genil (Córdoba), 1976   43

6 Pilgrim to Santiago de Compostela, c. 1995   44

7 The people of Piornal (Cáceres) throw turnips and snowballs
at "El Jarramplas," Carnival 1980   59

8 *La Maya* (May Girl), Colmenar Viejo (Madrid), 1989   60

9 Entrance of Moors at the annual celebration of *Moros y
cristianos* (Moors and Christians), Alcoy (Alicante), 1976   61

10 Children laying out a carpet of flowers for Corpus Christi,
Sitges (Barcelona), 1987   63

11 *Fiesta* of San Fermín, Pamplona, July 6, 1995   64

12 *Cabezudo* (fathead) "Vinegar-Face" and child, *fiesta* of San
Fermín, Pamplona, July 1983   65

13 Child and drunken man, celebration of *Moros y cristianos*, Alcoy (Alicante), 1981   66

14 Spectators and bullfight, Bilbao, 1994   69

15 *Recortador* (bull-dodger), San Sebastián de los Reyes (Madrid), February 1996   71

16 *Bous de la mar* (bulls of the sea), Denia (Alicante), 1987   72

17 The Basque Perurena lifts a stone weighing 261 kilos (574 pounds), *fiesta* of San Fermín, Lesaca (Navarra), 1988   74

18 Fans of Athletic of Bilbao celebrate a victory in their home stadium, 1989   75

19 The proper way to pour *sidra* or cider, Moreda de Aller (Asturias), 1988   80

20 *Cochinillo* (roast suckling pig) and other foods, Botín, Madrid, 2001   83

21 Torrespaña ("Spaintower"), headquarters of TVE (Televisión Española), popularly known as *El Pirulí* (The Lollipop), c. 1995   103

22 Asturian *gaitas* or bagpipes, Moreda de Aller (Asturias), 1988   154

23 Catalans perform their national dance, the *sardana*, Barcelona, 1988   163

24 Museo Nacional Centro de Arte Reina Sofía, Madrid, 2001   168

25 Centre Julio González, Institut Valencià d'Art Modern (IVAM), 2001   172

Series Foreword

The Old World and the New World have maintained a fluid exchange of people, ideas, innovations, and styles. Even though the United States became the de facto world leader and economic superpower in the wake of a devastated Europe after World War II, Europe has remained for many the standard bearer of Western culture.

Millions of Americans can trace their ancestors to Europe. The United States as we know it was built on waves of European immigration, starting with the English who braved the seas to found the Jamestown Colony in 1607. Bosnian and Albanian immigrants are some of the latest new Americans.

In the Gilded Age of one of our great expatriates, the novelist Henry James, the Grand Tour of Europe was de rigueur for young American men of means, to prepare them for a life of refinement and taste. In a more recent democratic age, scores of American college students have Eurailed their way across Great Britain and the Continent, sampling the fabled capitals and bergs in a mad, great adventure, or have benefited from a semester abroad. For other American vacationers and culture vultures, Europe is the prime destination.

What is the New Europe post-Cold War, post-Berlin Wall in the new millennium? Even with the different languages, rhythms, and rituals, Europeans have much in common: they are largely well educated, prosperous, and worldly. They also have similar goals and face common threats and form alliances. With the advent of the European Union, the open borders, and the Euro and considering globalization and the prospect of a homogenized Europe, an updated survey of the region is warranted.

Culture and Customs of Europe features individual volumes on the countries most studied and for which fresh information is in demand from students and other readers. The Series casts a wide net, inclusive of not only the expected countries, such as Spain, France, England, and Germany, but also countries such as Poland and Greece that lie outside Western Europe proper. Each volume is written by a country specialist, with intimate knowledge of the contemporary dynamics of a people and culture. Sustained narrative chapters cover the land, people, and brief history; religion; social customs; gender roles, family, and marriage; literature and media; performing arts and cinema; and art and architecture. The national character and ongoing popular traditions of each country are framed in an historical context and celebrated along with the latest trends and major cultural figures. A country map, chronology, glossary, and evocative photos enhance the text.

The historied and enlightened Europeans will continue to fascinate Americans. Our futures are strongly linked politically, economically, and culturally.

Preface

Spain is more like a small continent than a country. It has endless variety in landscapes, peoples and cultures, and regions with their own languages, traditions and cuisines. Some Spaniards speak of many "Spains." Yet the country also has its own kind of unity, a vigorous personality that makes it unlike any other place in the world.

It surprises nearly everyone. Before traveling there, most foreigners imagine it as an exotic Mediterranean country with brilliant sun, good beaches, bull-fights and flamenco: what a great poet summed up as "the Spain of brass bands and tambourines." This romantic stereotype was created a long time ago by travelers from cold, grey cities in northern Europe. Similar travelers continue to descend on Spain every year, still seeking sunny beaches and local color. What they find is often very different. It may even change their lives.

An English writer once confessed that his first sight of the Castilian landscape, the Spanish heartland, made him a different person forever. Many others have had similar experiences. Spain fills your eyes, your ears, your senses of touch, taste and smell. It has a way of getting under your skin and deeper.

Few Western countries have changed as profoundly as Spain in the last quarter-century, perhaps as much as in the previous five hundred years. Since 1975 it has been transformed from a dictatorship to a democracy, from a poor country to the ninth industrial power in the world, from a cultural backwater to a dynamic modern nation, a member of the European Union and NATO. This radical transformation obliges us to speak of the old and the new Spain, the old and the new Spaniards.

José Saramago, a winner of the Nobel Prize from neighboring Portugal, has written a novel about an earthquake that splits off the Iberian Peninsula from the rest of Europe. The story is a fable of the two countries that have usually been considered the strangest and most backward in western Europe. In Saramago's tale, some Europeans rejoice when the Peninsula sails out into the Atlantic Ocean, delighted to rid themselves of Spain and Portugal, those baffling Hispanic nations. Others sympathize with the floating countries and its peoples, staging demonstrations and crying "We too are Iberians."

Saramago's story is a parable for his country and Spain: on the one hand they have always been considered very different from the rest of the continent; on the other hand they are ancient European cultures, perhaps the most ancient of all. These two thoughts will guide us as we cross the Atlantic Ocean and explore Spain.

Acknowledgments

I would like to thank Claudio Boquet; Prof. Ramón Buckley; Prof. Susan Carvalho Chumney; Prof. Marvin D'Lugo; Emilio López González, Restaurante Botín, Madrid; Cristina García Rodero, Madrid; Beth Guynn, Getty Research Center, Los Angeles; the photographer Iñaki of *El Mundo del País Vasco*; Prof. Margaret Jones; Prof. José Labrador; Prof. Douglas LaPrade, always a faithful reader; Manuel Martín Ramos, Director of the Photographic Archive, Televisión Española, Madrid, and his assistant, Pilar López; my scrupulous editor, Wendi Schnaufer; Prof. Gretchen Starr-Lebeau; Prof. Roger D. Tinnell; Prof. Sherry Velasco; and Germán Yanke of *El Mundo*.

Chronology

Prehistory

c. 800,000 BCE	Hominids in north-central Iberian Peninsula
20,000–9000 BCE	Cave paintings, especially in northern Peninsula
c. 1600 BCE	Iberians immigrate to Peninsula
c. 1100 BCE	Phoenicians trade and found colonies on Mediterranean coast
c. 800 BCE	Carthaginians arrive as heirs to Phoenician trading empire
c. 750 BCE	Celts appear
c. 600 BCE	Greeks trade and found colonies on Mediterranean coast

Ancient Iberia

264–146 BCE	Punic Wars: Carthage and Rome struggle for dominion of Mediterranean Basin
217–19 BCE	Romans conquer Iberia

143–133 BCE	Romans lay siege to Numantia
19 BCE–450 CE	Roman Hispania; first Jews arrive; Christianity becomes official religion of Empire
409 CE	Germanic tribes (Vandals, Alans, Suevi, Visigoths) invade
480–711 CE	Visigothic kingdom

MUSLIM IBERIA

711–718	Moors (north African Muslims) invade and conquer nearly all of Peninsula
718–1492	Al-Andalus (Muslim Iberia)
929–1031	Caliphate of Córdoba; al-Andalus flourishes
1008–1086	Al-Andalus splinters into small kingdoms (*taifas*)
1096–1143	Almoravids from Morocco rescue and partially reunite al-Andalus
1143	Almoravid empire disintegrates; *taifa* kingdoms reemerge
1156	Almohads from Morocco subjugate *taifa* kingdoms
1252–1492	Last Muslim kingdom of Granada

"RECONQUEST"

718	Pelayo stops Moors at Covadonga, becomes king of Christian Asturias
751–763	Galicia joins Asturias
c. 813	Apostle St. James the Elder's tomb purportedly discovered, Santiago de Compostela

c. 840	Navarra achieves independence
c. 850	Christians reoccupy north-central Peninsula
910	León becomes kingdom
1035	Castile and Aragón become kingdoms
c. 1043–1099	Rodrigo Díaz de Vivar (El Cid) lives
1073	Castile annexes Galicia
1143	Castile and León recognize Portugal as sovereign kingdom
1162	Aragón and Catalonia unite in kingdom of greater Aragón
1212	Kings of Castile, Navarra, Aragón and Portugal defeat Moors at Las Navas de Tolosa
1229–1276	Jaime I of Aragón conquers Valencia and Balearic Islands from Moors
1230	Castile and León unite
1236–1252	Fernando III conquers Córdoba, Murcia, Jaén and Seville

UNITED SPAIN

1469	Isabel of Castile marries Ferdinand of Aragón, uniting most of Catholic Spain
1478–1480	Spanish Inquisition established
1482–1492	"Catholic Kings" besiege and conquer Granada
1492	Jews forced to choose between conversion to Christianity or expulsion from Spain. Columbus reaches New World under Spanish flag; Europeans settle Americas

1494	Treaty of Tordesillas divides non-European world between Spain and Portugal
1502	Muslims forced to convert or be expelled
1512	Fernando takes Navarra by force, uniting it with Spain

HABSBURGS

1516–1556	Charles I rules in Spain, becomes Charles V of Holy Roman Empire (1519)
1521	Juan Sebastián Elcano brings Magellan's round-the-world voyage home
1539	Ignacio de Loyola founds Society of Jesus (Jesuits)
1545–1563	Council of Trent initiates Counter-Reformation
1556–1598	Philip II reigns
1561	Philip II establishes Madrid as capital of Spain
1565	Spaniards begin conquest of Philippines
1568–1570	Moriscos (baptized descendants of Spanish Muslims) revolt in Alpujarras Mountains
1571	Battle of Lepanto: Spain, Venice and Papal States defeat Turkish navy
1580–1640	Portugal and its empire join Spain
1588	England and bad weather defeat Spanish Armada
1609–1612	Remaining Moriscos expelled
1640	Portugal revolts and achieves lasting independence
1640–1655	Catalans rebel

BOURBONS

1700–1713	War of the Spanish Succession between Habsburg and Bourbon claimants to throne
1700–1746	Philip V reigns (first Bourbon king of Spain)
1704–present	Great Britain occupies Gibraltar
1713	Treaty of Utrecht: Spain forfeits Flanders, Milan and Naples
1714	Aragón, Catalonia and Valencia lose autonomy; first unitary Spanish state
1759–1788	Carlos III reigns
1766	*Motín de Esquilache* (people of Madrid revolt against dress code imposed by state)
1767	Charles III expels Jesuits from Spain
1773	Pope suppresses Jesuits
1796–1802	Spain joins France against England; ruin of Spain's American trade
1805	British all but destroy Spanish naval power at Trafalgar
1805–1808	Spain allies with Napoleon
1808	Napoleon invades and installs brother Joseph Bonaparte on Spanish throne
1808–1814	Peninsular Wars (known as War of Independence in Spain)
1810–1826	Spain loses all colonies on mainland Latin America
1812	Liberals draft Constitution in Cádiz
1814	Spaniards defeat and drive French from Spain

1814	Pope restores Jesuits Fernando VII abolishes Constitution of 1812
1820	First pronunciamento brings Spanish army into politics
1833–1839	First Carlist War (rural Catholic revolt against central government)
1835	*Desamortización* or confiscation of Church property; religious orders disbanded temporarily
1848–1852	Second Carlist War
1872–1876	Third and last Carlist War
1873–1874	King abdicates, First Spanish Republic; Cubans revolt against Spain
1874	Restoration of monarchy
1898	Spanish-American War: Spain loses Cuba, Puerto Rico, Philippines, Guam
1909	*Semana Trágica*, bloody week of revolt and repression in Barcelona
1912	Spanish protectorate established over northwestern Morocco
1914–1918	World War I; Spain remains neutral and prospers
1921	Military disaster at Annual in Morocco
1923–1930	Dictatorship of Primo de Rivera
1925	War in Morocco ends
1928	Opus Dei (lay Catholic organization) founded in Spain
1931	Alfonso XIII abdicates

MODERN SPAIN

1931–1936	Second Spanish Republic
1936	"Nationalists" revolt against legal Republican government
1936–1939	Spanish Civil War
1939–1975	Dictatorship of General Francisco Franco
1939–1945	World War II; Spain "neutral" but sympathizes with Axis
1941	Franco bans public use of minority or foreign languages
1946	United Nations boycotts Spain
1950	United Nations lifts boycott
1953	Spain signs Corcordat with Vatican Spain signs treaty with United States, receiving economic aid in return for military bases
1955	United Nations admits Spain
1956	Moroccan independence ends Spanish protectorate; Spain keeps enclaves of Ceuta and Melilla
1959	Founding of ETA, Basque separatist group
c. 1960	Tourist boom begins, economic boom follows
1975	Franco dies, Juan Carlos I becomes king, restoring Bourbon dynasty
1977	First democratic elections since 1936
1978	Constitution ratified, establishing parliamentary monarchy
1979	Statutes of autonomy (home rule) introduced for Basque Country and

	Catalonia, with Galicia and other regions to follow
1981 (February 23)	Right-wing coup attempt fails
1981	Divorce law approved
1982	Spain joins North Atlantic Treaty Organization (NATO)
1982–1996	Socialist Felipe González governs as Prime Minister
1985	Government authorizes abortion in limited circumstances
1986	Spain becomes member of European Economic Community (later European Union)
1987	End of treaty between Spain and United States
1992	Olympic Games held in Barcelona; World Expo-92 in Seville; celebration of Quincentenary of 1492; Madrid named Cultural Capital of Europe
1996	Center-right Popular Party wins elections, José María Aznar becomes Prime Minister
1999	European Monetary Union: Spain and other members of EU adopt common currency (euro); "double circulation" of euro and national currencies
2002	Peseta ceases to be legal tender

1

Context

Spain is the very best country of all.

—Ernest Hemingway[1]

At the beginning of the new millennium, Spain is a country with almost forty million people and a stable democratic government. It has the world's ninth largest economy; a prosperous middle class is evident almost everywhere. It belongs to the European Union and the North Atlantic Treaty Organization. As the "mother country" of some 300 million Spanish-speakers, the nation has the potential to exert immense cultural influence throughout the world.

At the same time Spain is a country that clings tenaciously to its traditions, where people feel more loyalty to their town and region than to the national government. It is divided into seventeen semiautonomous regions that speak four different languages, have ancient rivalries and compete with each other for resources and power. About 15 percent of the workforce is unemployed. Prostitutes and beggars walk the streets. Bribery and cronyism infect both business and government; in the public perception of corrupt practices, the country ranks third among the fifteen members of the European Union.[2]

How can we explain these contrasts and paradoxes? Many writers have tried; most have failed. When a reader accused him of not understanding Spain, Ernest Hemingway replied that it is a difficult country to write about.[3]

We will try to understand Spain by looking at the place, the people, their past and present. We will draw on the work of scholars and travelers, experts and artists, Spaniards and foreigners. We will take the high road and the low road. As a Spanish poet wrote,

> Walker, there is no road,
> We make the road by walking . . .

THE PLACE

"In variety, strangeness, and grandeur the Spanish landscape is unequalled in Europe," declared a British writer who knew it well.[4] All of this in an area only a little larger than Texas. In fact Americans tend to feel more at home in the country than do many Europeans, who are sometimes shocked by the bigness and bareness of Spain, the second largest nation in western Europe. Another British writer noted:

> What most delights the traveller from northern Europe as he makes his way through Spain is its emptiness. Bare mountain ranges, bone-coloured rocks and hills, flat heaths and *páramos* [bleak plateaus], hardly a house. In such a country one can breathe.[5]

Americans are used to breathing in their country, and they recognize parts of their own landscape in Spain. If you took away the buildings and the people, at times you could not tell if you were in California or Catalonia, Montana or Aragón, Wyoming or Navarra, Arizona or Almería.

Spain has been described as a rocky castle with a few lovely valleys. It has also been compared to an ugly picture with a beautiful frame, referring to the fact that the coasts tend to be wetter and greener than the dry, brown hinterland. This depends on your taste. Some travelers find the vast, lion-colored *meseta* or plateau to be the most invigorating part of the country: it is a landscape that changes lives. It is also the terrain of religion and the Spanish mystics, where the flat, barren earth, ribbed by high sierras, leads the eye directly to the starched blue sky.

Few would guess that Spain has a higher average elevation than any country in Europe except Switzerland. About 70 percent of its surface stands above 1,500 feet. The central plateau rises steeply from the coastline then levels off quickly, giving an overall impression of flatness broken by a few mountain ranges. The country's climate is as varied as the landscape. Some mountains have snow almost the year around; some deserts hardly know rain. The weather on the great central *meseta* is best summarized by the Castilian proverb, "*Nueve meses de invierno y tres de infierno*" (Nine months of winter and three of hell). The change from cold to heat is usually abrupt, with hardly any spring or fall in between. The sun rules over Castile like an unforgiving god. On the other hand the northern tier of the country, from Galicia in the west through the Asturias, Cantabria and the Basque Country to the east, has many days of mist, fog, drizzle and rain, with no more sunshine than coastal Washington and Oregon. The Castilian proverb clearly does not apply to this part of the Peninsula.

From this, you can see that Spain is a country of variety and contrasts. The Iberian Peninsula contains many landscapes, from the rocky shores of the Costa Brava along the northern Mediterranean to the bleached sands of the southern beaches, from the green forests of Galicia and Navarra to the endless vineyards of La Mancha and the olive groves of Andalusia, from the snowy Pyrenees and Picos de Europa to the citrus groves of Valencia and the palm trees of the Levant. Between all these areas lies the great stretch of the yellow *meseta*, crossed by green stripes of trees along the rivers.

The Peninsula is split apart by mountains that divided the peoples into small independent kingdoms and cultures. This geographical isolation has been largely responsible for the most deeply rooted of all Spanish traditions, the one that determines nearly all others: separatism. Separate villages, towns, provinces, regions. It has been said that a Spaniard is loyal first of all to a *pueblo* or town, then to a province or region and finally, if at all, to the nation.

Until modern times, geographical boundaries, poor communications and illiteracy contributed to the people's suspicion of everything beyond the community. Speaking of Castile, the country's heartland, a poet said "she despises everything she doesn't know." Residents of one village may avoid speaking to those of another. Jokes make fun of rival towns, cities, provinces, regions. Rhyming slander is popular, along the lines of "*Loja, la que no es puta es coja*" (In Loja, women are either whores or cripples), "*Buena es Granada, pero junto a Sevilla no vale nada*" (Granada is all right, but nothing compared to Sevilla). If Spain is a country broken up by geographical barriers and human suspicion, can we speak of a "Spanish" landscape? The writer Salvador de Madariaga found one quality that unified all others:

> A kind of primitive strength, static, unexpressed. A kind of passive vigor ... primitive fertility. ... Its quiet strength, its permanent vitality, is the source of that impression which the traveler finds everywhere. ... The Peninsula is, in itself, apart from the people who inhabit it, a great power and a great presence.[6]

Other Spaniards might argue that there is no common landscape.

The major regions of continental Spain, moving mostly from north to south and west to east, are Galicia, Asturias, Cantabria, the Basque Country, Navarra, La Rioja, Aragón, Catalonia, Valencia or Levante, Murcia, Old and New Castile, Madrid, Extremadura and Andalusia. The major island chains are the Canaries and the Balearics. Each semiautonomous region enjoys a degree of independence from the national government that is similar to that of the states in the American federal system. But the historic, linguistic and cultural differences are far greater than in the United States. Let us look at the country's seventeen autonomous regions with their fifty provinces.

Galicia is the wet, green corner of northwestern Spain that sits atop Portugal on the map and is sometimes called "the Spanish Ireland." Partly-submerged *rías* or fjords gash its long coastline, providing safe natural harbors and the breeding grounds for the most abundant shellfish in Europe. Half of Spain's fishing fleet—twenty thousand strong and the largest on the continent—has a home port in Galicia. The region's culture is markedly Celtic and its first language, Galician (*galego* or *gallego*), is closer to Portuguese than to Spanish. Galicia has four provinces; its regional capital is Santiago de Compostela, the city that for centuries has drawn pilgrims to the tomb of the apostle St. James the Elder, who is supposedly buried in the crypt of its cathedral. The population of the region is just under three million, most of whom speak Galician.

Along with Portugal and Galicia, Asturias is the other Celtic region in the Iberian Peninsula. It nestles between Galicia to the west and Cantabria to the east along the rugged northern coast. Frequent rain greens its hills, mountains, and valleys. Asturias was once rich in coal; today its mines are mostly depleted. It has a single province with its capital in Oviedo. Its other chief city, Gijón, is a fishing port that builds vessels and ships coal. The region has a little more than a million inhabitants. A small number speak Asturian (*bable*), an archaic dialect of Castilian, but modern Spanish is the language of the great majority.

To the east of Asturias lies Cantabria, another small, mountainous region on the Bay of Biscay. It too makes up a single province; the capital is Santander. It is tucked between the sea and the mountains, both of which carry its name. With its extensive coastal plain and its historic connection to Castile, Cantabria is more prosperous than either Asturias or Galicia. Its half-million inhabitants speak Castilian.

The Basque Country (Euzkadi) is the easternmost region on the Bay of Biscay. Slightly larger than Cantabria, it is more densely populated. Its three provinces have 2,130,000 people. About a quarter of them speak Basque (*euskera*), an ancient tongue that is the only non-Indo-European language spoken in Europe. By tradition the Basque people fished, farmed and herded sheep, but in modern times they have led the nation in banking and heavy industry. The iron ore in their mountains, smelted in furnaces fired with Asturian coal, made their region the center of the country's steel production. Bilbao, the only metropolis in the Basque area, has been revived in recent years by the spectacular Guggenheim Museum that has put the city and the region on the map again.

Navarra is a landlocked area rising to the east of the Basque Country, bounded by the Pyrenees Mountains to the north and the Ebro River basin to the south. Like neighboring Euzkadi, it has an ancient history of autonomy and *fueros*, traditional laws and privileges governing its special relationship to the Spanish state. Because of its historic ties to the Basque Country, some of its inhabitants speak *euskera*. Navarra makes up a single province with its capital in Pamplona, whose annual fiesta of San Fermín is arguably the world's greatest bash. The region's 500,000 people enjoy one of the highest standards of living in Spain. With its snow-topped Pyrenean summits and alpine forests to the north, its rich bottomlands along the Ebro River and its desert-like *meseta* to the south, it is a microcosm of the inland Peninsula.

To the south of the Basque Country and Navarra lies La Rioja, the smallest autonomous region in Spain. Although it lacks the ethnic and cultural distinctiveness of its neighbors, La Rioja possesses some of the richest agricultural land in the Peninsula and its most famous vineyards, cultivated at least since Roman times. The region's 250,000 people have one of the country's highest average incomes. La Rioja makes up a single province whose capital of Logroño sits on the Ebro, Spain's longest river and the only major one that empties into the Mediterranean.

Another landlocked region, Aragón, rolls south from the Pyrenees in steep valleys, then turns into parched tableland, split through the middle by a green swath of rich soil washed by the Ebro. It includes three provinces and one major city, Zaragoza, the regional capital. On balance Aragón is a prosperous area whose 1,200,000 inhabitants speak Castilian, with the exception of a few people in remote spots who preserve the region's ancient dialect (*aragonés*).

The Ebro River eventually flows into Catalonia and the Mediterranean Sea. This region flanks southern France to the north, the old kingdom of Aragón to the west and Valencia to the south. It could be called the Spanish California, which it resembles in geography and climate, showing similar contrasts between snowy mountains (eastern Pyrenees), jagged coastline (Costa Brava), gently-rolling farmland and thriving cities. The second largest autonomous region in the country, Catalonia has four provinces and one of the densest populations in the Iberian Peninsula. Six million people live here, 75 percent of them in the regional capital of Barcelona, the second largest city and the first port of Spain. Catalan is spoken by some five million people; it is a Romance tongue distinct from Castilian, with a rich cultural and literary tradition stretching back to the Middle Ages. Along with the Basque Country, Catalonia has been a leader in commerce and industry. The old proverb "In Castile, wheat; in Catalonia, cloth" sums up the contrast between the two powerful regions—constant rivals or enemies—one largely agricultural, the other industrial.

The Valencian Community stretches south of Catalonia along the Mediterranean coast. Known also as the Levant (*Levante*), it comprises three provinces with a population of four million in round figures. The regional capital, Valencia, is Spain's third largest city and home to more than half of the Community's inhabitants. Many people speak a dialect of Catalan (*valenciano*) but they have neither their neighbors' sense of cultural distinction nor the Basques' ethnic sense of separatism. The Levant thrives from Mediterranean trade, agriculture on some of the lushest soil in Europe—the famous Valencian *huerta* or irrigated orchards—and tourism on its crowded beaches.

South of Valencia lies Murcia—flatter, hotter, and drier. A region with a single province, it has become the Imperial Valley of Spain by turning its arid terrain into productive farmland through irrigation. Agriculture and light industry have transformed Murcia from one of the poorest areas in Spain into a relatively prosperous one. The city of Cartagena, once a port of call for Carthaginians (who named it), Romans and Arabs, is Spain's chief naval base.

Inland from Murcia and Valencia rolls Castile, the great Spanish hinterland. A steppe that tilts to the west, its rivers—the Duero, the Tagus and the Guadiana—flow into the Atlantic Ocean. Divided into the autonomous regions of Old and New Castile, the area contains no less than a third of Spain's territory and more than half of its provinces. If we include Madrid—which lies in the middle of the area but constitutes a separate autonomous "region"—the Castiles have nine million people, about 25 percent of the country's population, all Spanish-speakers. The pockmarked tableland of New Castile is just as ancient as Old Castile's; its name refers to the fact that it was reclaimed from the Moors (Muslims from Africa) later than its northern neighbor. La Mancha, the parched land of Don Quixote, belongs to this autonomous region while the ancient kingdom of León forms part of Old Castile. "*Ancha es Castilla*" (Broad is Castile) runs a Spanish proverb, reminding us that there is room for everyone's point of view in the wide world, a spirit of tolerance that has not always been respected in the area's bloody past. Castile can rightly be called the cradle of Spain. Its dusty old castles and cities evoke centuries of battle between Moors and Christians, Moors and Moors, Christians and Christians: León, Zamora, Valladolid, Burgos, Soria, Segovia, Ávila, Salamanca, Toledo. León is the regional capital of Old Castile and Toledo of New Castile.

Madrid sits smack in the middle of the Iberian Peninsula, and this is the only reason for its being. It does not lie on a major river nor on rich farmland. At 2,134 feet, it is the highest capital city in Europe, with almost three million inhabitants, all Spanish-speaking. Like its perennial rival Barcelona, it is as glitzy, vigorous and seedy as any metropolis in Europe.

The rolling plateau of Extremadura, stretching between the Castiles and Portugal, forms a buffer region that is the poorest in Spain. Many of its crumbling villages have been emptied by emigration to Madrid, Barcelona and other cities. Extremadura has three provinces with its regional capital in Badajoz. Its one million people speak Castilian. Livestock, olives, cork, tobacco and mining are the main sources of income.

South of Extremadura and Castile lies Andalusia, a vast area with eight provinces and seven million people whose language is a dialect of Castilian. Its capital is Sevilla, the fourth largest city in the nation. With Extremadura, Andalusia has always been one of the country's most impoverished regions. Its wealth has traditionally been concentrated in the hands of a landholding elite whose large estates contrast with the small farms of northern Spain. The Sierra Morena Mountains separate the region from Castile, while the towering Sierra Nevada forms an internal barrier. The 410-mile-long Guadalquivir River is the area's backbone, draining an immense basin and providing water for drinking, power and irrigation. Like nearly all the country's major rivers, it empties into the Atlantic. Most of the region's people live along the Guadalquivir or on the coast. Like the rest of Spain, Andalusia is an area of great contrasts. Only about a hundred miles separate the snow-capped Sierra Nevada, the most southerly skiing area in Europe, from the moonscape of Tabernas in the province of Almería, a desert with close to zero rainfall.

Most foreigners forget that Gibraltar is also a part of Andalusia, although it has been occupied by Great Britain for three hundred years. Spaniards never forget. Guardian of the strait between Europe and Africa, the Rock may lose some of its strategic importance as Spain and the United Kingdom draw closer together in the European Union. Gib's several thousand inhabitants speak both Andalusian Spanish and a peculiar variety of English. Their political loyalties are overwhelmingly in favor of the United Kingdom: they enjoy special status as British subjects who profit from the economic benefits of a free port.

Spain also has two major archipelagos that make up separate autonomous regions. The Balearic Islands are due east of Valencia and have always fallen under the Catalonian sphere of influence. Their distance from the Spanish mainland ranges from 75 to 190 miles. The islands' 800,000 people speak an unusual dialect of Catalan. Thanks to tourists in search of its lovely inlets and beaches, the *mallorquines* enjoy Spain's highest per capita income. The archipelago includes Mallorca, Menorca, Ibiza and thirteen smaller, mostly uninhabited islands. The capital is Palma de Mallorca.

The other island region, the Canaries, lies 680 miles south of continental Spain in the Atlantic Ocean, a mere sixty-five miles west of the African coast. The main islands are Gran Canaria, with the capital city of Las Palmas; Tenerife, with Spain's highest peak of Teide; Fuerteventura; Lanzarote; and La Palma. While the islands have important fisheries and subtropical farms, tourism—both Spanish and foreign—is the chief industry. Unique among the autonomous regions of Spain, the Canary Islands are a free-trade area outside of the European Union (EU). The 1,600,000 *canarios* speak Spanish with an accent and rhythm that resemble those of the Caribbean, where many of their ancestors emigrated.

While we are so close to Africa, we should make brief calls in the white-washed ports of Ceuta and Melilla, Spain's two enclaves clinging to the coast of Morocco. They survive as the last fortresses erected more than five hundred years ago to protect the Straits of Gibraltar from Barbary pirates. Unlike the Canary and Balearic Islands, these outposts do not form autonomous regions, and their population is less Spanish than Moroccan. Their status could be compared to that of Puerto Rico in relation to the United States, although their tie is legally more secure, since both Ceuta and Melilla have a deputy with full voting rights in the Spanish *Cortes* or Congress. The great difference between Puerto Rico, on the one hand, and the two enclaves on the other is the presence of a third protagonist looming in the background, the kingdom of Morocco, which does not recognize Spain's sovereignty over the cities. When Spain joined the European Economic Community in 1986, the two sleepy North African ports suddenly acquired new importance as the southernmost territories of the EU. Since that time hundreds of thousands of Africans have tried to enter Ceuta and Melilla legally or illegally, with the hope of finding a livelihood in continental Europe. The small size of these outposts—a combined total of thirty-two square miles with a population of 138,000—and the large, rapidly-growing Muslim population make the

Spanish future of Ceuta and Melilla precarious. About one in four Spaniards believes the enclaves should be ceded to Morocco, and only one in twenty would support a war to defend them.

THE PEOPLE

Who are the Spanish? With so many unique areas, languages and cultures, must we refer only to local attributes, or can we speak of qualities that cut across regional boundaries?

When Spaniards refer to Spain, they may mean the region where they live, but definitely Castile, which covers only a third of the national territory. Other peoples, like the Basques, Catalans and Galicians, often do not consider their historic homelands as part of a larger nation. (Some 35 percent of Basques and Catalans, and 12 percent of Galicians desire full independence.) Curiously, most Spaniards, from whatever region, refer to Europe as a place beyond the national border: for them, the continent does not include Spain. Odd? Yes. Where are we then? We are in a country unlike any other; we must be wary of words and clichés that fail to capture the complexity and uniqueness of the land, the inhabitants and their cultures.

The Spaniards are an old people, perhaps the oldest in Europe. Recent excavations in Castile have uncovered evidence of hominids as far back as 800,000 years ago. The Iberian Peninsula has been a crossroads of migration and invasion from Europe in the north and from Africa in the south; Spain's destiny will always lie between these two continents. Seven-eighths of the Peninsula—more than 3,000 miles of coastline—are washed by the sea, the other main avenue of penetration by foreign tribes, peoples, and armies. Modern Spaniards carry in their veins the blood of many peoples both from Europe and Africa. This accounts for the great variety in physical types, from brunettes to blonds, their eyes ranging in color from deepest black to brown, hazel, grey, green and palest blue (see Photographs 1 and 2). In general, the northern tier of the country has a larger proportion of people with fair complexions.

Spaniards tend to be shorter than northern Europeans or Americans, but the younger generations tower over their parents. One sees overweight men and women in Spain but very few are obese. A writer noticed that "Only the old, bent, and ill carry themselves badly. Round shoulders are rarely seen."[7] By and large, Spaniards are a vigorous, attractive people who give an overall impression of dignity and pride.

Until recent times, the only major ethnic group that stood out from the general population were the gypsies (Roma), who migrated from India to

1. Gypsy girls in Maceda, Baños de Holgas (Orense, Galicia), 1986. Photograph by Cristina García Rodero, Getty Research Institute, Research Library, 90.R.34.

2. Two young girls, Pamplona, July 2000. Photograph by Gonzalo de la Serna.

Spain in the sixteenth century (see Photograph 2). The gypsies now number approximately 3 percent of the population; they are concentrated mostly in Andalusia. They cling bravely to their own folkways, refusing to be integrated into the mainstream of Spanish society. It is well known that the gypsies, like many tribal peoples, have a double set of ethical standards, one for themselves and another for everyone else. For this and other reasons, they have often exploited and been exploited by other Spaniards. As recently as 1984, the inhabitants of Torredonjimeno (Jaén) tried to lynch a gypsy family; five people were badly burned when the mob torched their house.

After the gypsies, the Basques are probably the most uniform ethnic group in modern Spain. Their roots go much deeper. Some scholars believe that they could be descendants of the original inhabitants of the Iberian Peninsula. They have the highest frequency of types O and Rh-negative blood of any European population, a fact that has been marshalled as evidence for their uniqueness. Basque or *euskera*, with its lack of prepositions and long, virtually unpronounceable words—Belausteguigoitia, Zumalacárregui—is unrelated to any other language in the world. Some linguists claim that this tongue is a close relative to the supposedly aboriginal speech of the Peninsula. If this is true, the Basques may be a sort of proto-Iberian or proto-Spanish people. Since the early 1900s, tens of thousands of Spaniards have moved to Euzkadi in search of jobs. Their intermarriage with Basques may have altered the area's gene pool more than the previous twenty-five thousand years.

As in other countries of western Europe, immigration from the Maghreb (northwestern Africa) has changed the face of Spanish society in recent years. Just as Cuban *balsas* try to make their way to Florida, Moroccan *pateras* struggle to reach the southern Spanish shore, often without success. It is estimated that some 200,000 Arabs now live in Spain, most of them Muslims from Morocco. They work in agriculture, construction and street vending, often illegally. Although many Spaniards claim that racism does not exist in their country, nearly all outsiders disagree. Pejorative words like *moro* (Moor) and *kafir* are often heard on the streets and cheerfully bandied about in comic books and cheap novels. In February 2000, thousands of Spaniards rioted against Arabs and burned the local mosque in the Andalusian town of El Ejido, leaving hundreds of immigrants homeless in the worst racial violence in modern Spain.[8] After northern Africans, Latin Americans form the largest group of immigrants, many for political reasons. Those who are educated profess to being treated well; others may be slighted and called *sudacas*, roughly translatable as "spics" or "greasers."

We have talked about the appearance of Spaniards; what about their inner lives? Because there are so many regional differences, it is again safer to speak of Castilians, Catalans, Basques, Galicians and so forth. We have already done this in our rapid tour of the Peninsula. But are there any common traits among all Spaniards?

In *Death in the Afternoon*, Hemingway wrote a passage that will give us a place to start. The American author used the bullfight as a yardstick to measure Spanish attitudes toward life and the taking away of life:

If the people of Spain have one common trait it is pride and if they have another it is common sense and if they have a third it is impracticality. Because they have pride they do not mind killing; feeling that they are worthy to give this gift. As they have common sense they are interested in death and do not spend their lives avoiding the thought of it and hoping it does not exist only to discover it when they come to die. This common sense that they possess is as hard and dry as the plains and mesas of Castille and it diminishes in hardness and dryness as it goes away from Castille. At its best it is combined with a complete impracticality.[9]

Most observers might agree that pride is still a common trait among Spaniards from many regions. More than the testy *pundonor* or point of honor evoked in the plays of Spain's classic drama, it is a kind of innate sense of personal dignity. You can often see it in the people's bearing and behavior. Yet pride is not always a virtue; in fact, it used to be considered the source of all vices. American writer James Michener used the Spanish phrase "*¡Viva yo!*" (Hurray for me and to hell with everyone else!). He tells the story of a contest for the cartoon that best revealed the national character, won by an artist who drew a little boy peeing in the middle of the street and spelling out the words "*¡Viva yo!*" Michener goes on:

A comprehension of the Spaniards's addiction to Viva yo will help anyone trying to make his way in Spain. When the little car barrels right down the middle of the highway, forcing everyone else into the ditch, you don't swear at the driver. You say "Viva yo" and you understand what happened and why.[10]

When Spaniards speak of their individualism, they mean something quite different from the Americans or the British, for whom the word may suggest a degree of eccentricity. You will see plenty of flamboyant and outspoken individuals in Spain, but few of them could be called eccentric. There is powerful social pressure to move within the limits of what is considered to be correct, what the Spaniards refer to as "*serio,*" not exactly serious but dignified and responsible. There is no surer way for parents to disapprove of their daughter's boyfriend, for example, than by stating that the unfortunate young man is not *serio*, not the kind of person they want in the family. A person who is *serio* acts with restraint and good manners, since after all he must deal with other Spaniards who are equally proud and dignified. Each person is like an armed warrior, except that the weapons are invisible. One warrior must reassure the other that weapons will not be needed, at least for the time being. This situation applies mostly to men, but Spanish women can also weigh in for battle.

Hemingway mentioned the Spaniards' commonsense acceptance of death. Unlike most Americans, they do not attempt to conceal mortality or consider it to be in bad taste. As the poet Federico García Lorca said, a dead Spaniard is more dead than anyone else, since he has so much life to lose. Because people are so aware of death, they seem to live more intensely. This can be seen in daily life, in the country's 138,000 cafés or bars, almost as many as in all other members of the EU. There, ten Spaniards can make as much noise as a hundred Americans. Unlike so many modern people, they haven't lost the art of communal singing; everyone from young children to old men and women seems to know the words and tunes. Nightclubs and discos usually open around midnight and do not close until dawn. There can be traffic jams at four o'clock in the morning on winter weekends in Madrid; during the summer, on weeknights too. In 1993, a bad year for the economy, Spaniards spent $750,000,000—three-quarters of a billion dollars—on the annual explosion of their local *fiestas*.

This is the impracticality mentioned by Hemingway. It may be revealed in some of the noble expressions of the Spanish people throughout the centuries, their idealism, self-sacrifice, devotion and mysticism. In short, the qualities embodied in the character of Don Quixote, the creation of Spain's best-known writer, Cervantes. But impracticality may also show itself in bad organization, poor planning, slipshod work, reckless spending, careless driving and other traits that distress so many foreigners. Yet millions return to the country in spite of these problems. Spain gives them something they find nowhere else.

THE PAST

Spanish civilization is probably the most complex in Europe. This brief discussion will only make a few flashbacks to illuminate some decisive historical events. (See also Chronology.)

As we said before, the Spanish are an old people. Excavations at the archeological site of Atapuerca, in the province of Burgos, have found evidence of pre-human communities from about 800,000 BCE, more than half-a-million years before the emergence of homo sapiens. This *homo antecessor* was probably a forerunner of the Neanderthals, and is the most ancient hominid to be discovered in Europe.

Spain possesses one of the world's most impressive memorials of primitive humans, the stunning cave paintings at Altamira in the Cantabrian region. There artists used natural dyes to paint bison, deer, and human beings, taking advantage of the conformation of the rock to produce three-dimensional effects. Altamira shows us that in the history of art, the earliest expressions may be the very best.

For at least a thousand years before Christ, various civilizations explored, settled and fought to dominate the Iberian Peninsula: Phoenicians, Greeks, Carthaginians, Romans. While Rome conquered Gaul in a single campaign, it took over two centuries to subdue the Iberians or Celt–Iberians, as the ancient inhabitants of the central Peninsula are called. The symbol of that struggle is the site of Numantia in what is now Old Castile, whose people held out against the Romans for twenty years, finally committing collective suicide rather than submit to the invaders. Some scholars cite the fierce resistance of the Numantians as an early example of the xenophobia and isolation that would characterize the Iberian peoples for most of their history.

Rome gave Iberia a name—Hispania, root of the modern *España* or Spain—a law, and a faith, Christianity, which became the official religion of the Empire. Latin formed the basis for modern Castilian, Catalan, Galician and Portuguese, four of the five languages spoken in the Peninsula. The Romans also left roads, bridges and buildings. Some still stand, like Segovia's sturdy aqueduct, the graceful bridge over the Tagus River at Alcántara, the splendid amphitheaters at Mérida and Tarragona.

During the slow decay of the Roman Empire, Germanic tribes invaded, crossed the Peninsula and migrated as far south as Africa. The Visigoths, one of the most civilized of these peoples, had already been converted to Christianity when they settled south of the Pyrenees. They made the old Roman city of Toledo their capital and adopted the Latin language. During these dark centuries, their culture was one of the brightest in western Europe. The Visigothic contribution to Spanish culture consisted of a revised legal code, hundreds of place names, some everyday words and a handful of Christian names that still ring with Teutonic valor. Alfonso means "all-prepared," Fernando is a compound of "peace" and "daring," Rodrigo combines "fame" and "powerful," Gonzalo signifies "strife." Ever since, Spanish kings and nobles have shown a preference for Germanic names.

The Moors invaded from northern Africa and swiftly conquered most of the Peninsula in the year 711, a key date in Iberian history. While other European countries can claim a Celtic, Roman and Germanic past, none— not even neighboring Portugal—had seven centuries of continuous Islamic presence. This is the great division, the parting of the waters that separates Spanish culture from the mainstream of European history.

The Muslims brought few women, so they took Christians as wives, much as the Spaniards themselves would do with the natives in the New World. Many Christians willingly converted to the victorious religion; by the year 1000 about three-quarters of the people were Muslim. Other Christians were allowed to continue practicing their faith as long as they agreed to pay taxes and did not cause trouble. The same held for the Jews since they too were "people of the Book." For several centuries, then, Iberia was a land of three religions living on the most intimate terms, in both peace and war in a land known as al-Andalus (later Andalusia). The civilization of the Iberian Peninsula was the most glorious in the world at a time when the rest of Europe was living in benighted conditions. The Moors turned the arid *meseta* green through irrigation, built wonderful mosques and palaces, opened the best universities in the world, produced eminent philosophers, mathematicians, astronomers, botanists, historians, poets, mystics. In one of the smallest courts of al-Andalus in Almería, some five thousand looms weaved silk, cotton and wool; one minister amassed a library of 400,000 manuscripts. This could be called the supreme moment in Iberia's history, the only time it has led the rest of the world in refinement and culture.

The rich legacy of Muslim Spain includes irrigation systems that are still in use and some of the most beautiful buildings in the world—the Great Mosque in Córdoba, the Alhambra in Granada, the Giralda tower and the Alcázar in Sevilla, the Aljafería palace in Zaragoza. The Arabic language gave Spanish about 10 percent of its vocabulary, words that reflect the skills of the Moors in farming, irrigation, architecture, construction, carpentry, leatherworking, ceramics, pottery and other crafts. Place names include no less than Madrid, the national capital; Guadarrama, the most important mountain range in central Spain; Guadalquivir, the longest river in Andalusia, and hundreds more.

The long, slow Christian victory over the Moors took no less than seven hundred and eighty-one years. Spanish historians used to glorify it as the "Reconquest." The word is misleading for at least two reasons. First of all, a process that takes so long could hardly be described by a word that suggests a brief, unified campaign. More than a jihad or blitzkrieg, it was an ebb and flow, two steps forward and one backward, a war of attrition. Second, as we have seen, warfare was not steady, but interrupted by long periods of truce, even centuries of peace in some of the great Muslim strongholds in southern al-Andalus.

There is no accepted word to replace the misnomer of "reconquest." Whatever we call it, the process was crucial, one that resulted in the creation of the country. In fact, some historians believe that the word "Spain" should not be employed until the Christian kingdoms of Castile and Aragón contracted their dynastic union in 1469. Other scholars point out that a unitary state was not achieved until 1714, when Aragón, Catalonia and Valencia lost their autonomy.

In 1492, Ferdinand and Isabel, named the "Catholic Monarchs" by the pope, finally conquered Granada, the last Muslim kingdom in the Peninsula. This year changed the future of Spain in more than one way. Of course Columbus took the Spanish flag to the New World, an event that led to a revolution in the way human beings thought about themselves, the earth and the universe. The Spanish Empire would soon extend all the way from Europe to Asia. In that same year of 1492, the Catholic Kings gave the large Jewish population—perhaps 500,000—the choice between conversion to Christianity or expulsion from the country. Although Ferdinand and Isabel promised the defeated Muslims that they would be allowed to continue in their faith, within ten years the sovereigns had broken their word, giving their defeated enemies the terrible choice between conversion and expulsion. Imagine what it would have been like for a Jewish or Muslim family, whose ancestors might have been in the Iberian Peninsula for seven hundred to a thousand years, to change the faith of their fathers or leave the country that they rightly considered to be their own. To this day, the descendants of the expelled Jews and Moors still refer to their lost homeland with yearning, as their Sepharad or al-Andalus. The expulsion was one of the most poignant injustices in history, what one writer calls "a permanent scar on the Spanish soul."[11] The country lost a huge class of skilled laborers, artisans, merchants and professionals who would not be replaced, if ever, until the last quarter of the twentieth century. In between lay a century of power and ascendancy, followed by 300 years of decline, tyranny, ignorance and isolation.

Of course this sounds like the vision of Spanish history known as the *leyenda negra* (Black Legend), an interpretation based largely on the work of English historians. Since Spain and England would be archrivals for three centuries, struggling for control of the sea lanes between Europe and America, bad blood flowed between the two countries. The English saw Spain as the home of fanaticism, poverty, the Inquisition, backwardness, the Counter-Reformation and barbarous customs like the bullfight; the Spanish saw England as "perfidious Albion," the home of pirates, skeptics and heretics, and beginning in 1704, the illegal occupiers of Gibraltar, a piece of their national soil.

The Black Legend exaggerated the evils of Spain: the long Spanish decline, from about 1600 to 1900, also included some of the greatest creations in the history of art and literature. Yet in recent times, some Spanish scholars have come to see the expulsion of the Moors and Jews, with the subsequent centuries of religious intolerance, as the fatal flaw in their country's history, a pattern that would be repeated again and again in later years. Freethinkers were persecuted in the seventeenth century, followers of the Enlightenment in the eighteenth, liberals in the nineteenth, and democrats, socialists, communists and separatists in the twentieth. As a Roman historian noted long before Spain existed as a political body, if the people have no foreign enemy, they look for one at home. One writer says:

> Spain is the great producer of exiles, a country unable to tolerate its own people. The Moors, the Jews, the Protestants, the reformers—out with them; and out, at different periods, with the liberals, the atheists, the priests, the kings, the presidents, the generals, the socialists, the anarchists, fascists, and communists.[12]

Let nobody think that intolerance emanated only from the Spanish right, from Catholics, conservatives, and traditionalists; the Spanish left, socialists, communists, anarchists and separatists, also perpetrated violence and murder in the Civil War (1936–1939) and later. Spanish history is not a pretty tale.

Although this book deals above all with contemporary Spain, we will refer frequently to the Civil War and its aftermath. In some ways it was as much a watershed as the American War between the States. In the United States the conflict led to a unified country and a freer polity; in Spain it led to forty years of fascism and dictatorship. The great wonder of modern Spanish history is that the nation has been able to move so surely from tyranny to democracy in the last quarter-century, a transition that is the envy of most countries in eastern Europe and Latin America. Only since the death of General Francisco Franco in 1975 has Spain restored its buried tradition of religious tolerance after a hiatus of almost five hundred years. The descendants of expelled Muslims and Jews have been invited back to their former homeland; those whose ancestors stayed have been granted the freedom to practice their former religions. In one of the great ironies of modern history, King Juan Carlos and Queen Sofia, like a reverse Ferdinand and Isabel, have personally dedicated mosques and synagogues, just as the Catholic Monarchs closed them. At the same time, Protestants and other Christian denominations are now free to worship alongside Catholics, Muslims, Jews and adherents of other religions.

THE PRESENT

What kind of country is Spain today, in the early years of the new millennium? One scholar has said that "it is so new and so young that it is
different every day."[13] Never has the nation been as prosperous and free—
freer than the United States in many ways, for example. More than twenty-
five years after the death of Franco, the memory of his long dictatorship is
alive enough for Spaniards to recoil at displays of puritanical repression.

No longer is Spain a land of extremes in wealth and poverty, with little
in between. A large middle class thrives. By the mid-1990s, the average
household income was around $26,000, 70 percent of the figure for the
United States.[14] Thanks to the unsung efforts of educators, the country's
literacy rate rose from 50 percent to more than 90 percent between 1900
and 2000. In the last twenty years the number of university students has
doubled. Although they are the continent's heaviest drinkers and smokers,
Spaniards enjoy the longest life expectancy in western Europe. Their longevity may be explained by a diet of abundant fresh food and a climate that is
generally benign. The public health system offers free care to all residents
and the number of physicians is the highest per capita in the world.

After forty years of tyranny under Franco, Spain held free elections in
1978, drafted one of the most liberal constitutions in Europe, and became a
parliamentary monarchy. King Juan Carlos is a descendant of the Bourbon
dynasty that has ruled the country with few interruptions since 1700. Unlike
most of his ancestors, not known for their democratic leanings or virtuous
habits, he has been an exemplary ruler and leader. When the Army attempted
a coup d'état in 1981, he opposed the rebellion and personally guaranteed
the survival of the fledgling democracy.

Spain has a parliamentary, multiparty system of government that encour-
ages ideological debate more than does the American two-party system, which
tends toward compromise in the middle. To the despair of foreigners, Spaniards refer to their political parties by their initials. From 1982–1996, the
Socialists (PSOE, Partido Socialista Obrero Español) ruled; since then, the
Popular Party (PP, Partido Popular or Conservatives) has held power. Although these two groups have dominated elections in the past twenty years,
a handful of smaller parties can sometimes make or unmake governments:
the United Left (IU, Izquierda Unida), composed of fragmented communists
and disaffected Socialists; the moderate Catalan Convergence and Union
(CiU, Convergència i Unió), and the Basque National Party (PNV, Partido
Nacionalista Vasco).

Separatism poses the greatest threat to the unity of the Spanish state. In all three of the minority language regions—the Basque Country, Catalonia and Galicia—strong nationalistic groups exist. Separatism is especially virulent in the Basque area, although it enjoys more autonomy than any other region in Europe. Euzkadi has been called "more than a region but less than a state." The Basque independence movement ETA has killed some eight hundred people, injured thousands and caused millions of dollars in damages over the last forty years. The great majority of Basques and Spaniards are opposed to this brutal organization, which kills innocent bystanders as well as chosen enemies.

With the exception of a few terrorists, Spaniards have taken to political freedom like ducks to water. In few countries has a people changed from dictatorship to democracy so well. Thousands of everyday decisions, once routinely made by fiat from above, are now shared by groups of voters, workers and students. All seem to flourish in their new freedom. On the other hand, most Spaniards remain pessimistic about politics at home and abroad. Criticizing the government is a national pastime. Now that the country belongs to the EU, a new breed of critic has emerged, the "euroskeptic." Some observers have joked that Spaniards would complain even if they lived in paradise.

The rain in Spain is mostly European nowadays. In 1986 the country joined the European Economic Community (EEC), in 1999 the European Monetary Union. The national currency, the *peseta*, circulated jointly with the euro between 1999 and 2002. On July 1, 2002, the *peseta* will cease to be legal tender and the euro will become the only official currency in Spain and the entire EEC. Maybe Spaniards will now consider themselves to be true members of the continent; perhaps the French will no longer claim that Africa begins beyond the Pyrenees.

Spain belongs to the "Europe of regions." As in many neighboring countries, it was split apart by separatism at the very time it was entering the EU. The nineteenth-century English traveler Richard Ford said, "Spain is today, as it always has been, a bundle of small bodies tied together by a rope of sand, and, being without union, is also without strength."[15] The difference today is that the rope comes from Brussels, not Madrid, and it is being tugged by the whole weight of the EU and NATO, the most powerful economic and military blocs in the world. That weight may be the only force strong enough to keep the nation from being torn apart by regional tensions. The prosperity of Spain and Europe will require a delicate balance between regionalism and globalism.

The country's problems are not only political or economic, but moral. Polls have shown that the great majority of Spaniards feel little loyalty to the nation and would not be willing to give up their lives for it. On the other hand, most would be willing to sacrifice themselves for their families, still the cement of Spanish society. As we will see later, the family is changing and will probably weaken in the future. The Church and the Army, the nation's other two traditional pillars, lost much of their prestige during their long collaboration with Franco. The military has been largely absorbed by NATO; the draft has been eliminated. Catholicism is no longer the country's official faith and has been enfeebled by secularization. Although most people continue to be nominal Catholics, they clearly do not follow the pope's advice on birth control or other issues: Spain now has the lowest birthrate in the world.[16] Like other modern nations, it lacks a moral consensus.

Let us end the way we started, looking once more at the place and the people. Spain is still the wildest country in Europe, but we cannot truly speak of wilderness as we do in North or South America. After all, the Peninsula is not much larger than Texas and it has been inhabited continuously for almost a million years. Yet Spain is a paradise for hikers, trekkers, cyclists, birdwatchers and everyone who enjoys the outdoor life. Just as the Peninsula formed an historical bridge between Europe and Africa, it is the major flyway for the annual migration of birds between the two continents. Its most famous natural sanctuary, the Coto Doñana in the province of Cádiz, is recognized as one of the most important in Europe and has been classified by UNESCO as a "Biosphere Reserve."

For centuries Spaniards had little interest in nature. Until the 1980s, exercise meant walking to the local bar for a cup of coffee or a glass of wine. The Spanish blindness to nature was embodied in the long, dark night of the Franco regime, when uncontrolled speculation did permanent damage to the Mediterranean coast and the skylines of venerable towns and cities. The sea turned into an open sewer, pollution poisoned the air and rivers, ecological outrages were committed with impunity. Drought and soil erosion harmed the land as they have under all regimes. Since Spain's entry in the European Union, the country has been forced to clean up its dirty act. Although some seven hundred conservationist groups are active, the country still lags behind most industrialized countries; it was the last member of the EU to establish a full Ministry of the Environment. Responsibility for ecological issues is divided among a labyrinth of agencies. Development usually wins out over conservation, as in the notorious case of the AVE (Alta Velocidad Española) or high-speed train between Madrid and Andalusia, a pet project of the Socialist regime. Not by chance was it completed in 1992, the "Spanish year" when Barcelona hosted the Olympic Games, Sevilla held World's Fair Expo-92, the nation celebrated the Quincentenary of 1492, and Madrid was named Cultural Capital of Europe. The AVE wrought irreparable damage to the environment along its three hundred miles of track.

If Spain is the wildest country in Europe, the Spaniards are its wildest people. While the work ethic has pervaded the industrial world, the country remains a bastion of the festive sense of life: good food, wine and other pleasures, with lots of time to enjoy them. The nation shuts down in August when many people take a four-week vacation, except for those in the tourist industry. Not by chance, this is the month of many patronal feasts or local *fiestas*, the most elaborate in the world. Many Spaniards also take off a week or more at Easter, when clogged roads make travel more dangerous than any time of year. Public holidays include New Year's, Epiphany (January 6), Easter and Corpus Christi (variable dates), Assumption (August 15), Columbus Day (*Día de la Hispanidad*) or Hispanic Day (October 12), All Souls' (November 2), Day of the Constitution (December 6), Immaculate Conception (December 8), Christmas, the Day of the Holy Innocents (December 28). Other holidays are celebrated in certain regions, such as St. Joseph's Day (March 19) and St. James' Day (July 25). To extend these celebrations, Spaniards creatively devise "*puentes*" or bridges, a public holiday connecting with a weekend. No industrial country in the world has so many holidays.

Until recent times, those who enjoyed *fiestas*, holidays and vacations were mostly men, whose mothers, wives and sisters stayed home to cook, wash and clean. Like so many other customs, this one changed after Franco's death. Now Spanish women take to the streets along with men and boys. Their enjoyment of leisure time is an example of their improved situation. The Constitution of 1978 formally granted equal rights to both sexes. In 1985 abortion was decriminalized under certain conditions: when pregnancy is the result of rape, when the mother's health is in danger or when the fetus is deformed. From the outset many Catholic doctors and nurses refused to follow the law; some pharmacists still ban birth control devices.

Although the word *machismo* derives from Spanish, it is more prevalent in Latin America than in Spain itself. Nevertheless, the phenomenon is part of the Hispanic heritage. The treatment of women has also been extraordinarily severe in the "mother country," an historical product of both Islam and Catholicism. Repression went hand in hand with the idealization of women as manifested in the worship of the Virgin Mary, and a strict honor code based on female chastity. For centuries women had few choices but to be nuns, wives or whores.

Some believe that Spain is patriarchal in appearance only, and profoundly matriarchal beneath the surface. The poet Antonio Machado, one of the country's most trenchant critics, says,

> Where a woman stays . . . at home, near the hearth and devoted to the care of her children, she is in control and she puts the stamp of her will on the whole society. The true problem is the emancipation of men, subjected to a rigid maternal regime. The woman who is silent in public life has the leading part and the decisive vote in everything else.[17]

Machado knew: he lived in his mother's house for many years and died at her side. While some might dispute his words, few would fail to recognize the familiar sight of the Spanish man who is lost without women, who has never cooked a meal or washed a dish in his life, who will go to his grave in the care of a mother, sister or spouse. This helpless character still survives, although he is now the exception rather than the rule.

In the New Spain, men are finally sharing domestic work with women. They are also sharing work outside the home. The same is true of higher education; since 1987 there have been more female than male students in Spanish universities. Yet huge inequalities still exist. Centuries-old attitudes will not change quickly. The country's greater European involvement will help to improve the position of women. Equal rights between the sexes, along with unemployment, separatism, the environment and integration with Europe are the greatest challenges for Spain in the twenty-first century.

SELECTED READINGS

Anuario El País 2002. Madrid: Ediciones El País, 2002. An annual report published by Spain's leading newspaper.

Baker, Carlos, ed. *Ernest Hemingway: Selected Letters 1917–1961*. New York: Scribner's, 1981.

Brenan, Gerald. *Thoughts in a Dry Season*. Cambridge: Cambridge University Press, 1978.

De Miguel, Amando. *La sociedad española, 1996–97*. Madrid: Editorial Complutense, 1997.

Ford, Richard. *Gatherings from Spain*. 1846; reprint London: J. M. Dent & Sons, 1970.

Gibson, Ian. *Fire in the Blood: The New Spain*. London: Faber and Faber, 1992.

Gies, David T., ed. *The Cambridge Companion to Modern Spanish Culture*. Cambridge: Cambridge University Press, 1999.

Graham, Helen, and Jo Labanyi, eds. *Spanish Cultural Studies: An Introduction. The Struggle for Modernity.* Oxford: Oxford University Press, 1995.

Grunfeld, Frederich V., and Teresa Farino. *Wild Spain: A Traveller's Guide.* New York: Interlink Books, 2000.

Hemingway, Ernest. *Death in the Afternoon.* 1932; reprint New York: Scribner's, 1960.

Hooper, John. *The New Spaniards.* London: Penguin, 1995.

Jones, Anny Brooksbank. *Women in Contemporary Spain.* Manchester: Manchester University Press, 1997.

Kern, Robert W. *The Regions of Spain: A Reference Guide to History and Culture.* Westport, CT: Greenwood Press, 1995.

Machado, Antonio. *Juan de Mairena: Sentencias, donaires, apuntes y recuerdos de un profesor apócrifo.* 1936; reprint Madrid: Castalia, 1971.

Machado, Antonio, and Manuel Machado. *Obras completas.* Madrid: Editorial Biblioteca Nueva, 1984.

Madariaga, Salvador. *Spain: A Modern History.* New York: Praeger, 1960.

Mar-Molinero, Clare, and Angel Smith, eds. *Nationalism and the Nation in the Iberian Peninsula: Competing and Conflicting Identities.* Oxford: Berg, 1996.

Michener, James. *Iberia: Spanish Travels and Reflections.* New York: Random House, 1968.

Mulero Mendigorri, Alfonso. *Introducción al medio ambiente en España. Procesos de degradación y actuaciones protectoras básicas.* Barcelona: Ariel, 1999.

Pierson, Peter. *The History of Spain.* Westport, CT: Greenwood Press, 1999.

Pritchett, V. S. *The Spanish Temper.* New York: Knopf, 1955.

Spain: 2001–2002. London: The Economist Intelligence Unit, 2000. One of a series of useful "country profiles," updated regularly.

Stanton, Edward F. *Handbook of Spanish Popular Culture.* Westport, CT: Greenwood Press, 1999.

Stolz, George. "Europe's Back Doors" [on Ceuta and Melilla]. *The Atlantic Monthly* (January 2000): 26, 28–33.

The Statesman's Yearbook 2002. The Politics, Cultures and Economies of the World. New York: St. Martin's Press, 2000. A useful source for up-to-date facts on population, economy, society and so forth.

OTHER SOURCES

The Instituto Cervantes, created by the Socialist government for the purpose of fomenting Spanish language and culture throughout the world (similar to France's Alliance Française), can be reached by mail at 122 East 42nd Street, Suite 807, New York, NY 10168; telephone (212) 689–4232; telefax (212) 545–8837; E-mail <cervanny@class.org>. The Instituto Cervantes also has websites based in the United States (<http://www.users.interport.net/~cervante/>) and in Spain (<http://www.cervantes.es/>).

Agencia Efe, the largest press agency in the Spanish-speaking world, has some very helpful and up-to-date services available online. Its website is <http://www.efe.es>.

The following search engines specialize in Spanish topics: "Buscador," <http://www.buscador.clarin.com>; "Olé," <http://www.ole.es>; "Sí, Spain," <http://www.sispain.org>; "Go Spain," <http://www.clark.net/pub/jumpsam/>; "Yahoo! España," <http://www.es.yahoo.com>.

2

Religion

We have run into the Church, Sancho.
> —Miguel de Cervantes, *Don Quixote*[1]

Our people . . . either walked behind priests with candles or chased them with torches.
> —Antonio Gala, *La casa sosegada* (The Quiet House)[2]

The story of religion in Spain is one of extremes. For centuries the country was called "more Catholic than the Pope." It produced great mystics like St. Teresa of Avila and St. John of the Cross, religious orders like the Dominicans and Jesuits. It has also been home to the most virulent iconoclasm and the bloodiest slaughter of priests, monks and nuns in the history of Christianity. How can we explain these extremes?

For eight hundred years, Christians, Muslims and Jews lived in peace or war in the Iberian Peninsula. During this long stretch between the eighth and fifteenth centuries, they identified themselves—and were identified by others—not by their language or nationality, but by their religion. When the Christians finally expelled the Moors and Hebrews after the long "reconquest," they were in no mood to tolerate heretics or dissenters. The Inquisition ensured that believers did not stray from orthodoxy and that the remaining Muslims and Jews did not return to the faith of their fathers. The country then turned its vast energy to another conquest, this time in the New World where the indigenous populations replaced the Semites as the infidels and targets for conversion. For Spaniards religion has usually resembled a jihad, a crusade or a holy war.

If believers have tended toward fanaticism, nonbelievers have almost matched them. "There is nothing more fearful than the priestly zeal of unbelievers,"[3] wrote the poet Antonio Machado, a man not known for sympathy toward official religion. The same persecutory behavior that was once used in the name of faith in the Middle Ages and early modern period, was later used in the name of progress in the nineteenth and twentieth centuries. Liberal or republican governments expropriated Church properties and condoned the burning of temples, monasteries and convents. To offer only the most extreme example, some 8,000 priests, monks and nuns were tortured and assassinated when the Spanish Civil War exploded in the summer of 1936.

Religion has continued to be a fundamental part of modern Spanish identity. When the workers at one of the sherry houses in Andalusia mounted a strike in the late 1960s to demand vacation for christenings, the head of the company asked a union leader why "a bunch of commies" should need time for church. "You might not believe in God," replied the union man, "but you had to believe in baptism otherwise your kids would be Moors, wouldn't they?"[4] Five hundred years after the defeat of the Muslims, the word *moro* is still synonymous with the barbarian, unbaptized infidel, while many unbelievers insist on having their children christened in the Catholic Church and sending them to parochial schools. Spanish atheists have a strangely spiritual quality. Some of them have been known to ask for a confessor on their deathbed; others have gone into that dark night cursing all priests, saints and the mothers that bore them. The famous filmmaker Luis Buñuel is said to have declared "I am an atheist by the grace of God."

Religious instincts are buried deeply in Spanish culture. The language itself has profound sacred roots. Perhaps no other modern tongue identifies Christianity and correctness so intimately: "*Habla en cristiano*" (Say it in Christian), one Spaniard might tell another who is not speaking clearly. When one wants to certify that a person is reliable, one says "*va a misa*" (he or she attends Mass). When one wants to be sure that something is done in the right way, one stipulates "*como Dios manda*" (as God commands). When a terrible calamity is mentioned, like a terrorist attack or a nuclear war, a Spaniard might say "*Que Dios nos coja confesados*" (Let's hope we've confessed our sins). When the world's first test-tube baby was born, a faultlessly secular newspaper, *Cambio 16*, ran this headline: "Born without Original Sin."

The Spanish language also reveals the country's profane traditions. This folk-poem demonstrates the worldy leanings of many Spaniards:

Lo primero y principal,
oir misa y almorzar;
pero si algo corre prisa
antes almorzar que misa.
(First and foremost,
go to Mass and eat lunch;
but if pressed for time,
food instead of church.)

Popular sayings reflect anticlerical feeling: "*Vivir junto al cura es gran locura*" (To live next to a priest is madness), "*Ni por lumbre a casa del cura va la moza segura*" (Not even for firewood should a young girl visit a priest's house), "*Al fraile no le hagas la cama, ni le des a tu mujer por ama*" (Don't ever make a priest's bed or give him your wife as maid). For centuries in both Spain and Spanish America, a "niece" or "nephew" has been the accepted euphemism for a priest's illegitimate child.

Traditional festivals in Spain continue to recall the religious struggles that formed the nation's identity. Every year in towns throughout the country and even in Spanish America, reenactments called "*Moros y cristianos*" (Moors and Christians) are staged—the battles won by the good guys against the evil villains, that is. In other fiestas, Spaniards smash a Judas figure in the head; he represents the Jews, the other people with ancient roots in the Iberian Peninsula. In recent years the Spanish government has also demonized terrorist groups like ETA (Basque Land and Liberty), using illegal tactics to capture and frame its members. In turn ETA has brutally killed not only representatives of the national government but its own members who have decided to abandon the use of political violence. The circle of persecution seems almost inevitable in Spain, whether from right or left, the center or the periphery, Catholics or communists.

Fanaticism is still alive in the memory of many Spaniards. As we have seen, the Spanish Civil War (1936–1939) unleashed terrible barbarity against priests by supporters of the Spanish Republic. What we have not mentioned is that their enemies, the Nationalists or followers of Generalissimo Francisco Franco, tortured and executed their enemies with equal or greater brutality, since they won the war and prolonged repression for nearly forty years. During this long night in Spanish history, the Church was granted a monopoly over the country's religious life in a conscious, futile effort to revive the power of the Spanish empire under the Catholic Monarchs and their descendants. When the winds of change finally began to blow during the Second Vatican Council (1962–1965), the Spanish Church relented, plagued by a bad conscience for its shameless collusion with the Franco regime. In this way the institution played a key role in the slow transition from dictatorship to democracy, which gathered full steam after the Generalissimo's death in 1975. Some historians call this dramatic process the "Spanish Reformation," one as significant for the nation as the Counter-Reformation of the sixteenth century.

CATHOLICISM

Under the new Constitution of 1978, the Catholic Church ceased to be the official religion of the Spanish state, yet continues to enjoy special privileges. Citizens may contribute about 0.5 percent of their taxes to the Church. Approximately 40 percent of Spaniards have chosen this option in recent years. If they do not check this box on their tax returns, their money goes to "objectives of social interest" (charities). What few citizens realize is that even if they decline to pay the so-called "religious tax," the state still grants the Church a fixed amount established during the Franco regime, adjusted annually for inflation. Some have criticized this cozy arrangement, noting that Protestants, Muslims, Jews, atheists and agnostics help maintain a religion in which they do not believe, and which for centuries subjected them to the most heinous discrimination. They also point out that a taxpayer's most ethical choice is not to check the box for the Church but the one for "objectives of social interest," because this does not subtract from the Church's endowment and increases the public contribution to charities.

Although figures on the national level are not available, individual dioceses may disclose their budgets. These show that the Church is not as dependent on taxpayers as some suppose. In the Barcelona diocese, for example, only 17 percent of their income derived from the state in 1988, while the figure rose to 36 percent in the Madrid diocese the following year.[5] The numbers indicate disparity in various parts of the country. Other diocesan income derives from return on assets, loans, sales and donations from the faithful.

The Catholic press and media are another source of earnings and influence for the Church. The situation is far different from that in the United States and other English-speaking countries. In addition to its many bulletins, weeklies, monthly magazines and publishing houses, the Catholic Church also controls radio stations and enjoys space on both public and private television. An extensive radio network, COPE or Cadena de Ondas Populares Españolas (literally Network of Popular Spanish Radio Waves), had no less than 111 stations in 1992 (45 medium-wave and 66 FM). Since the demise of the daily newspaper *Ya*, for years the mouthpiece of the Spanish Bishops'

Conference, the Church has strengthened its ties with the venerable monarchist daily *ABC*, the second most widely-read periodical in the country.

Education is another example of the Byzantine world of religion in Spain. The Church monopolized teaching until the nineteenth century when the first secular schools were established. The most famous example was the Institución Libre de Enseñanza (Institute of Free Education), founded by Francisco Giner de los Ríos in 1876. Through the Institución's doors passed some of the greatest minds of modern Spain, including several winners of the Nobel Prize. The Second Spanish Republic (1931–1936) attempted to loosen the Church's grip on education further, but the victory of the fascists in the Civil War set back the clock by half a century. One detail tells all: during almost forty years of Franco's dictatorship (1939–1975), Spanish classrooms were required by law to display both a crucifix and a portrait of the Generalissimo.

After the new Constitution of 1978, the Church lost much of its control over education: compulsory teaching of Catholicism disappeared from public schools, a logical consequence of the separation of Church and state. But nothing ever changes completely in Spain. The national government continues to finance parochial schools and to underwrite the teaching of religion in public classrooms.

About one-third of students from K–12 attend Catholic schools. If the Church has lost its former monopoly, it still owns some of the leading educational institutions in the country. Many parents, whatever their own beliefs, want their children to study with priests and nuns. In fact, enrollment in religious schools is highest in Madrid and Barcelona, the two most secularized cities in Spain. A Catholic education still carries a lot of prestige among the faithful and unbelievers alike.

The Church also administers some of the most reputable universities in the country, such as Deusto (Bilbao) and Navarra (Pamplona). Like other private institutions of learning, they are run by religious orders. Spain has given birth to three of the most influential orders in the history of Christianity, all of them involved in education to one degree or another—the Dominicans, the Jesuits and Opus Dei. The Dominicans, founded by the Castilian priest St. Dominic in the early thirteenth century, stamped out heresy and were active in the Inquisition. The second order, the Society of Jesus, established by the Basque soldier Ignacio de Loyola in the sixteenth century, became the Papacy's private army and specialized in missionary work and education. The third, Opus Dei, founded by the Catalan priest Josemaría Escrivá de Balaguer in 1928, differs from the other two in that its members are both men and women, clerical and lay, and in its use of business and politics to further its goals. Three organizations were founded: one by a Castilian, one by a Basque, one by a Catalan, but they were all characterized by

> their zealous defense of the faith, their missionary thrust and, above all, their capacity to resolve the perennial problem confronted by all churches: the necessary adaptation to a changing world. In three different and crucial historic junctures, Spanish civilization has generated brilliant rescue operations, each in tune with the times. The first [Dominican Order] eliminated medieval heresy through the Inquisition; the second [Society of Jesus] assimilated the consequences of the Renaissance and the Reformation; the third [Opus Dei], no doubt with more modest achievements, has managed to make the spirit of capitalism its own.[6]

We should take a closer look at the Opus Dei for several reasons: it possesses enormous wealth and influence, it may be the most powerful religious organization in modern Spain, and more than one-third of its members are Spanish. Called simply *La Obra* (The Work) by its members, it is surrounded by an air of mystery and remains virtually unknown in the United States. Opus Dei is not a religious order according to canon law, since the majority of its members are not ordained, do not wear a special habit and do not live in seclusion; they work in normal professions in the outside world. In almost every other way, however, it functions like a religious order, with a hierarchal structure and many members who take vows of poverty, celibacy and obedience. The small number of priests in the organization—about 1,500—wield disproportionate power compared to the 75,000 lay members. Next come the "numeraries," who are required to have a college degree and to observe the rule of celibacy, like the "associates" below them. Finally, the "supernumeraries" and the "auxiliaries," who perform most of the menial tasks in the group's residences, are not required to take vows of chastity. Reports from ex-members suggest that censorship is exercised over personal correspondence and reading matter. Those who leave Opus Dei may be pressured to withhold information about their experience; there have even been allegations of smear campaigns against them. In favor of the *opusdeístas*, some Spaniards claim that they are hard-working, responsible and devoted family members.

Unlike most Dominicans and Jesuits, the members of Opus Dei hold positions in government and business as well as in education and the media. They have occupied important posts in every conservative government from the 1960s to the present. They control banks, corporations, newspapers and radio stations, in addition to publishing houses, schools and universities. In other words, the organization has not excluded its members from secular power; in this lies its originality, the key both to its success and the suspicions it awakens among many critics. Unlike the Jesuits—their most implacable enemies—*opusdeístas* can be found on the editorial staffs of magazines or on the boards of private companies.[7]

What bothers many Spaniards is that Opus Dei seems to be the only Catholic organization in the country that has failed to respond to the liberalizing trends of Vatican II and the new democracy. In contemporary, open, European Spain, it persists as a reminder of the old, secret, isolated country of the Franco era. Many critics, inside as well as outside the Catholic Church, are also concerned by the privileged ties between Opus and the papacy. The members of the group have been called the pope's shock troops, similar to the Jesuits in the sixteenth century. John Paul II has done everything in his power to advance the organization; it is now virtually free of supervision by local bishops. The pope helped expedite the beatification of Escrivá de Balaguer, the fastest in the Church's long history. His personal spokesman, Joaquín Navarro Valls, is typically both Spanish and *opusdeísta*. As we will see below, the antipathy felt by many Spaniards for John Paul II is related to their dislike of Opus Dei.

An extraordinary fact about the new, secularized Spain is that it still has more monks and nuns than any other nation in the world. If we bear in mind that the total population is only 40 million—less than that of nearly all the major industrial nations—we realize that Spain continues to be one of the most religious countries in the West, at least in this dimension and in missionary work. (The country has some seven thousand missionaries abroad.) In 1989 there were 918 closed monastic communities, 60 percent of the world's total number. Three years later it was estimated that there were eighteen thousand monks—both ordained and unordained—and no fewer than fifty-five thousand nuns. Although these numbers seem high, they have fallen dramatically. COARESE, a group representing the secularized clergy, estimates that more than six thousand monks and ten thousand nuns as well as three thousand parish priests chose to renounce holy orders in Spain between 1960 and 1990.[8] Most decided to leave the Church in order to live with a partner or be married. It has been reckoned that there are more secularized clergy in Spain than in any other nation except Brazil and Holland.

The drop in vocations is the greatest crisis facing the Church, a symptom of what Catholic scholars have called "galloping secularization." The average

age of Spanish priests is fifty-seven and rising. A survey carried out by the Episcopal Conference in 1995 showed that there were twenty-two thousand parishes in Spain, manned by only twenty thousand clergymen, with some help from the ordained members of the monastic orders. Less than two thousand seminarians were preparing for the priesthood; many of them would wash out before completing the rigorous seven-year training. In other words, there is a severe shortage of clergy and no evidence that the situation will improve.

If there is a crisis in vocations, does this mean that there is also a crisis in belief? While Catholicism ceased to be the official religion of Spain with the Constitution of 1978, it is still the faith of the overwhelming majority of Spaniards—between 80 and 90 percent, depending on the source. But belief is not the same as practice: only about 30 percent attend Mass with any regularity, while some 45 percent attend rarely or not at all. The decline is even greater in the younger age groups.[9] In 1997 a poll by the Institute of Spanish Youth (INJUVE) indicated that for the first time, more than half of the population (54 percent) between the ages of fifteen and twenty-nine did not believe in God. Only 19 percent attended Mass while 23 percent declared themselves indifferent to religion, and 2 percent believed in other faiths. Since these figures are shy of 100 percent, the other respondents must have been indifferent to polls as well as to religion.[10] Of course we should always be cautious about statistics, especially on such a private matter. Figures vary widely and should be taken with a grain of baptismal salt.

One of the most reliable sources, the annual survey by the sociologist Amando de Miguel, showed the following results in 1996: practicing Catholics 27 percent; nonpracticing Catholics 53 percent; nonreligious 19 percent; another religion 1 percent. These figures changed little throughout the 1980s and 1990s, indicating that they reflect a stable situation in which approximately one-fourth of the population attends church, one-half considers itself Catholic but does not worship in public, and one-quarter is either nonreligious or believes in another faith.[11] We will discuss other religions below.

De Miguel notes that 27 percent does not seem like a very large proportion of practicing Catholics in a country that was once considered more devout than the pope. But he also points out that no other organization in Spain, whether religious, political or recreational, can approach this figure. In other words, practicing Catholics outnumber any other social group in the country, and still form a coherent, powerful constituency. Religion remains the single most important determinant in Spanish society: if we know a person's religious practices, they are a fairly reliable predictor of gender, age, education and politics. In general the most religious segments of the population are women and the elderly; young girls are raised in the faith of their mothers (see Photograph 3). The least religious Spaniards are those with a university education and liberal politics. These trends vary from region to region but remain consistent overall. To sum up, we can say that females of all age groups are more pious than their male counterparts; the older a Spaniard, the more likely that she is religious; the less educated a person and the farther to the right in politics, the more likely that she attends Mass. One social factor unrelated to religious belief is socioeconomic status. While for centuries the ruling elite had an intimate relation with Catholicism, in contemporary Spain, dominated by a large middle class, religiosity is distributed evenly over the social spectrum. If anything, the pendulum may have swung in the opposite direction: most Spaniards now believe that the Church is largely on the side of the poor.

Based on his surveys over many years, De Miguel thinks Spaniards worship less but retain a diffuse sense of spirituality, perhaps as great as before. Another of his recent surveys shows that more than half of the respondents believed that "Each person understands God in his or her own way." With his usual wit, the sociologist calls this an "à la carte God," one that is probably even more prevalent in younger people. In the same poll, only about one-fourth of the respondents accepted God as portrayed in the Bible. Another example of how much Spaniards are diverging from official dogma is a poll in which 64 percent held that women should have the right to be ordained, and 68 percent that priests should have the right to marry and continue serving the Church. "If we had solicited their opinion on divorce and birth control," adds De Miguel, "orthodoxy would have been even lower."[12] His statement is confirmed indirectly by current fertility rates in Spain, near the lowest in the world. Clearly there is an abyss between what the Church prescribes and what people do.

This fact was made clear in a famous birth control campaign launched by the Socialists in 1990. Motivated by an increasingly higher incidence of AIDS (among the worst in Europe), unwanted pregnancies and abortions, as well as by young people's reluctance to use contraception, the ministries of Health and Social Affairs came up with a rhyming motto—"*Póntelo. Pónselo*" (Put one on. Put one on him)—widely propagated on radio and television to the accompaniment of pop songs. Tens of thousands of posters also conveyed the message and 1,600,000 free, attractively presented condoms were distributed to teenagers. A spokeswoman for the government explained that the motto was an attempt to change sexual stereotypes for males and females:

3. Religion as a feminine institution in Spain. Contest among girls for *cruces de mayo* (May crosses), Badajoz, 1986. Photograph by Cristina García Rodero, Getty Research Institute, Research Library, 90.R.34.

while young men carried condoms in their pockets as a matter of macho pride—even though they rarely used them—young women were considered to be "naughty" if they took the precaution of carrying the sheath.

The "Condom Campaign" offended many traditional Catholics. Hoodlums in the city of Valladolid smashed public telephone booths that carried the rhyming slogan. The secretary general of the Spanish Bishops' Conference issued an angry statement in which he charged that the government's program was "a political, materialistic, agnostic and atheistic project aimed at depriving human beings of their transcendent dimension," at reducing sexuality to "a biological function," love to "the mutual attraction of bodies," and making sexual pleasure "the fundamental thing in life."[13] It would be hard to imagine a statement this inflammatory by a bishop in another Western nation. Not only were the Spanish clerics out of touch with their flock, but with their own ranks. A survey published earlier in the same year indicated that almost as many priests opposed the Church's birth control policy as supported it. Although similar situations exist in other parts of the world, the gap between Rome and the faithful is wider in Spain than in most countries.

MINORITY RELIGIONS

After suffering harsh repression during the Franco regime, Protestants and other Christians finally won full rights to worship under the Constitution of 1978. Since then they have grown from thirty thousand members to sixty thousand according to some sources, 300,000 according to others. The wild fluctuation in numbers suggests that the situation remains controversial. In spite of their new freedoms, some Protestants complain that the Catholic Church as well as the media still portray all competing religions as sects. In fact it is not uncommon to hear evangelicals lumped together with Hare Krishnas and other marginal groups. More than four centuries after the Counter-Reformation, Protestants are routinely depicted as heretical cult members. Newer evangelizing religions like Jehovah's Witnesses have discovered that some Spaniards, especially in the rural areas, do not understand that it is possible to be a Christian without also being Catholic.

Strangely enough, it may have been harder for Protestants than for Muslims and Jews to make inroads in democratic Spain. Ancient prejudice against the Semitic faiths persists, yet some Spaniards consider them to be an integral part of the country's heritage. A distinguished Catholic theologian says "Spain was once a country of three religions, but nowadays the young know nothing about Islam or Judaism, let alone Catholicism, and their part in the making of Spain."[14] A guilt factor may be involved too: the dramatic expulsion of Moors and Jews is impressed on the national consciousness more than the tedious wars of attrition against the Protestants. As if to make historical amends, King Juan Carlos and Queen Sofía have personally dedicated mosques and synagogues. Madrid now has a park named after its Moorish founder, Emir Mohammed. Under Franco as well as the Socialists and the Conservatives, Spanish governments have nurtured a special relationship with the Arabic world.

There are approximately 500,000 Muslims in Spain. The numbers are deceptive because one-fourth reside in Ceuta and Melilla, the two Spanish enclaves on the Moroccan coast. Most of the remainder are naturalized Spaniards who were born in other countries. An estimated one thousand are native-born converts who live largely in Andalusian cities once ruled by Muslims. In the Albaicín, the old Moorish quarter of Granada, for example, lives a community of several hundred converts. As of October 1999, students in public schools have the right to study Islam as well as Catholicism. The only problem is that the estimated fifty thousand Muslim students have only eighty qualified teachers in the whole country.

The Islamic presence in continental Spain has two widely divergent sources. One is the flood of mostly illegal immigrants from northern Africa, who pass through Ceuta or Melilla or brave the Straits of Gibraltar on flimsy rafts, often succumbing either to the weather or the Spanish Coast Guard. The other source is much smaller but more influential, the wealthy Arabs from the Gulf States who have bought choice properties along the fashionable Costa del Sol in the provinces of Málaga and Cádiz. Members of the Saudi royal family have luxurious homes in the area, for example. An immaculate white mosque has been erected in the coastal resort of Marbella. While driving a car in this cosmopolitan region, one sees street signs in Spanish, English and Arabic.

The Jewish presence in Spain is much smaller, an estimated twenty thousand. The country's close ties to the Muslim world have made relations with Israel problematic. In popular language, *judío* (Jew) or *hebreo* (Hebrew) are still synonymous with a selfish, stingy person. However, many Spaniards recognize the ancient debt their country owes to its Judaic heritage. Throughout the world, thousands of Sephardim, whose ancestors were sent packing from the Peninsula five hundred years ago, continue speaking an ancient dialect of Spanish. The government's foreign radio service now broadcasts in *djudeoespanyol* (Judeo–Spanish) as well as in Arabic and other modern tongues. Just as a small number of Catholics have converted to Islam, others have chosen Judaism, some of whose ancestors were once expelled from the country or obliged to become Christians. In small ways, Spain is recovering its multicultural heritage of three faiths (Christian, Muslim, Jewish), a theme promoted at the World's Fair Expo '92 in Sevilla.

In addition to the minority religions, cults and sects seem to be quite common. Reliable numbers are hard to come by, but some believe these groups are proportionately larger than in other European countries, owing to a reaction against decades of monolithic Catholicism. Most sects are international, like Alpha Omega, Hare Krishna, the Raelian Movement and the Unification Church ("Moonies"). Others have native origins, such as Palmar de Troya (Trojan Palm Grove), Rachimura and Arco Iris (Rainbow). These groups thrive mostly in large cities, above all Madrid, Barcelona and Valencia.

Diffuse superstition and New Age mysticism are probably more significant than cults or sects in Spain. In a visit to the country in 1991, Pope John Paul II referred to a "new paganism." A recent survey showed that three out of every four young Spaniards trust in astrology, one-half believe in UFOs, one-third in reincarnation and spiritualism. The authors of this study conclude that religious belief is not in crisis, but that Spanish culture is passing through a period of uncertainty, "open to the idolatry of the inner life, with genuine manifestations that defy the scientific-technical canons of Western rationality."[15]

POPULAR RELIGION

As we will see many times in this book, popular culture has been a greater force in Spanish life than in other Western countries. Many historians and critics claim that the most original expressions of Hispanic civilization derive from the people, not the elite. This argument would be hard to refute in the field of religion. The most characteristic forms of devotion in Spain seem to have a life of their own beyond the walls of the Church, and are frequently opposed to Catholic dogma. Some notable examples would be the country's shocking tradition of blasphemy; superstition and witchcraft; exaggerated forms of penitence; the extreme cults of the Virgin Mary, the crucified Jesus, the saints and the dead, usually to the detriment of orthodoxy. We will look briefly at these phenomena as well as other forms of popular religion.

Blasphemy and cursing are so widespread in Spain that they have attracted the attention of anthropologists. Even Spanish Americans, who speak the same language, may be offended. The English traveler Richard Ford attributed this phenomenon to a combination of linguistic influences—the family and ancestor insults from the Arabs, Christian blasphemy and sexual allusions from northern Europe. The result is not recommended for delicate ears. One example would be the many variants of the expression "*Me cago en . . .* " (I shit on . . .), followed by the name of a divine figure or sacred element, whether God, the Virgin, the nails of the cross, the saints or the dead. One could cite the phrase "*Me cago en los piececitos del Niño Jesús*" (I shit on the Baby Jesus' little toes), an expression that reveals an extraordinary fusion of irreverence and intimacy. Only a people as religious as the Spaniards could curse with such flair.

Superstition and witchcraft are probably more widespread in Spain than in most European countries. This is only partially due to contacts between the Peninsula and Latin America, where the occult is a part of everyday life in some places. Superstition and magic also form an ancient part of Mediterranean civilization. These practices remain strongest in rural Spain, yet recent surveys indicate that they also flourish in the cities. Superstition is not only a prerogative of peasants and the proletariat, but extends to all social classes. A poll by Amando de Miguel shows that about three-fourths of the population believes in good or bad luck and a third still believes in *gafes*, hoodoos or people who are supposed to cause misfortune.[16] Female practitioners of healing or witchcraft go by different names in various parts of the country: *meiga* (sorceress) in Galicia, *xorguiña* (witch) in the Basque Country, *sabia* (wise woman) and *echadora* (fortune-teller) in the Castiles and Andalusia.

Popular religion in Spain is most exuberant in the yearly cycle of sacred festivals and patronal feasts, in which people in towns across the country celebrate their local or regional saints, Christ or the Virgin. As we have seen in Chapter 1 (Context), Spaniards spend a fortune every year on these festivities, probably more per capita than any other nation in the world. Very little of this money pays for durable goods and much of it literally goes up in smoke or flames. From a utilitarian point of view, this seems wasteful. But let nobody—not even God, Christ or the Virgin—try to take these celebrations away from the Spanish people. They cling to them tenaciously. In Chapter 3 (Customs) we will see these festivals in their secular or nonreligious dimensions, although it can be very hard to distinguish between the sacred and the profane.

Popular religious celebrations have an extraordinary richness and variety in Spain. A significant number of people work the year around organizing and preparing the special clothing, icons, ornaments, fireworks, foods and drinks for these occasions. A scholar of popular religion has evoked the abundant physical elements involved: "images, banners, insignias, emblems, coats of arms, precious objects, reliquaries, urns, tapers, lights, candles, lanterns, lamps, oil lamps, torches, candelabras, rockets, illuminations, palm leaves, branches, flowers, perfumes, incenses, costumes, ornaments, disguises, delicacies, drinks."[17] Visitors from Protestant countries often find it difficult to understand this sensual display, not to mention the hearty eating and drinking that are an indispensable part of popular religious festivals in Spain.

Spaniards celebrate their saints, Christs and Virgins with no holds barred. We must use the plural because many villages, towns and cities have their own particular denomination for Jesus or Mary: the Christ of Anguish, the Expiration, the Five Wounds, the Great Power, Humility—sticking only to the first part of the alphabet. Then there is the Virgin of the Mount, Pass, the Oaks, the Olive Grove, the Rosemary Patch, the Spring, the Stream, the Valley, to cover the second part of the alphabet. To each one of these divine figures, and thousands more, corresponds a specific icon or image which may be removed from its cathedral, church, chapel or sanctuary at designated times, often for elaborate processions. The most famous example is probably the Virgen del Rocío (Our Lady of the Dew)—also known as the White Dove, Queen of the Marshes and Mother of Andalusia—in the small town of Almonte in the province of Huelva. Each year at Pentecost, tens of thousands of Spaniards head for Almonte from more than sixty points of departure, traveling for hours or days on foot, horseback, in ox-drawn carts, trucks, cars and trailers across the marshy southwestern corner of the Peninsula. En route the faithful sing, dance and consume incalculable amounts of food and wine. When they reach Almonte at the appointed time, the local men "take out" the Virgin of the Dew from her chapel; a frenzy ensues in which people are trampled and wounded every year (see Photograph 4). This is popular religion at its most intense and mysterious, almost incomprehensible to people from the United States or northern Europe.

The Rocío pilgrimage combines various elements of collective religiosity in Spain: worship of the Virgin Mary, devotional fervor, religious brotherhoods, pilgrimage. Marianism thrives throughout the Peninsula but is strongest in Andalusia, where the festive, emotional display of devout feelings contrasts with the more sober faith of the Castiles and León; yet in both north and south, Catholics may fast, maintain long vigils, flagellate themselves and endure unimaginable hardships on special occasions like Lent, Maundy Thursday or Good Friday. Visions of the Virgin Mary, often with elaborate messages for her audience, are almost a cottage industry in Spain. *Cofradías* or religious brotherhoods play an important role in celebrations of Mary, Christ and the saints. They can be powerful social groups whose influence surpasses the realm of religion. The *cofradías* are almost exclusively male (see Photograph 5). Finally, pilgrimages and *romerías*—shorter, more

4. The *Virgen del Rocío* (Virgin of the Dawn), Almonte (Huelva), 1978. Photograph by Cristina García Rodero, Getty Research Institute, Research Library, 90.R.34.

5. Penitents, Good Friday, Puente Genil (Córdoba), 1976. Photograph by Cristina García Rodero, Getty Research Institute, Research Library, 90.R.34.

6. Pilgrim to Santiago de Compostela, c. 1995. This pilgrim wears the traditional scallop shell around his neck and walks with a staff. The sign to the left indicates the direction of Santiago and warns motorists to beware of pilgrims. Photograph reproduced courtesy TVE (Televisión Española).

festive trips to a local shrine or sanctuary—exist in every part of the country. The most famous pilgrimage is the thousand-year-old *Camino de Santiago* or Way of St. James, traversing northern Spain and leading to the cathedral in Santiago de Compostela, where the apostle James the Elder is said to be buried (see Photograph 6).

It is fitting that we have concluded this chapter with a summary of popular religion in Spain. While official devotion there has many similarities to that in other Catholic countries, popular celebrations are startlingly varied and original, with few parallels anywhere in the world.

SELECTED READINGS

Caro Baroja, Julio. *Introducción a una historia contemporánea del anticlericalismo español*. Madrid: Istmo, 1980.

Cervantes, Miguel de. *Don Quijote de la Mancha*. 2 vols. [1605, 1615]; reprint, edited by John J. Allen. Madrid: Cátedra, 1989.

Christian, William A., Jr. "Folk Religion: An Overview." In *The Encyclopedia of Religion*, edited by Mircea Eliade, 5: 270–74. 16 vols. New York: Macmillan, 1987.

Crain, Mary M. "Pilgrims, Yuppies and Media-Men: The Transformation of an Andalusian Pilgrimage." In *Revitalizing European Rituals*, edited by Jeremy Boissevain, 95–112. London: Routledge, 1992.

De Miguel, Amando. "Religión." In *La sociedad española, 1996–1997*, edited by Amando De Miguel, 205–246. Madrid: Editorial Complutense, 1997.

Delgado, Manuel. *La ira sagrada. Anticlericalismo, iconoclastia y antirritualismo en la España contemporánea*. Barcelona: Editorial Humanidades, 1992.

Díaz-Salazar, Rafael, and Salvador Giner, eds. *Religión y sociedad en España*. Madrid: Centro de Investigaciones Sociológicas, 1993.

Duffy, David G.P.R. "A Pilgrim's Rewards, Step by Step" [on the *Camino de Santiago*]. *New York Times* (May 30, 1999): Section S, pp. 10, 12.

"En España hay ya más jóvenes no creyentes que católicos practicantes." *El Mundo* (August 3, 1997): 26.

Gala, Antonio. *La casa sosegada*. Barcelona: Planeta, 1998.

García Rodero, Cristina. *España Oculta: Public Celebrations in Spain, 1974–1989*. Foreword by Julio Caro Baroja. Introduction by Mary M. Crain. Washington, DC: Smithsonian Institution Press, 1990.

Gibson, Ian. *Fire in the Blood: The New Spain*. London: Faber and Faber, 1992.

Gironella, José María. *Nuevos 100 españoles y Dios*. Barcelona: Planeta, 1994.

Hooper, John. *The New Spaniards*. London: Penguin, 1995.

Josephs, Allen. *White Wall of Spain: The Mysteries of Andalusian Culture*. Ames: Iowa State University Press, 1983.

Lannon, Frances. "The Social Praxis and Cultural Politics of Spanish Catholicism."

In *Spanish Cultural Studies: An Introduction. The Struggle for Modernity*, edited by Helen Graham and Jo Labanyi, 40–45. Oxford: Oxford University Press, 1995.

Machado, Antonio. *Juan de Mairena. Sentencias, donaires, apuntes y recuerdos de un profesor apócrifo*. 1936; reprint. Madrid: Castalia, 1971.

Maldonado, Luis. *Para comprender el catolicismo popular*. Estella, Spain: Verbo Divino, 1990.

———. *Religiosidad popular. Nostaligia de lo mágico*. Madrid: Editorial Cristiandad, 1975.

Mitchell, Timothy. *Betrayal of the Innocents: Desire, Power, and the Catholic Church in Spain*. Philadelphia: University of Pennsylvania Press, 1998.

———. *Passional Culture: Emotion, Religion and Society in Southern Spain*. Philadelphia: University of Pennsylvania Press, 1990.

Payne, Stanley. *Spanish Catholicism: An Historical Overview*. Madison: University of Wisconsin Press, 1984.

Puente Ojea, Gonzalo. *Ateísmo y religiosidad. Reflexiones sobre un debate*. Madrid: Siglo XXI, 1997.

Rodgers, Eamonn. "Religion," "Roman Catholicism." In *Encyclopedia of Contemporary Spanish Culture*, edited by Eamonn Rodgers, 445–447, 456–457. London and New York: Routledge, 1999.

Sádaba, Javier, and others. *La influencia de la religion en la sociedad española*. Madrid: Libertarias, Prodhufi, 1994.

Sánchez, José. *The Spanish Civil War as a Religious Tragedy*. South Bend, IN: University of Notre Dame Press, 1987.

Sellers, Jeff M. "Evangelicals Wary of Religious 'Cult' Label." *Christianity Today* 40, no. 11 (October 7, 1996): 89.

Stanton, Edward F. "Religion." In *Handbook of Spanish Popular Culture*, edited by Edward F. Stanton, 23–49. Westport, CT: Greenwood Press, 1999.

Walsh, Michael. *Opus Dei: An Investigation into the Secret Society Struggling for Power within the Roman Catholic Church*. New York: HarperCollins, 1992.

OTHER SOURCES

The Spanish search engine "Olé" has dozens of religious websites, including *Centro Bíblico* (Biblical Center—evangelical), *Conozca la Historia de su Santo* (Know the Story of Your Saint), *Diakonia* (Orthodox), *Estudio Teológico Agustiniano Tagaste* (Tagaste Agustinian Theological Study), *Grupos Bíblicos Universitarios* (College Biblical Groups), *Información sobre el Catolicismo* (Information on Catholicism), *Siempre Fiel* (Always Faithful—Catholic), *Religión*, and so forth: <http://www.ole.es>. On these and other sites, one can find anything from the Bible, biblical commentaries and theology to dictations by angels and the Virgin Mary. See also other search engines like "Buscador," "Go Spain," and "Sí, Spain" (listed under "Other Sources" at the end of Chapter 1).

3

Customs

A cada terra el seu ús (To each land its own custom).
—Catalan proverb

En todas partes cuecen habas (They cook beans everywhere).
—Castilian proverb

The peoples of Spain once belonged to separate kingdoms, still speak various languages, and cling tightly to their unique ways of life. In this chapter we will look at the exuberant variety of traditions in the country's diverse areas. Sometimes we will see a common Mediterranean, European or Catholic culture behind these local customs.

What strikes a foreigner who visits Spain? If the visitor is from the United States or northern Europe, she will be overwhelmed by the vitality of life on the streets. Although an Englishman's castle is his house, a Spaniard's is the street, or perhaps his local bar on that street. The foreigner will feel the sheer human energy. Sights, sounds and smells will assault her senses, tempting her to stop at the café where the aroma of dark-roasted coffee wafts to the street, or at the bakery where the fragrance of fresh bread and pastries allures the passersby. Many pedestrians are well dressed and display their clothes with dash and style. At the same time a beggar may be asking passersby for alms, a mangy cur may slink across the sidewalk, a pair of youths may be dealing drugs and toss a used syringe in the gutter. Life is there in front of the visitor's eyes, in all its extremes, without the barriers she would normally find in her own country.

A Spaniard may seem to be in a hurry, but not for the same reasons as an American, Canadian or German. If these people rush to work, the Spaniard could be rushing to play. He will ride a bus, subway or taxi across town in order to have a cup of coffee or a glass of wine at a particular bar—what he would call "my bar"—to read the newspaper, talk to friends or simply do nothing, *nada*. He takes his leisure seriously. If other peoples often live in order to work, the Spaniard may work in order to live. If a foreigner asks him, "Do you enjoy your job?" he will look at the person as if she were crazy. Of course he does not enjoy his job; nobody does, he says. All that matters is life before and after work, free time, sweet nothing, here and now. The cry of lottery vendors on the streets of Spanish cities, those blind men or women with their strident nasal twang, seems to be reminding all to seize the moment, the hour, the day: "*Tiras para hoy . . . para hoy . . . para hóooy!*" (Tickets for today . . . today . . . today!).

All of this applies to most regions of Spain except Catalonia, where a strong work ethic has made the region the country's most prosperous. To the bewilderment of other Spaniards, Catalans may live for work and even enjoy it. Not only do they labor hard but they also save their money in a nation where extravagant generosity is a code of life. Needless to say there are many jokes about tightwad Catalans, who counter with stories about spendthrift Castilians. Like nearly all jokes, they deal in generalities. Obviously there are many exceptions: industrious Castilians, indolent Catalans and everything in between.

The sense of time is different in Spain. Historians have recorded the country's lag of years, decades or centuries behind other nations. Although the gap has narrowed during the last quarter-century, the visitor often has the impression that she is living in another age. She will find stores where shoes, clothes, needlework, wineskins, pastries or candies are made as they were in the Middle Ages; yet the owners of these shops may use the latest model of cellular telephone. Past and present, tradition and technology live side by side. Spaniards move from one to the other in a split second.

Time seems to pass slower in Spain. The country's historical lag may have its origins in the delayed schedule of daily life. Everything seems to start later than in other western countries. Most people rise later in the morning, have breakfast, lunch and dinner later, start and finish work later. By the time they go to bed, it is naturally far into the night.

Let us look at a schematic daily schedule based around meals. If we appear to grant excessive importance to eating, that is only because the Spaniards do the same (see Wines and Foods, below). The people's lives revolve around meals much more than in the United States and other western countries.

8–9 A.M.	light breakfast
11 A.M.	late breakfast or *merienda* (snack)
1 P.M.	*tapas* (appetizers)
2 P.M.	three-course lunch
3–5 P.M.	*siesta*
5–6 P.M.	tea, coffee, pastries or *merienda*
8–10 P.M.	*tapas*
10–11 P.M.	supper

Spaniards have been following this rhythm for centuries. During the long lunch hour, when many stores close and most people go home to eat, villages and cities resemble ghost towns. There are exceptions to the pattern but in this as in so many things, the majority follows a similar schedule. In Spain there is a right way to do almost everything, and that is the way the Spaniards do it, of course.

The influence of tourism and the European Union has put pressure on Spanish companies to adopt the *jornada intensiva*, the American-style schedule without a long lunch break. Some stores now stay open straight through from 9 or 10 in the morning until 5 or 6 in the afternoon. But resistance to change is stubborn. The leisurely three-course lunch remains the main meal of the day for most Spaniards; no amount of foreign influence will destroy this entrenched custom. The Spanish *comida* or lunch works on the principle of the python: gorging followed by lethargy and repose. The *siesta* is not a sign of laziness, but a necessary interval for digesting food while staying out of the merciless afternoon sun, the *sol de justicia*.

The delayed rhythms of meals also explain the country's stupendous night-life, unmatched anywhere in the world. Foreigners often wonder how Spaniards can work all day yet party all night. One answer is that many work neither long nor hard, and nearly all have prepared for the evening with a long *siesta*. Frequent doses of *torrefacto*, the dark-roasted coffee preferred by the Spanish, help to keep them awake too. Finally, a diet of fresh fish, chicken, veal, game, produce and fruit, widely preferred to canned or frozen foods, gives them the energy for those long days' journeys into night.

Unlike Americans or the British, the Spaniard usually does not entertain at home, but at his favorite bar. Spain has approximately one café or bar for every three hundred inhabitants, more than any country in the world. Even so, these locales often seem to be bursting with clients, especially during the peak hours before and after lunch and dinner. Along with restaurants, nightclubs and discos, bars and cafés are the main venues for the country's ongoing party.

Living life in the streets and exhausting the night are cultural traits shared by the people of most regions in Spain. Here too the notable exception is Catalonia, where devotion to work makes reveling impractical. If one compares the adjacent towns along the Catalan–French border, most people retire to their homes early in both places. If one follows the border to the north through Aragón, Navarra and the Basque Country, however, the contrast between the two nations is stunning. In Hendaye (France), for example, the streets are mostly deserted by 8 p.m., while across the international line in Irún (Spain), the Basques are just warming up for a long night, no matter what time of year.[1]

The Spaniards' nocturnal life is another aspect of what one observer has called a "cult of excess" or "cult of addiction."[2] They drink more alcohol per capita than any other people in the European Union. (See Wines and Foods, below.) In smoking they are second only to the Greeks. Ever since the Spanish and Portuguese introduced tobacco to Europe in the mid-sixteenth century, they have been passionate smokers. It has been said that a Spaniard without a cigar would resemble a house without a chimney. Some things do not change; the Spanish government has a special arrangement with Cuba to import the world's best cigars with a markup of around 20 percent, miniscule compared to that in Canada, Mexico and other less favored trading partners. As a result, Spain is a cigar smoker's paradise, where more than thirty million *habanos* are consumed every year, along with millions of cigars from other parts of the world, including the Canary Islands. One saying sums up the mating of the three Spanish drugs of choice—tobacco, alcohol, and coffee: "*café, copa y puro*" (coffee, liqueur and cigar), the classic way to round off a large meal.

The state has conducted lackluster campaigns against abuse of legal drugs. The same could be said of the government's efforts to curtail the consumption of illegal substances. Trafficking has always been prohibited, but strangely enough, private use was perfectly legal until 1992. The police are amazingly tolerant in the amount of lawlessness they permit in public. Evidence of use is probably more obvious than in any other western country: one sees addicts and pushers everywhere in the larger cities, where discarded syringes and needles litter the streets. There is a large population of heroin and cocaine addicts; the so-called soft drugs like LSD, Ecstasy and amphetamines are used widely by young people. Drug use has been related to the country's crime rate, which has more than doubled in the last twenty years. Although the government can be held accountable for weak enforcement, it increased its budget to combat trafficking by 42 percent between 1996 and 2000.[3] Spain's geographical location, a mere eight miles across the Strait of Gibraltar from Morocco, makes it the natural bridge for international traffic between Africa and Europe. More than one-half of the drugs that follow this route are destined for points beyond the Spanish border.

Gambling is another aspect of the cult of excess and addiction. Spaniards are the biggest betters in Europe and third in the world, surpassed only by Americans and Filipinos; they spent an average of $571 per person in 1997. The country's bars and cafés host games of cards and dominoes, and ring with the sound of fruit (slot) machines. Bingo halls and casinos are common sites for large-scale gambling. The highest stakes are played in football lotteries and the *Lotería Nacional* run by the National Organization of Blind Spaniards (O.N.C.E.), a powerful institution, supported by the state, that is a major investor in banking, tourism and the media. Its Christmas prize, fittingly called "*El Gordo*" (The Fat One), is held to be the world's richest drawing. Every Spaniard dreams of winning; the expression "*Me tocó la lotería*" (I won the lottery) is used to express any stroke of good luck. It has been estimated that the Spanish spend about ten times more on lottery tickets than on insurance policies. Net income from the *Lotería Nacional* would cover the entire budget of the country's diplomatic corps overseas.

By this time the reader's impression may be that Spain is a nest of vice and corruption. One of the great paradoxes of Spanish life is that the people manage to maintain close-knit families in spite of their night life and their cult of excess. One survey after another has shown that for more than three-quarters of the population, the family continues to be paramount.[4] In fact it may be the only enduring institution in a fast-changing society, an anchor in a sea of change. Continuing loyalty to the family unit accounts in part for the low suicide rate and the generally cohesive structure of Spanish society.

SEX, MARRIAGE AND FAMILY

During the long, dark night of Generalissimo Francisco Franco's dictatorship (1939–1975), Spain and neighboring Portugal were the most puritanical countries in Europe. A rigid formality governed every aspect of relations between the sexes. The cult of female virginity encouraged young men to find a sexual outlet in brothels, which were finally made illegal but continued to be tolerated by the authorities. (In fact they were called *casas de tolerancia*, "houses of tolerance.") Incredible as it sounds, numerous brides actually entered marriage believing that "babies come from Paris," a Spanish version of the stork legend.

After Franco's death, a double revolution shook the country: a political reaction to forty years of repression within the country, combined with the erotic liberation that had rocked the West since the 1960s. The result was an explosive mixture of politics and pornography. One journalist said of the period: "In our imaginations and innocence we would fuse things so respectable yet so different as bare arses and democracy."[5]

Twenty-five years later, Spain has buried the prudish legacy of the dictatorship and outgrown the excesses of the late 1970s and 1980s. In most ways it now resembles other European countries. The old connection between marriage, sex and procreation has been transformed. Cohabitation and premarital sex are no longer frowned upon, which has led to a spectacular increase in births out of wedlock. Yet at 10 percent overall the figures remain at less than half the rate in other European countries, not to mention the United States. On the other hand, married couples are having fewer children, so much so that Spain now has one of the lowest birth rates in the world and is approaching zero population growth. UNICEF has called the situation "drastic." Statistics vary, but hover around 1.36. (The figure in the United States is 1.85.) Only one in every five families has four children or more. Some demographers have suggested a return to postwar childbirth incentives.

The overall level of sexual activity—both inside and outside of marriage—may be surprisingly low. The average age for initiating sexual relations is about nineteen for men and twenty-one for women—about a year later than other Europeans—suggesting that young Spaniards are freer than their parents and grandparents, but hardly precocious or promiscuous.[6] There may be less love-making in the land of Don Juan than in any other western European country.[7] This could be a residue of forty years of repression.

Pornography is far more common in Spain than in the United States. After a brief trip to the country, the American writer Paul Theroux thought it was "worse than German varieties, [which are] possibly the most repellent in the world."[8] Like most Anglo–Saxon tourists, he was surprised to learn that pornography is not considered taboo: "In the primmest little districts in Alicante or Murcia or Mallorca . . . [porno] films were on view next to the candy store or the hairdresser. . . . Help! *Socorro!*"[9]

The fall of the birth rate is one of the two revolutionary changes in the population. The other is a rise in longevity. Average life expectancy is the highest in Europe: eighty-one years for women and seventy-five for men (higher also than in the United States). Combined with plunging birth rates, soaring longevity has led to a population with a scarcity of children and middle-aged adults and an excess of older people. The spread in ages has caused some of the country's most pressing social problems, such as extremely high unemployment, especially among women and youth, and shrinking resources to finance old-age pensions and retirement.

Longer education, later entry into a difficult market and housing shortages are forcing young people to live with their parents until an older age, around twenty-five for women and twenty-eight for men. (Whereas the only legitimate reason for departure used to be marriage, now it may be a desire for independence.) This means that they still lack the privacy enjoyed by most of their counterparts in northern Europe and the United States. A popular song tells of making love in a Simca 1000 car; one poll indicated that almost 10 percent of Spaniards have their first intercourse in an automobile. Another 15 percent lose their virginity in the countryside, 9 percent in a hotel. The poll does not account for the remaining 66 percent; one assumes that they are less original.

About 70 percent of all adults believe that fidelity to one's partner is fundamental. According to most statistics, men continue to be more unfaithful than women, but both sexes are frequently jealous of their partners. The country's leading pollster on sexual subjects says wittily: "In Spain 47% are Othellos and 43% claim not to feel this passion; but with respect to the latter, we can ask ourselves if they are the ones who provoke it."[10]

Of course we should probably be skeptical of statistics on intimate subjects. One report, for example, shows that 5 percent of heterosexual Spanish men claim to make love every day, compared to 3 percent of heterosexual women. If the sample is a representative one, as its author assures us, then either 3 percent of the women are overworked or 2 percent of the men are Don Juans in their imaginations only.[11]

There is a general belief in Spain that young people don't want to get married. "Marriage with papers" (con papeles), they believe, can wait until the proper time. That time comes sooner than later for most couples, because less than 2 percent of Spanish men and women live together outside of marriage. The neoconservative trend in most western countries seems to be present in Spain too: young people between the ages of eighteen and twenty-four are more inclined to a religious wedding than those between twenty-five and twenty-nine. The two infantas or princesses of the royal family led the way in the 1990s with opulent weddings in the cathedrals of Sevilla and Barcelona. But the number of people of all ages who choose to be married outside the Catholic Church—either in another faith or in a civil ceremony—has grown to 20 percent of the population.

One Spanish sociologist argues that there is a gender split in attitudes toward sex. He believes that most young Spanish women still hold to the "Prince Charming myth," according to which they will be emancipated by love and marriage. In contrast, most young men seek sexual pleasure rather than love, preferring to elude or postpone marriage. In spite of all the advances that women have achieved in civil rights, in education and the workplace, they continue to follow some of the same patterns as their mothers and grandmothers. "While young men worship pleasure," this scholar says, "young ladies worship love; therefore, all the men have to do is make them fall in love."[12] An American reader is reminded of the dynamic represented in the recent bestseller, *The Rules: Time-Tested Secrets for Capturing the Heart of Mr. Right* and its satiric response, *The Code: Time-Tested Secrets for Getting What You Want from Women—Without Marrying Them!* Don Juan dies hard, in Spain and elsewhere.

Spanish society continues to be basically monogamous: a full 74 percent of the population prefers a relationship with a single person. After the initial euphoria of legalized divorce in 1981, rates climbed much less than in neighboring countries. In fact Spain has the third lowest divorce rate on the continent (0.7 percent), just above Greece and Italy. The low incidence can be explained in part by the agonizing duration of the process: divorce is only granted after a separation of two to five years. Separation has the same privileges as divorce except the right to remarry—full autonomy for the man and woman, division of property, visitation and custody arrangements for children, child support and alimony. The main causes of divorce are desertion (91 percent), mistreatment (87 percent), adultery by the wife (75 percent), adultery by the husband (74 percent), homosexuality (74 percent) and "lack of love and conjugal harmony"—what we would call incompatibility (73 percent). The figures show that most divorces have multiple causes.

Gay and lesbian culture has been part of the sexual revolution in democratic Spain. During the fascist regime, homosexuals were repressed more violently than in any country in Europe, with the possible exception of Portugal under Franco's ally, Antonio Salazar. For years the greatest insult in the Spanish language, notoriously rich in vituperation, was to call a man *maricón* (fag). During the 1960s and 1970s, alternative tourism in places like Sitges (Barcelona) and Ibiza gradually began to expose Spanish men to foreign gays. The Catalan-speaking areas of the country, above all Barcelona and Valencia, formed the front line of sexual politics. Other centers were Madrid, especially during the time of its *movida* or cultural movement in the late 1970s and early 1980s, and Bilbao, now one of the most radical sites in Spain.

The new Constitution of 1978 guarantees equality for all citizens, including gay men and lesbians of course. About 700,000 Spaniards (less than 2 percent of the population) consider themselves to be homosexual, while approximately the same number are bisexual. Even gay culture—*el mundo gai* as it is known in Spain—has been unable to escape the primal power of the family model: some 80 percent of Spanish homosexuals live or have lived as couples.

Attitudes of the general population have changed from condemnation to acceptance during the last two decades. Some 60 percent of Spaniards believe that homosexuals are normal, 18 percent that they are abnormal, 8 percent that they are degenerate. They tend to be more accepted by women than by men. Although gay and lesbian rights organizations are years behind their northern European and North American counterparts, the private sphere is reported to be almost as free.

The visibility of gays and transvestites in the major cities of Spain often gives the impression that they are more numerous than is actually the case. The alternative press has an extremely small circulation, and active members in homosexual rights organizations are few. Women's studies remain undeveloped in Spanish universities while gay and lesbian studies are inconceivable. Some of this may be changing as AIDS and HIV-related problems have revitalized sexual politics and led to public demonstrations in Madrid and other cities.

Lesbianism lags far behind gay culture in Spain and remains taboo in most circles. A notorious example is Carlos A. Malo de Molina's best-selling book, *Spaniards and Sexuality*: although its author makes repeated claims to openmindedness, his chapter on homosexuality does not include a single reference to lesbians. *Nosotras*, the magazine of the Madrid Colectivo de Feministas Lesbianas (Collective of Feminist Lesbians), is one of a small number of publications that is trying to redress the situation.

As in most other countries, artistic expression in Spain has surged ahead of popular attitudes toward homosexuality. Subversion of traditional values is common, especially in the arts, theater and cinema. The camp films of Pedro Almodóvar (see Chapter 5), for example, satirize everything from straight bourgeois sexuality and *machismo* to the nuclear family. Other directors like José Luis Borau, Jaime Chávarri, Eloy de la Iglesia, Manuel Gutiérrez Aragón, Ventura Pons and Gonzalo Suárez have treated homosexual themes less hysterically than Almodóvar. Writers such as Esther Tusquets and Juan Goytisolo in the pre–Civil War generation, and Luis Antonio de Villena and Jordi Petit in more recent years, have used radical textual strategies to represent homoerotic desire.

Another change in Spanish sexual habits is the decreased importance of prostitution. Although paid sex may be more visual than ever—one only has to read the classified ads in major newspapers like *El País* (see Chapter 4)—it is much less widespread than it was under Franco. Greater sexual freedom among the younger generations has limited the social function of prostitution as an escape valve for adolescent males. A mere 2 percent of Spanish men now receive their sexual initiation in brothels. Male prostitution, anathema under fascism, remains less common than in most other European countries.

The sexual revolution has not damaged home life in Spain. The Center of Sociological Research has published a report showing that the family is more highly valued than ever, notwithstanding trends that would seem to militate against it: abortion, a falling birth rate, divorce, lower attendance at church. Family values are holding together the social fabric much more than government, religion or any other institution.

In the Center's report, Spaniards gave the family 9.37 points out of a possible 10 as the most important aspect of their lives, followed far behind by work (7.95), economic well-being (7.78), fitness (6.95), religion (5.69) and politics (3.20). A full 81 percent of the population would be willing to sacrifice anything else for the family, even their own lives. On the other hand, only 51 percent would give their lives to save another human being—outside the family, one assumes.

In 1985 Spaniards showed an 89 percent level of satisfaction with their family lives; by 1994 the percentage had risen two points. Six out of every ten people agreed with the statement that "In our time, the only place where one can be completely happy and live in peace is at home with the family."[13]

It is fashionable to speak of "the crisis of the family" in the West. Despite tumultuous change during the last quarter-century, the institution has shown great resilience in Spain. We can predict safely that the family will continue to be the greatest source of stability in Spanish life.

FIESTAS

Spain is the land of *fiestas*. It spends more time and money on collective celebrations than any country in the world. Although summer is the high season, festivities are held throughout the year. Masked revelers dance through the streets of Cádiz in Carnival; giant floats go up in flames during the springtime *fallas* in Valencia; young girls adorn themselves with flowers from head to toe during the May festival in Almería; bonfires burn on Atlantic and Mediterranean beaches for St. John's or Midsummer's Night; people pelt each other in the *Tomatina* or tomato-battle each August in Buñol; pastry shops bake thousands of special *roscos* (biscuits) and *panelles* (sweet rolls) in Galicia and Asturias on All Saints' Day; crowds all over the country swallow twelve grapes with each stroke of the clock at midnight on

New Year's Eve; *carantoñas* or figures with grotesque masks and animal skins take to the streets for the *fiesta* of St. Sebastian in Acehuche in late January; and then the whole cycle begins anew.

Most of these celebrations are obviously related to the calendar of the Catholic Church with its annual cycle of holidays and saints' days. Other festivities are partially or wholly secular. As we have seen in Chapter 2 (Religion), it may be hard to draw the line between the sacred and the profane.

Every town and city in Spain has its own feast or celebration in honor of its patron saint, who might also be Jesus Christ or the Virgin Mary. Even abandoned villages retain their *fiestas*, coming to life once a year as former inhabitants return from the cities where they have migrated for work. Spaniards feel a great attachment to their *pueblo* and to their *patria chica*, their hometown and local region in contrast to the *patria grande*, the nation. Their loyalties are almost tribal: first and foremost they belong to a family, then to a town or region, lastly to Spain.

Anthropologists speak of Spaniards' "festive sense of life." They believe it evolved from primitive rites that probably fused dance, orgy and feast—that is to say, *fiesta*. The bullfight, with its ritual sacrifice of an animal-god, would be the most authentic survival of these ancient mysteries, which often involved blood, wine, revelry and feasting. In fact most bullfights are celebrated during patronal feasts in spring and summer.

The festive spirit creates a breakdown of everyday norms and inhibitions, a freeing of the body and senses, a renewed sense of fellowship and a closer identity to the community and its traditions. After a true *fiesta*, life is never the same. Many witnesses have attested to the fact, but it can only be understood through direct participation. For centuries this was limited to adult males; the last twenty years have brought equality to the festive world. Now young girls, boys and women take to the streets for celebrations.

The only way to comprehend the stunning power, joy and wildness of a Spanish *fiesta* is to be there, to live through the whole celebration from sweet beginning to bitter end. Some revelries last less than twenty-four hours, others several days or a week and more, at times almost overlapping with the next event on the festive calendar.

Short of being there in person, the best way to perceive a Spanish *fiesta* is to look at the stupendous photographs taken by Cristina García Rodero, who traveled the length and breadth of the Peninsula in search of sacred and profane celebrations, mostly in the 1970s and 1980s. These photos constitute a brilliant record of her people's festive sense of life. Although we cannot see all of her ten-thousand-plus plates in black-and-white and color, a select few, mixed with an occasional shot by other photographers, will give us an idea.

We will begin our visual journey in the winter, continue through the spring and end in the full explosion of summer *fiestas*.

Carnival celebrations were prohibited during Franco's dictatorship, since they were considered to be pagan rites that threatened public order and morality. Spaniards rejoiced in private until the new democracy allowed these festivities to be reborn out of their lenten ashes. They are now celebrated in hundreds of towns with abundant eating and drinking, grotesque costumes and the playful triumph and final death of personages who represent Carnival itself. In the snowy mountain village of Piornal in the province of Cáceres (Extremadura), we see such a personage, here called *Jarramplas*—an untranslatable name suggesting playful wickedness—being pelted with turnips after Mass in the local church (see Photograph 7).

At winter's end in Valencia, elaborate floats or *fallas* are constructed out of wood, cardboard and papier mâché; they usually depict contemporary figures and events in a humorous and satirical way. Neighborhood organizations spend months designing and building the *fallas* at enormous expense, in competition with similar groups in other parts of the city. At midnight on March 19, in honor of the city's patron St. Joseph, in the midst of deafening fireworks and the smell of burnt powder, surrounded by seething crowds, the Valencians torch the floats in the famous *cremá* as the work of months goes up in flames. Few *fiestas* represent so well the Spanish sense of reckless, devil-may-care enjoyment of the moment with no consideration for practical matters.

May rites in Spain are pan-European festivities that celebrate spring, flowers and fertility. They probably have their origins in pre-Christian beliefs and practices. In some regions, a *Maya* or May Girl is chosen by the people. They deck her out in wildflowers, jewelry and embroidered silk shawls (see Photograph 8).

In the Levantine town of Alcoy, a very different celebration occurs later in the spring. Citizens dress up as *moros y cristianos* (Moors and Christians), the two peoples who fought for control of this land during the Middle Ages. On the first day, twenty-eight groups or *comparsas*, evenly divided between the two contending armies, parade their lavish costumes through the downtown streets (see Photograph 9). On the second day, Masses and processions are held (Catholic only, of course). On the third and final day, the two armies meet in battle amid the clash of swords and the smoke of matchlock guns. Naturally the good guys (Christians) always win. The *fiesta* closes with the apparition of a child representing the young San Jorge (St. George), patron saint of Alcoy, shooting arrows from the turrets of the town's castle.

Toward the end of spring at the moveable feast of Corpus Christi, diverse

7. The people of Piornal (Cáceres) throw turnips and snowballs at "El Jarramplas," Carnival 1980. Photograph by Cristina García Rodero, Getty Research Institute, Research Library, 90.R.34.

8. *La Maya* (May Girl), Colmenar Viejo (Madrid), 1989. Photograph by Cristina García Rodero.

9. Entrance of Moors at the annual celebration of *Moros y cristianos* (Moors and Christians), Alcoy (Alicante), 1976. Photograph by Cristina García Rodero, Getty Research Institute, Research Library, 90.R.34.

rites are celebrated throughout the country. The streets of Toledo are carpeted with tons of fresh thyme; when a religious procession walks through the town, the trampled herbs release a pungent fragrance as people watch from balconies draped with lovely *mantones de Manila*, silk shawls that are saved all year for this unique occasion. In the Mediterranean town of Sitges, children lay out carpets of flowers instead of herbs, creating brilliant displays that fill the air with sweet aromas (Photograph 10). In both towns we can see the relationship between the festivities and the rebirth of nature in the spring.

All Spain seems to explode during the high season of patronal feasts in the summer months. The most famous of all is the festival of San Fermín in Pamplona (Navarra), a *fiesta* made famous once and for all by Hemingway (see Photograph 11). In fact little has changed since the novelist evoked the celebration in *The Sun Also Rises* (1926). San Fermín is a sort of Carnival and Mardi Gras rolled up into eight days of continuous eating, drinking, dancing and revelry in what has been called the world's greatest party. Photograph 12 does not show the well-known *encierro* or running of the bulls through the town's streets, nor the bullfights, nor the *peñas* or folk clubs dancing the *riau-riau* down the streets of Pamplona, but something very different: one of the beautiful pauses that punctuate the festivities. We see a *cabezudo* or fathead, this one nicknamed "Vinegar-Face," leaning against a mailbox, while a little boy does the same on the other side. This shot captures the playful aspect of *fiestas* and the special role of children, for whom these celebrations are unforgettable rites of passage.

Photograph 13 catches a similar moment involving another child, this time a little girl who runs along the sidewalk where a man sleeps off a hangover. Here we see how the inhibitions of everyday life are suspended during *fiesta*, allowing a luminous time and space to come into being, reborn at the next celebration.

These events seem to be reminders of a bygone age. For this reason, some have predicted the inevitable demise of festive life in contemporary society. Spanish *fiestas* are wasteful and do not seem compatible with rational politics, science and the global economy. Or could these same forces be driving Spaniards to hold onto their annual rituals more tenaciously? Studies suggest that this may be the case. Some anthropologists speak of "festive escalation": rather than declining, *fiestas* in Spain have acquired new vitality. Towns and regions have sought to retain their identities by renewing old traditions. A few have even invented new festivities. At the same time, commercialization and tourism have corrupted ancient customs while producing the revenue that favors their survival. In this sense, the world of Spanish *fiestas* is a model

10. Children laying out a carpet of flowers for Corpus Christi, Sitges (Barcelona), 1987. Photograph by Cristina García Rodero, Getty Research Institute, Research Library, 90.R.34.

11. *Fiesta* of San Fermín, Pamplona, July 6, 1995. Photograph by Rafa Rivas, courtesy *El Mundo del País Vasco*.

12. *Cabezudo* (fathead) "Vinegar-Face" and child, *fiesta* of San Fermín, Pamplona, July 1983. Photograph by Cristina García Rodero, Getty Research Institute, Research Library, 90.R.34.

13. Child and drunken man, celebration of *Moros y cristianos*, Alcoy (Alicante), 1981. Photograph by Cristina García Rodero, Getty Research Institute, Research Library, 90.R.34.

of the country's predicament between past and present, local traditions and global influences. In spite of these opposing forces, the festive sense of life remains as strong as ever in Spain. A brief survey like this one fails to capture the variety, power and complexities of Spanish *fiestas*.

BULLS

If Spain is the most festive country in the world, it may also be one of the most tragic. Just as some writers speak of the Spaniard's festive sense, others (or the same) invoke his tragic sense of life, a phrase made permanent by the philosopher Miguel de Unamuno's essay of the same title.[14] The two points of view are not contradictory but complementary: since the Spanish live so hard, they have more to lose in death. Rather than ignore mortality as we do in the English-speaking countries, they seem to exalt it in their funerary rites, their devotion to ancestors and cemeteries, their preference for the Crucifixion over the Resurrection, and above all, in the *corrida de toros* or bullfight.

To begin, the bullfight is not a sport involving two evenly matched opponents who face each other in a spirit of fair play. These are Anglo–Saxon notions that will only distract us from comprehending the true nature of this uniquely Hispanic spectacle. The very word "bullfight" is a misnomer and a false translation from the Spanish *corrida de toros*, which means "running," not combating bulls. The English term fosters a mistaken mentality in which *toro* and *torero* are supposedly locked in mortal struggle. Knowledgeable aficionados realize that this is not the case. Some *matadores* have said that their art resembles dancing or lovemaking more than combat, man and animal participating together in a prescribed ritual.

The bullfight is a tragedy, for the animal must die and the man must expose himself to mortal danger. The sight of a tourist attending a *corrida* and rooting for the bull is a pathetic image of misunderstanding, of falsely imposing the values of one culture on another, in fact, of failing to understand the tragic sense of life. If the bull does not die, as in Portugal, there is no tragedy and the spectacle loses its drama and its reason for being.

Tragedy requires dignity, and the *toro bravo* or fighting bull is an animal of great dignity. The men making their living as *toreros* may perform with dignity too. As in any event involving humans and animals, however, there is great temptation for foul play. The abuses in the *corrida* are multitude. Some writers see them as part and parcel of the corruption that has plagued Spanish life for centuries.[15]

Some 4,500 books have been written about the bullfight in Spanish alone.

A few are good, most are not; there is something about the *corrida* that seems to attract the very best and the very worst in human nature. All we can do here is dispel a few misconceptions, cite the best sources and hope the reader will avoid the clichés that surround the subject. As we have done with regard to *fiestas*, we might be tempted to advise the reader to attend as many *corridas* as possible. Unfortunately it would take months of travel and great expense to penetrate the arcane world of the bullfight, and the adventurer would have to endure many terrible afternoons in order to enjoy a few moments of beauty on the sand.

We have already dispelled the first misconception, that the *corrida* is a sport. The second misconception is that the *toro bravo* is no more than a bovine in a bullring. It is much more—the descendant of a species related to the wild animals that once roamed the primitive forests of Europe. They were hunted for thousands of years and were finally reduced to one place in the world, the Iberian Peninsula. As Hemingway said, the *toro bravo* is as different from a domestic bull as a wolf from a dog. He is the true king of beasts: in gory Roman circuses, the fighting bull was set against bears, lions, tigers, elephants and other wild creatures, usually destroying them. If *toreros* did not possess weapons of guile and steel, there would be no tragedy or dignity, only wanton slaughter of man by beast.

Misconception number three is that all Spaniards are enamored of the *corrida*. The American Paul Theroux says: "Bullfights are as frequent on Spanish television as football games. . . . Spaniards, not a people noted for finding common agreement on anything, are almost unanimous in their enthusiasm for bullfighting."[16] In fact less than half the population consider themselves to be aficionados, and no more than a third actually go to the bullring. These figures plunge even lower in certain parts of the country like Galicia and Asturias, where *corridas* are almost as out of place as they would be in Scotland and Wales. However, we should note that there has been increasing enthusiasm in the last twenty years. While the spectacle used to be a typical male prerogative, women have joined men at the *plaza de toros* under the new democracy (see Photograph 14). The recent popularity of the *corrida* parallels the greater enthusiasm for *fiestas* and other customs, caused by a similar reaction to the conformity of modern life.

In spite of increased attendance in recent years, the spectacle also has more vocal enemies. Spain's animal rights lobby regularly conducts campaigns against the *corrida*. Its members have persuaded some local governments to outlaw bullfights; this has been done almost exclusively in regions without a strong taurine tradition, like Catalonia and the Canary Islands. Criticism from inside the country, combined with attacks by northern European del-

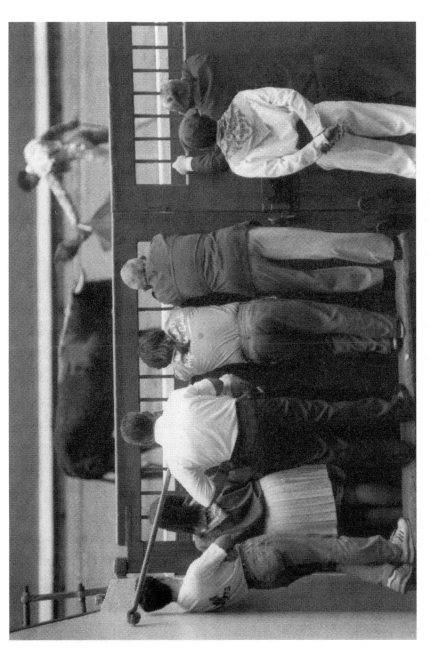

14. Spectators and bullfight, Bilbao, 1994. Photograph by Iñaki, courtesy *El Mundo del País Vasco.*

egates to the European Union, have submitted bullfighting to more pressure than ever before.

The fourth and last misconception is that brave bulls only appear in formal *corridas*. Actually only about 5 percent of taurine events are professional events for full-grown animals (five years old). Other events include *becerradas* for one-year-old calves; *novilladas* for three or four-year-old bulls; festivals for charity; *recortadores* who practice the art of bull-dodging; *capeas* and *encierros*, the running of brave calves, cows or bulls in thousands of cities, towns and villages, nearly always during patronal celebrations (see Photograph 15). Cristina García Rodero shows one of these events during the annual *fiesta* in the port of Denia (Alicante), in which a magnificent fighting bull has pursued the men and boys right down to the seawall (see Photograph 16).

SPORTS AND GAMES

Modern sports developed slowly in Spain. Until the early 1900s, "sport" referred to hunting and fishing. Most people were sedentary, with the exception of farmers and manual laborers. Exercise for Spaniards meant going to their local bar for a cup of coffee or a glass of wine. But most people also participated in the customary *paseo* or stroll, in which males and females walked in opposite directions around the town square in the late afternoon or early evening. This continues to be the most popular physical activity in the country, with no less than 90 percent of the population still taking the *paseo* daily or several times a week.

Democracy has brought greater participation in sports by all, men and women, young and old. The Constitution of 1978 gave the country's seventeen semiautonomous regions the responsibility for promoting sports, physical education and leisure. Like all modern countries, Spain now has a culture of sports.

Traditional games have survived more than in most western countries. These activities developed in relation to the festive calendar. *Chapas* or "coins," for example, similar to the game of marbles, was played most commonly during Easter Week; *taba* or knucklebones was seen during the feast of St. Casilda in May; and *calva*, a primitive form of bowling, was practiced around the feast of St. Anthony in June. Nowadays these games, if played at all, can be observed any time of year, weather permitting. The same could be said of two pre-Spanish activities in the Canary Islands, sailing lateen-rigged boats and *lucha canaria* (wrestling).

The Basque area, which overlaps the border between Spain and France, has preserved traditional sports and games more than any other region in

15. *Recortador* (bull-dodger), San Sebastián de los Reyes (Madrid), February 1996. Copyright © Fernando Manuel Durán Blázquez.

16. *Bous de la mar* (bulls of the sea), Denia (Alicante), 1987. Photograph by Cristina García Rodero, Getty Research Institute, Research Library, 90.R.34.

the Peninsula. They are still performed in conjunction with patronal feasts. Many involve some form of betting, even more of a passion in this area than in other parts of the country.

Basque sports and games show their agricultural origins. Men compete in chopping down beech trees with an axe; mowing grass with a scythe; lifting bales of hay, wooden carts, or quarry stones weighing as much as 650 pounds (see Photograph 17); in tug-of-wars and in pulling oxen or bulls with a rope. Farm animals have their own contests: dogs herd sheep and oxen drag huge stones that weigh up to three thousand three hundred pounds. These competitions all require strength, in both men and animals; they derive from the daily chores of farmers, shepherds and loggers.

The only traditional Basque sport to spread beyond the region is *pelota* or *jai alai*, reputedly the fastest ball game in the world. It has been likened to squash, but this is like comparing tennis to ping-pong: the *jai alai* court is much larger (about fifty meters in length), the play faster and more spectacular. The Basque word *jai alai* means "sprightly" or "lively" game—a perfectly accurate description. It developed as a loose, informal competition that followed archaic rules and the honor system, but has grown in modern times into a formal, regulated sport with immense sums of money at stake. Although its international headquarters is located in Madrid, *jai alai* can be seen in Spanish America (Mexico, Argentina and Uruguay) and the United States (especially in Florida) as well as Spain. Basque and Navarrese players dominate the game worldwide.

Pelota (ball) in various forms is also popular in other parts of northern Spain. It is often played without the characteristic *txistera* or wicker basket of *jai alai*, and resembles handball. One survey counted 1,422 courts in Castile-León, 891 in Valencia, 616 in the Basque Country and 483 in Navarra. *Pelota* may be the closest thing to a national sport in Spain, although it is played very little in the south.

Soccer is the world's most popular sport and Spain is no exception. It is played, watched and read about far more than the *corrida*. Matches routinely attract crowds of 100,000 fans. The "beautiful game" sustains weekly and daily newspapers, supports multimillion-dollar betting pools and fills hours of radio and television programming. Spain is a country of *fútbol* (soccer) fever (see Photograph 18).

Although Spain has never won a World Cup or even played in the finals, it ranks seventh in the historical ranking of teams throughout the world. The country's premiere club, Real Madrid, has won more European Cups than any other team. Its great rival, Fútbol Club Barcelona, has participated in more European championships than any other club.

17. The Basque Perurena lifts a stone weighing 261 kilos (574 pounds), *fiesta* of San Fermín, Lesaca (Navarra), 1988. Photograph by Cristina García Rodero, Getty Research Institute, Research Library, 90.R.34.

18. *Fútbol* fever. Fans of Athletic of Bilbao celebrate a victory in their home stadium, 1989. Photograph by Iñaki, courtesy *El Mundo del País Vasco.*

Real Madrid and "Barça" dominate Spanish soccer. Their rivalry reflects the ancient competition between Castile and Catalonia, the most powerful regions in the country. Each club has some 100,000 members. Joking about the two, a writer said parents "make their babies members while they are still hanging from their umbilical cords."[17] In Catalonia, supporting Barça is a matter of regional pride; in fact the team's dark-blue and deep-red jerseys closely resemble the Catalan flag. "To see Catalan patriotism in full collective cry," noted one observer, "go to the stadium one night when a big soccer game—Barça versus Madrid, ideally—is on, and 120,000 throats are bawling in chorus for the home team while the heraldic figures dash and dodge on the unnaturally green field and tiny frantic bats skitter through the arc-lighted air."[18]

A memorable truce between the two giants of Spanish soccer occurred in the 1992 Olympic Games held in Barcelona. Spain met Poland in the finals. To their own surprise, many Catalans waved Spanish flags and pulled for the national team that fielded players from both Barça and Real Madrid. Castilians were equally surprised to find themselves rooting for the same team as their habitual rivals, in the Camp Nou stadium no less. The Spaniards took the match and one of a record thirteen gold medals in their best Olympic effort in history. The Barcelona Games were Spain's coming of age in athletics. (Four years later Spanish athletes collected seventeen medals in the Atlanta Olympics, followed in 2000 by eleven in Sydney.)

The country has also excelled in other sports. Miguel Indurain prevailed in cycling for almost fifteen years, winning an incredible five Tour de France, two Giro d'Italia, one Vuelta a España, a World Championship in 1995 and an Olympic gold medal in 1996. The Navarrese superstar has been called the greatest Spanish athlete of all time.

Tennis is the other major sport in which Spain has excelled on the international level. Players like Arantxa Sánchez Vicario, Conchita Martínez and Sergi Bruguera have won major tournaments and made the sport more popular among Spanish youth. At the 1994 French Open, Spanish tennis probably had its highest moment: Bruguera beat his compatriot Alberto Berasategui in the men's finals, Sánchez Vicario took the women's and Jacobo Díaz won the men's junior title. When Martínez took the women's singles at Wimbledon that year, journalists spoke of a new "Spanish Armada" invading England on the tennis courts rather than on the high seas. At the French Open in 2000, Spain showed the depth of its talent by placing no less than five out of eight men and women in the singles quarterfinals, although none ended as a winner.

Golf has gained new popularity in Spain—the first country other than the United States or the United Kingdom to host the Ryder Cup. The country has produced several international champions in the 1980s and 1990s: Severiano Ballesteros, José María Olazábal and Sergio García. Ballesteros won the Masters twice and the British Open three times, Olazábal also took the Masters twice, and García is sometimes called the next Tiger Woods.

WINES AND FOODS

Most books speak of foods and wines in that order. We will reverse the terms, using the Spanish order: first a little wine to wet the palate, followed by some *tapas* or snacks to stimulate the appetite for a full meal.

Spaniards do nothing in moderation; their drinking habits are no exception. The country is among the world's two or three largest producers of grapes. Its wines have the sun and soil in them, and they bring great happiness to the people.

Drinking habits impose a special rhythm on daily life, closely linked to eating. As in most wine-producing countries, Spaniards place a high value on food. They spend more time and money on eating and drinking than the peoples of most western nations.

The incidence of alcoholism is very low for a country that consumes so much wine, beer and distilled beverages. People usually drink with others; the solitary alcoholic rarely makes a scene. Imbibing is an essential part of the daily schedule described early in this chapter, especially during the periods before lunch and supper. Drinks are usually accompanied by *tapas*, the "small foods" or snacks that have become the rage in restaurants throughout the world. As in other predominantly wine-producing nations, the people of Spain suffer from heart ailments less than the inhabitants of milk-producing countries: between 1960 and 1990, for example, the incidence was only half as high as Denmark's and a third as high as Britain's.

In his classic *Notes on a Cellar-Book*, George Saintsbury says, "No reasonable person should quarrel if we begin with Sherry, even as the truly good and wise usually do at dinner."[19] We will do the same. Sherry in fact is the country's prime glory of the grape, a drink that was created and perfected in Spain. To be more precise, we should say Andalusia, the only region in the country allowed to use the official name of *jerez*, or sherry (from the city of Jerez de la Frontera in the province of Cádiz). While vintners in several countries have been able to match some of the legendary table wines of Europe, nobody has come close to making sherries like those of the venerable *bodegas* in southwestern Spain, known as "the cathedrals of wine." Their cellars contain about one million casks, each containing five hundred liters of the liquid gold.

Even more than the viticulture of red, white and rosé wines, sherry-making is an art that requires ample time and expertise. *Jerez* is fortified, which means that the natural process of fermentation is halted by the addition of brandy. Before bottling, sherries age in oak barrels and are continually blended with other wines of various ages in a complex technique known as the *solera* system. (*Solera* means "wine lees," "tradition" or "quality.") Strictly speaking then, there are no vintage sherries; nearly all are blends. The resulting nectar ranges from slightly salty, bone-dry *manzanilla* made only on the coast, to dry, straw-pale *fino*, older, nuttier *amontillado*, fuller, darker *oloroso* and opaque, rich cream or "old brown." There is a time and a place for every variety. The drier sherries, preferably served chilled, can be drunk alone or with *tapas* to whet the appetite, and some gourmands use them to accompany a first course of hors d'oeuvres, soup, or salad. The medium-bodied wines of Jerez are extremely versatile and go well with almost any snack. Finally, the sweet, full-bodied sherries can accompany dessert or be enjoyed like an after-dinner liqueur.

More than a mere drink, sherry is a way of life in southern Spain. Its apotheosis comes every year at the famous *feria* in Sevilla, which could be described as a *fiesta* of sherry. Untold amounts of *fino* flow during this week-long, springtime celebration of flamenco, bullfighting and *jerez*, the supreme creations of Andalusian culture.

Like sherry, Spanish "table" wines are commonly drunk before the main repasts of lunch and dinner, as well as during meals. Most of the country's production is mediocre, "three-man" wine because it takes two men to hold down a third to make him drink it. But a growing number of regions have *denominación de origen* or mark of origin, the Spanish equivalent of the French *appellation contrôlée* that guarantees the source and quality of the product. La Rioja, the smallest autonomous region in Spain, once made the best table wines in the country—especially reds. They are quite similar to French Bordeaux, with their deep color, rich bouquet, complex flavors and abundant tannins for aging. Other areas of Spain now compete with La Rioja at home and abroad: Old Castile with its prestigious Rueda and Ribera del Duero, including Vega Sicilia, the most famous winery in Spain; New Castile with the more plebeian Valdepeñas, mother's milk to Sancho Panza; Aragón with Cariñena; Navarra with clear rosés; Galicia with purplish Ribeiro and golden Albariño; the Levant with hearty, sun-filled wines from Utiel-Requena, Yecla and Jumilla; Catalonia with fine reds and whites from Penedès, Priorato and other areas. Nearly all of Spain's *cavas* or sparkling wines also come from the Catalan region, which produces more bubbly than any other place in the world. The European Union has recognized *cava* as the first mark of origin that is not the name of a geographical region.

After a hearty three-course meal washed down with wine, the Spaniard may finish with a liqueur or spirit: brandy from Jerez de la Frontera; Basque *pacharán* made with sloes or blackthorn berries; *anís* or *anisette*; Galician *orujo* or *marc*, a firewater derived from the residue of wine grapes. We should not forget the many elixirs made from herbs by monks who follow ancient, secret recipes.

No discussion of drinking habits in Spain should omit *sangría*, the refreshing mixture of red wine, *gaseosa* (sweet carbonated soda), sugar and chopped fruits that is normally imbibed during the long summers. Spaniards are also drinking more beer all the time, in bottle or in draft. In Asturias, the regional drink is *sidra*, a cloudy hard cider that is poured with the drinker holding the bottle high in the air with one hand and pouring into a glass extended below the waist in the other hand, with the purpose of creating effervescence (see Photograph 19). The Asturians have a proverb that says, "We may have lost paradise because of the apple, but we'll get it back with cider."

Spain is one of the world's last paradises of food. It has been so for a long time. Eight hundred years ago, King Alfonso the Wise declared "Spain is rich in honeys, abundant in fruits, teeming with fish, well provided with milk . . . filled with deer and hunt, covered with cattle, merry with good wine, happy with an abundance of bread and sugar . . . well stocked with oil and fragrant with saffron."[20]

The people of Spain spare no effort to find, prepare and eat the most diverse fare imaginable. Fishing fleets spend months on the high seas catching cod, hake and other prized species; Asturian scuba divers plunge for sea urchins on wave-pounded shores; Galicians descend on ropes to gather goose barnacles on sea-lashed rocks; Catalans hunt for precious truffles, jewels of the forest, with trained dogs; Castilians, Basques and Navarrese scour woods and fields for wild mushrooms, which cause deaths every year; Manchegan peasants patiently separate the reddish pistils from six hundred crocus flowers to obtain a single ounce of saffron, the world's most precious spice, worth its weight in gold.

A country's cuisine is its landscape in a cooking pot, said the Catalan writer Josep Pla.[21] The remarkable fare of his native region, combining fish or crustaceans with meat or poultry, is expressed in the saying "*mar i muntanya*" (sea and mountain). The fish and shellfish of Galicia remind us of its deep *rías* and rocky coast. The wild salmon and *fabada* of Asturias evoke its

19. The proper way to pour *sidra* or cider, Moreda de Aller (Asturias), 1988. Photograph by Cristina García Rodero, Getty Research Institute, Research Library, 90.R.34.

streams and smokehouses. The fish, crustaceans, mushrooms and cheeses of the Basque Country recall its fishing ports and mountain villages. The trout and red peppers of Navarra bring to mind its rushing creeks and lush alluvial plains. The crusty breads and *cocido* of Castile contain its golden fields of wheat and acres of chickpeas. The *paella*, oranges and lemons of the Levant evoke the ricefields of the Albufera and the citrus groves of the *Huerta*. The fried fish and *gazpacho* of Andalusia are its sandy beaches and endless olive groves in a pan or bowl.

Before we overstimulate our appetites, we should dispel two general misconceptions about the foods of Spain. From the outset, *Spanish* cooking must be distinguished from *Spanish-American*. Spanish-American foods are often hot and spicy; Spanish viands rarely so. The New World's contribution to the mother country lies not in recipes but in ingredients like tomatoes, peppers, potatoes, corn, coffee and chocolate. Penelope Casas, a leading authority on Spanish cuisine, states that she does not know of a single recipe in the Peninsula that imitates a dish from Mexico or South America.

A second misconception is that there is a single Spanish cuisine. As we have done before, we must look first to the *patria chica*, not the nation: most cooking follows local and regional lines. Casas says, "Each region of Spain is . . . a cultural and gastronomic world in itself, defying generalization."[22] Nevertheless, the globalization of eating habits in recent years has created a few dishes that can be found almost anywhere in the country: *gazpacho, paella* and *tortilla española* or omelette, for example. But each of these dishes began as a local specialty before expanding to other areas. *Gazpacho* is Andalusian in origin, *paella* Valencian, the "Spanish" omelette Castilian.

While the cuisines of Spain's regions are extremely diverse, they have some things in common. Daily eating follows a similar schedule in all parts of the country, though it tends to be still later in the South. The peoples of nearly every region share a taste for fresh fish; we have seen that Spain consumes more than any other nation except Japan. Spaniards from many areas also share a love of pork products in every imaginable form. As Richard Ford said, "Bacon throughout the length and breadth of the Peninsula is more honored . . . than any one or all the fathers of the Church in Rome; the hunger after the flesh of the pig is equalled only by the thirst for the contents of what is put afterwards into his skin."[23] In the Middle Ages, eating pork was proof that a person was not a Muslim or Jew; Christians loved bacon on both religious and gastronomic grounds. No other country offers such a vast range of pork, from tender, juicy suckling pig to fresh loin chops, a bewildering array of *chorizo* in all sizes and colors, *salchichón* or salami, *mor-*

cilla or blood sausage, *sobrasada* or sausage spread, white or black Catalan *butifarra* and finally the deep-red, finely-marbled, air-cured hams, made from Iberian pigs fed on acorns, a diet that gives their flesh a delicate, nutty taste that is unmatched by any other meat in the world. The best hams are cured from one to three years in mountain areas like the Sierra de Aracena in Andalusia, producer of Jabugo, the most cherished in Spain. These delicacies are known throughout the country as *jamón serrano* or mountain ham. Photograph 20 shows roast suckling pig, seasoned lightly with garlic, along with other delicacies. The best *cochinillo* is so tender that one can cut through its crunchy, golden skin with the side of a plate, without a knife.

Spaniards from all regions also share a taste for cheese. At the last count, the country had eleven varieties with mark of origin. Some of the best-known are mild Tetilla ("little tit") and San Simón (smoked) from Galicia; creamy Cabrales (veined blue) from Asturias; pungent Picón (three-milk blue) and Quesucos (smoked or plain) from Cantabria; prized Idiazábal (smoked or plain) from the Basque Country, ivory-colored Roncal from Navarre, Queso de la Serena from Extremadura and nutty Manchego from New Castile, all made from sheep's milk; Camerano (cottage cheese) from La Rioja; Mató (fresh goat) and Montsec (cured goat) from Catalonia; hard Tronchón from Aragón; buttery Mahón (preserved with oil and paprika) from the Balearic Islands; Herreño, Majorero and Palmero from the Canaries (goat cheeses).

Before the reader dies of hunger, we will end this chapter with a culinary tour of the Peninsula. Galicia has Europe's largest fishing fleet and some of the world's best fish and crustaceans, like *pulpo á feira* ("fairground octopus"), almost a national dish; the tastiest beef in the Peninsula, thanks to year-round green pastures; *caldo gallego*, a hearty potage made from cabbage, white beans, ham knuckle and *chorizo; lacón con grelos*, salted ham with turnip tops; *empanadas*, turnovers containing veal, fish or crustaceans with garlic, onions and peppers; round, white-frosted *tartas de Santiago*, almond tarts topped with a stamped red cross of St. James.

Asturias has its legendary *fabada*, a hearty winter stew made from white beans, cured pork, *chorizo* and blood sausage; wild salmon prepared with *serrano* ham; and *tarta de manzana*, a tart made from the best apples in Spain.

Cantabria has fresh or preserved sardines and anchovies, abundant shellfish, mountain stews with pork and venison, milk-based desserts like *flan* (caramel custard), *leche frita* (fried milk or deep-fried custard) and *arroz con leche* (rice pudding).

In a nation that boasts some of the world's most delicious foods, the Basque Country has the best in both quantity and quality: fresh fish, lamb or beef cooked outdoors over wooden fires; *marmitako* or fisherman's stew

20. *Cochinillo* (roast suckling pig) and other foods, Botín, Madrid, 2001. Hemingway describes this restaurant in *The Sun Also Rises*. Courtesy Antonio González, Jr.

made from fresh *bonito*, tomatoes, peppers and potatoes; Spain's greatest variety of cured fish; silvery, spaghetti-thin baby eels cooked with garlic and flecks of dried red peppers; terrines of rabbit; pigeons stuffed with *foie gras*; and *pastel vasco* or Basque tart filled with ice cream, or perhaps a *suspiro de Bilbao* ("sigh of Bilbao"), an airy almond meringue that will round off any meal.

Navarra does not lag behind its neighbor: trout prepared with cured ham; white asparagus as thick as thumbs, served with homemade mayonnaise; fresh artichokes with clams; the famous *pimientos del piquillo* or small, hot peppers grilled over an open fire, skinned, seeded and stuffed or cooked with fish, crustaceans or mushrooms; omelettes with tender green asparagus and salt cod (*bacalao*); enormous cutlets and braised steer made from fighting bulls; *chistorra*, a thin, spicy air-dried sausage fried and eaten by itself or with potatoes, green bell peppers or scrambled eggs; wild berries from the Pyrenees for dessert, topped with whipped crème fraîche. Like the neighboring Basques, Navarrese men take eating so seriously that they belong to gastronomic clubs (*txokos*).

La Rioja has meats and vegetables worthy of its noble wines—*calderete* or lamb stew; *pochas* or baby fava beans cooked with quail; trout roasted with wild mushrooms and red wine; desserts like *mazapanes de Soto*, marzipan balls prepared from almonds, boiled potatoes, sugar and lemon zest; peaches soaked in red Rioja; and wine sorbet.

Nearby Aragón is famous for its trout, game and *chilindrón* dishes—chicken, pork or lamb cooked with the region's red peppers, so tasty that they have been called "the shellfish of the hinterland." Other specialties include *ajoarriero*, a free-for-all dish normally cooked with dried cod, but with many choices for the remaining ingredients, from cauliflower to potatoes, lobster to dogfish, snails to crayfish. We could finish a meal in Aragón with some of the region's candied fruits, wrapped in foil and packed in little wooden boxes.

The cuisine of Catalonia is more like that of a country than a region: creative combinations of fish and meat; fish or crustaceans cooked with the startling *romesco* sauce of ground almonds and sweet red peppers, with truffles or wild mushrooms; *suquet de peix* or fish stew; snails and wild mushrooms; a *calçotada* of fresh green onions barbecued to a crisp then served on baked terra cotta in a *salbitxada* or piquant sauce of almonds and tomatoes; to finish, fresh strawberries served with *cava* and a hint of lemon, *crema catalana*—Catalan crème brûlée—or *mel i mató*, unsalted curd cheese with honey.

When we travel south from Catalonia, we move into Valencia where rice is a way of life. Here the world's best *paellas* are made, preferably on the beach over a wooden fire, with fish, crustaceans and vegetables; or an *arroz a la banda*, a simpler dish of rice and fish; rice cooked with fresh squid to give it an inky color; *fideua* or noodle *paella*; fish, chicken or duck prepared with the region's sweet oranges. We could have a *leche merengada* or lemon and cinnamon-flavored ice milk to digest the rice, or one of the many Levantine varieties of *turrón* or almond nougat, made according to ancient recipes inherited from the Arabs.

Further south in Murcia, we cross immense market gardens, Spain's equivalent to California, where vegetables can be harvested all year round: fresh capers the size of large olives, Europe's best artichokes, juicy tomatoes and onions for a mixed salad, or *ensalada murciana* of ripe tomatoes, red peppers, onions, capers and pickled tuna; *remojón de bacalao* with boiled cod, onions, olives and oranges; a sea salad with mussels, langostinos, squid, mushrooms and capers; salted tuna fillets (*mojama*) or the precious salted roe (*hueva*) from the Mar Menor or inland sea, priced at more than $50 a pound; fresh figs or mulberries for dessert, fruits of the Murcian *Huerta*.

Moving inland to La Mancha, we should eat a dish seasoned with the area's prized saffron, such as a *tojunto* made from beef or rabbit and tomatoes; game like wild boar, deer, rabbit, hare, partridge and quail; a *pisto manchego*, the Manchegan ratatouille or medley of tomatoes, red and green bell peppers, zucchini, onions and garlic; stuffed eggplants; mushrooms with garlic; sweet *bizcochos borrachos* or "tipsy sponge cakes." In other parts of Castile and León we can find the best suckling pig and lamb in Spain; León's famous *cecina* or smoked, air-dried beef, served in thin slices like *serrano* ham; the *olla podrida* or "rotten stew" containing everything from pig's ear and feet to bacon, cured ham, *chorizo, morcilla* and garbanzos; Madrid's abundant *cocido*, the city's staple diet, customarily served in three separate courses—soup, vegetables and meats; *callos a la madrileña* or tripe; fried calf's sweetbreads; a dozen varieties of omelette; traditional Castilian pastries like honey-soaked *pestiños* and cream-filled *bartolillos*. While near the capital, we should also indulge ourselves in *churros con chocolate*, deep-fried fritters with hot chocolate so thick that a wooden spoon, used to stir it, will stand up straight in the cup.

In neighboring Extremadura, we find the home of the Iberian pig, who feed on the region's plentiful acorns from cork and oak trees; some of Spain's most wonderful sausages; *migas* or fried breadcrumbs with peppers and bacon; a *frite* of fried lamb with onion, garlic, lemon and paprika; baked leg of kid; *caldereta* or Extremaduran meat stew; *pollo al padre Pero*, an alliterative dish of young chicken simmered in a spicy sauce of tomatoes and peppers; pastries soaked in honey.

Andalusia has been called the frying pan of Spain, both for its climate and its cuisine. Here we could start our meal with *pescaíto frito* or mixed fried fish (fresh anchovies, sardines, mullet and whiting), or a cold *gazpacho*; cured tuna; *pinchos morunos* or Moorish kebabs, either as a *tapa* or main dish; oxtail with prunes; stuffed partridges with anchovy fillets and *serrano* ham, baked in sherry wine. Perhaps more than any other region of Spain, Andalusia's convents offer heavenly temptations lovingly prepared by nuns who follow ancient recipes: puff pastries, almond cookies, lemon cakes, *canastillas* or little baskets with jelly and almonds, *mantecados* and *polvorones*, cakes and shortbread wrapped in thin white paper; *yemas* or confections made from egg yolks and sugar. Some of these treats still bear the names of famous nuns or convents: *yemas de Santa Teresa* from the Carmelite nuns of Avila, *yemas de San Leandro* from Sevilla, *yemas de San Pablo* from a religious order in Cáceres.

We will end our gastronomical tour of Spain in the two island chains. In the Balearics we should start the day with an *ensaimada*, a coiled pastry sprinkled with powdered sugar and taken with morning coffee. For lunch we could try squid with summer salad; a Russian salad made with diced vegetables and homemade mayonnaise, invented on the island of Mahón; a *tumbet* or layered potato and eggplant pie; *escaldums* or braised turkey with almonds; "dirty rice" with hare, liver and chicken; *sopes mallorquines* or one-pot cabbage stew; snails with paprika sausage; *coca* or Mallorcan pizza covered with vegetables, pine nuts or fresh sardines, or alternatively with a sweet filling as dessert.

Finally, on the Canary Islands we should take advantage of the exotic fruits like mango, papaya and prickly pears. We should also try the traditional *gofio* or poor man's bread, a versatile whole-grain meal that can be combined with broth for a first course, with pork cracklings as a main dish and with milk and honey as a dessert. Nor should we forget to try one of the islands' famous dishes with *mojo*, a cold red or green sauce based on oil, vinegar and spices to season potatoes, fish and meat. We could also order *carajacas* or marinated liver; a *puchero canario* or island stew. If it is Carnival time—the highlight of the year for many islanders—we could try *truchas*, crisp, golden yellow buns stuffed with sweet potatoes, almonds, lemon rind, cinnamon and almonds, sprinkled with confectioners' sugar. Then we would be ready to begin the Lenten season with a vow to eat less food.

Up to this point we have discussed traditional foods in the Peninsula. We will end with a brief mention of the new Spanish cuisine that has become an international sensation in the late 1990s and early 2000s. It all started in the Basque Country—that great bastion of eating—around 1975. A group of young, adventurous chefs tried applying the concepts of French *nouvelle cuisine* to their own region. Names like Arguiñano, Arzak, Berasategui and Subijana became known all over Europe. The second revolution commenced in Catalonia about ten years later, when another group of young cooks decided that their region could do something similar, but with a more Mediterranean accent. They went even farther than the Basques in deconstructing traditional cuisine, destroying the boundaries between courses and creating a remarkable new style based on foams, gelatins and savory ice creams. Food critics have compared some of these Catalan chefs to Spanish surrealist painter Salvador Dalí in their flamboyant creativity. The trend has now spread to other areas of Spain and is drawing thousands of gastronomic tourists to the country. There seems to be no limit to what can happen in Spanish kitchens today.

SELECTED READINGS

General

Ford, Richard. *Gatherings from Spain*. 1846; reprint London: J. M. Dent & Sons, 1970.

Gibson, Ian, *Fire in the Blood: The New Spain*. London: Faber and Faber, 1992.

Hooper, John. *The New Spaniards*. London: Penguin, 1995.

Josephs, Allen. *White Wall of Spain: The Mysteries of Andalusian Culture*. Ames: Iowa State University Press, 1983.

Rodgers, Eamonn, ed. *Encyclopedia of Contemporary Spanish Culture*. London and New York: Routledge, 1999.

Sex, Marriage and Family

De Miguel, Amando. *La sociedad española, 1996–97*. Madrid: Editorial Complutense, 2001.

Graham, Helen, and Jo Labanyi, eds. *Spanish Cultural Studies: An Introduction. The Struggle for Modernity*. Oxford: Oxford University Press, 1995.

Malo de Molina, Carlos A. *Los españoles y la sexualidad*. Madrid: Temas de Hoy, 1992.

Fiestas

Caro Baroja, Julio. *El estío festivo (Fiestas populares del verano)*. Madrid: Taurus, 1984.

García Rodero, Cristina. *España Oculta: Public Celebrations in Spain, 1974–1989*.

Foreword by Julio Caro Baroja. Introduction by Mary M. Crain. Washington, DC: Smithsonian Institution Press, 1990.

Stanton, Edward F. "Fiestas." In *Handbook of Spanish Popular Culture*, 51–79. Westport, CT: Greenwood Press, 1999.

Bulls

Claramunt, Fernando. *Historia ilustrada de la tauromaquia*. 2 vols. Madrid: Espasa Calpe, 1989.

Cossío, José María. *Los toros: tratado técnico e histórico*. 12 vols. Madrid: Espasa Calpe, 1943–1997. Known as the bible of bullfighting.

Douglass, Carrie B. *Bulls, Bullfighting, and Spanish Identities*. Tucson: University of Arizona Press, 1997.

Hemingway, Ernest. *Death in the Afternoon*. 1932; reprint New York: Scribner's, 1960.

Mitchell, Timothy. *Blood Sport: A Social History of Bullfighting*. Philadelphia: University of Pennsylvania Press, 1991.

Stanton, Edward F. "Bulls." In *Handbook of Spanish Popular Culture*, 81–109. Westport, CT: Greenwood Press, 1999.

Toros: Los toros hacia el tercer milenio. Madrid: Espasa Calpe, 2000.

Sports and Games

García Ferrando, Manuel. *Aspectos sociales del deporte. Una reflexión sociológica*. Madrid: Alianza, 1990.

London, John. "The Ideology and Practice of Sport." In *Spanish Cultural Studies: An Introduction: The Struggle for Modernity*, edited by Helen Graham and Jo Labanyi, 204–207. Oxford: Oxford University Press, 1995.

Moreno Palos, Cristóbal. *Juegos y deportes tradicionales en España*. Madrid: Alianza, 1999.

Stanton, Edward F. "Sports and Games." In *Handbook of Spanish Popular Culture*, 111–125. Westport, CT: Greenwood Press, 1999.

Wines and Foods

Casas, Penelope. *The Foods and Wines of Spain*. New York: Knopf, 1996.

De Miguel, Amando. *La sociedad española, 1996–97*. Madrid: Editorial Complutense, 1997.

Grimes, William. "The Trouble with Sherry: It's Misunderstood." *New York Times* (December 1, 1999): B10.

Spain (Eyewitness Travel Guides). New York: DK Publishing, 1996.

Trutter, Marion, ed. *Culinaria Spain*. Cologne: Könemann, 1998.

OTHER SOURCES

The search engines "Olé," "Sí, Spain" and the Iberian Studies Web from Brigham Young University have dozens of websites related to Spanish customs.

For *fiestas*, see "Cultura: España: Folklore" for an enormous list of towns, cities and regions with their celebrations: <http://www.ole.es/Paginas/Cultura/Esp@na/Folklore/>. The Getty Museum and Research Center in Los Angeles has more than six thousand of Cristina García Rodero's photographs; together, they make up an invaluable record of Spanish *fiestas*.

For bulls and bullfighting, the Los Angeles Public Library probably has the most extensive collection in the United States. On the World Wide Web, consult "El Web de PcToros; Mundo Taurino (Internet)," maintained by Stanley Conrad from San Diego, CA; "Tauromaquia," maintained by former matador Mario Carrión; "Torero, Torero," maintained by Rosa Jaramillo; and "Rough Guide to Bullfighting" at <http://mundo-taurino.org>. The World Society for the Protection of Animals (WSPA) has websites devoted to the issue of bullfighting: <http://www.way.net/wspa/zzbull.html> and <http://www.way.net/wspa/bullfact.html>. See also <http://www.peta-online.org/cmp/ccircfs6.html>.

For sports, see the website "Olé" and its special section on "Deportes": <http://www.terra.es>. The daily newspaper *Sport* can be reached through the Iberian Studies Web or directly at <http://ns.bon.servicom.es/sport>. Another site is <http://www.cybermundi.es/deportes.htm>.

For wines and foods, see the website "Olé" and its special section on gastronomy: <http://www.terra.es>.

4

Media

I share some of those peculiar and questionable qualities that mark those who practice this nocturnal and somewhat maligned trade [journalism], one that neither television nor the world of computers appears to be able to do away with.

—Juan Luis Cebrián[1]

Radio in Spain is something more than just radio.

—Manuel Vázquez Montalbán[2]

The very mention of the word television produces misgivings and reproofs.

—Eduardo Haro Tecglen[3]

The media in Spain are more visible and audible than in most western countries. The press constitutes a kind of "paper parliament" or "fourth estate" along with the three branches of government. It sets the agenda both for the state and the other media. Radio thrives in Spain's oral culture; it is the most popular in Europe and among the best in the world. Although Spaniards watch television more than any other Europeans except the British, this medium lags far behind the press and radio in originality and style. It has been plagued by political corruption from the outset.

The media have played an important role in Spain's conversion from dictatorship to democracy, yet the country still suffers from the totalitarian legacy of government control. More than twenty-five years after the death of dictator Francisco Franco, the state continues to be the country's largest media proprietor. The Catholic Church also intervenes in the press, radio and television, although its power has waned significantly. In recent years, multimedia groups have begun to compete with the state and Church. A small number of companies, abetted by foreign capital, now controls a large portion of the print and electronic media.

THE PRESS

One of the paradoxes of Spanish life is the visibility of the print media in a country where few people read. In the mid-1980s the government published a survey showing that more than half of all Spaniards had not read a single newspaper in their lives.[4] The same was true of books. "The best way to keep a secret in Spain is to publish it in a book," said former president Manuel Azaña.[5] The number of newspaper readers has grown in recent years—from 9 million in 1986 to 13 million in 1998—yet Spain still trails most of its European neighbors. This may be explained in part by the fact that people in the Mediterranean countries, with their strong oral culture, tend to read less than those in northern nations.

In spite of low readership, the press enjoys an extraordinary presence. One only has to walk around a Spanish city to see the colorful kiosks or newsstands located in strategic places on corners and sidewalks, in parks and plazas, in airports, train, bus and metro stations.

Every available space on the walls, the counter and on the opened-out doors is taken up with the vividly coloured covers of every conceivable kind of magazine. Usually there are so many on sale that the owner of the stall has to set out trestles at the front and sides to accommodate them. There are news magazines and general and special interest magazines, including a good number published in the States and elsewhere in Europe. There are humorous magazines, educational magazines, "adult" magazines . . . literary and scientific reviews . . . comics for children and comics for adults.[6]

In the nineteenth century these newsstands gave birth to *literatura de kiosko*—light, popular reading matter sold on the streets. The term now refers to any publication with mass appeal, whether sold at kiosks, in stationery shops or department stores.

Newsstands are a tribute to the Spanish genius for drama and display, for taking life to the streets. The common sight of people browsing, chatting and buying periodicals at kiosks serves as a healthy corrective to statistics on readership. Both are deceptive. On the one hand, Spaniards in fact read less than most Europeans. On the other, where they do read, in the major cities, they are very well informed, beneficiaries of superb writing and reporting.

The Spanish have never been in the habit of subscribing to newspapers and magazines. Since they live so much of their lives in public, it seems more sensible for them to purchase reading matter at a convenient newsstand. The act of buying a periodical at the neighborhood kiosk becomes a daily ritual like drinking coffee at the local café. What matters is not only the product but the process, the social interaction.

Because most periodicals are sold at kiosks and not by subscription, sales fluctuate wildly. This is especially true of magazines: their readers tend to be less loyal than those of dailies. One joke says that a Spanish man is more likely to change his wife or mistress than his newspaper, which may be closely related to his social, political and regional identity. Since men make up almost two-thirds of newspaper readers in Spain, the joke is no laughing matter. Women, by way of contrast, make up more than half of magazine readers. Their favorite periodicals belong to the so-called *prensa del corazón* (literally "press of the heart"), a genre that flourishes in the whole Spanish-speaking world. We will learn more about it later.

Once they purchase a periodical, Spaniards tend to share it with other readers more than consumers in other countries. In bars, cafés, offices and waiting rooms, one sees dog-eared copies of the daily press that have been read over and over by many people. This explains why only 10 percent of Spaniards buy newspapers while 25 percent manage to read them. Even nonreaders are eventually exposed to the main stories of the day when the radio and television report the news, taking the lead from the dailies, the real kings of the Spanish media. In fact there is a whole genre of radio and television shows called *revista de prensa* in which commentators review the headlines and editorials of the most important newspapers. In this and many other ways, the press is the most powerful branch of the media in Spain, and for this reason it has been called a "fourth estate" or "paper parliament." It establishes the content and tone of the national discourse that is one of the most exciting parts of Spanish life. It is much easier for a Spaniard to feel himself a part of this debate than in the United States, where power is diffused among many media, and television often exerts more influence than print journalism.

The primacy of the press has its good and bad sides. On the one hand, journalism can be sophisticated, comparable to the level of American news-papers like the *New York Times* and the *Washington Post*. Coverage tends to be extensive; dailies like *El País*, *El Mundo* and *ABC* run to seventy or eighty pages in their typical tabloid format. The space devoted to signed editorials may be the largest in the world, and constitutes the heart of each issue. The quality of reporting and writing is generally high; the separation between journalism and literature is not as distinct as in the Anglo-Saxon world. Most creative writers sooner or later earn a living as reporters or columnists. The most famous example is Francisco Umbral, who wrote for the liberal *El País* during the late 1970s and the 1980s, then shifted to the more conservative *El Mundo*, perhaps sensing Spain's drift to the right. He is a well-known novelist and essayist who displays a consistently brilliant use of the Spanish language in his column, day after day, week after week. It is as if a distin-guished American writer like Saul Bellow wrote six full-length articles a week for an American newspaper, nonstop for twenty-five years.

There is also a negative side to the press's sway over all other media. Journalism in Spain resembles a liberal profession more than a trade. News-papermen—males still dominate the field—comprise an intellectual elite who are fully aware of their prestige. They consider themselves intellectuals who write for other members of the intelligentsia.[7] Buying and reading the press in Spain is a bourgeois habit. This explains in part the contrast between mostly male, educated, middle-class consumers of the daily press and a larger underclass of poorly educated men and women who do not buy newspapers. There is really no equivalent of the populist press in Spain, nothing like the sensationalistic *New York Daily News*, the British *Sun* or the German *Bild Zeitung*. These down-market broadsheets do not contain the best journalism in the world, but they attract a large number of people who otherwise might read nothing at all. This is precisely what most of the poor and uneducated do in Spain—ignore newspapers and magazines.

Although it is easy to find fault with the Spanish press, we must remember that it has had less than thirty years to recover from the propaganda machine of Franco's reign (1939–1975). Even after the dictator's death, official sanc-tions and censorship hobbled the print and electronic media. The Consti-tution of 1978 finally recognized and protected freedom of expression (article 20) and helped to change the situation. The press played a fundamental role in moving the country through the transition to democracy. A new daily, *El País*, was launched in 1976 and soon became the voice of the new Spain under the brilliant leadership of Juan Luis Cebrián. More than a newspaper, it was a political, social and cultural arbiter. During the long Socialist sway

(1982–1996), *El País* turned into a quasi-official organ of the state, losing the moral high ground it held earlier. The way was opened for *El Mundo*, the most important phenomenon in the Spanish press of the 1990s. It played a role similar to that of the *Washington Post* during the Watergate scandal. *El Mundo* became the opposition paper of choice, a scourge of the Socialists that specialized in vigorous investigative journalism and muckraking. So far no new daily has emerged under the Conservatives (1996–present) to become the standard reference for contemporary Spain. The other leading newspapers are the staid *ABC*, based in Madrid, a monarchist tabloid with a contentious editorial line, and the venerable *La Vanguardia*, the most widely read daily in Barcelona, voice of the powerful Catalan bourgeoisie, now with a special edition in Madrid.

A list of the top twenty daily newspapers, with their headquarters and average daily circulation, reveals several surprises:[8]

Top Twenty Daily Spanish Newspapers

Marca (Madrid)	458,441
El País (Madrid)	440,628
ABC (Madrid)	301,054
El Mundo (Madrid)	284,519
La Vanguardia (Barcelona)	210,012
El Periódico de Catalunya (Barcelona)	207,772
El Correo Español-El Pueblo Vasco (Bilbao)	133,014
Sport (Barcelona)	131,140
As (Madrid)	123,447
La Voz de Galicia (La Coruña)	107,492
El Mundo Deportivo (Barcelona)	101,072
El Diario Vasco (San Sebastián)	93,553
Diario de Navarra (Pamplona)	63,212
Heraldo de Aragón (Zaragoza)	62,505
Las Provincias (Valencia)	58,068
Levante-El Mercantil Valenciano (Valencia)	53,676
La Nueva España (Oviedo)	53,566
Expansión (Madrid)	48,170
La Verdad (Murcia)	42,156
Información (Alicante)	41,110

Two dailies that fall just short of making the list, *Diario 16* and *La Razón*, both based in Madrid, are unusual in that they attract younger readers with their visual appeal and emphasis on social issues rather than politics: unemployment, drugs, immigration. They could represent a trend for the future.

The most remarkable fact about these figures is that three of the top ten dailies (*Marca, Sport* and *As*), including the most widely read newspaper in the country, belong to the sporting press. Spain may be the only nation in the world with such a love affair with sporting dailies; they account for 20 percent of total sales. This fact explains in part the large newspaper readership among males, who make up more than 80 percent of those who buy these publications. *Marca, Sport, As* and others devote most of their space to professional soccer. The location of the sporting dailies in the two great metropolises, Madrid and Barcelona, reflects the rivalry between the country's sports powerhouses, El Real Madrid and Fútbol Club de Barcelona (see Chapter 3). Most of the other leading dailies also have a largely regional distribution, one of the hallmarks of the press in Spain. *El País, ABC* and *El Mundo* circulate mostly in Madrid; *La Vanguardia* and *El Periódico* in Catalonia; *El Correo Español* and *El Diario Vasco* in the Basque Country; *La Voz de Galicia, Diario de Navarra* and *Heraldo de Aragón* in the regions for which they are named; *Las Provincias* and *Levante* in the Valencian Community; *La Nueva España* in Asturias; *La Verdad* in Murcia. Only three dailies, *El País, El Mundo* and *La Vanguardia*, publish regional editions and could be called truly national papers. Finally, we cannot fail to notice the absence of a single daily from Andalusia or Extremadura on the list, in spite of the fact that these regions have 20 percent of the national population. They are also two of the poorest parts of the country and suffer from low levels of education. Southerners tend to read less both inside of Spain and in the larger European context.

Sunday editions of Spanish newspapers enjoy a special popularity with slick, stylish magazines known as supplements. Their circulation may double weekday figures to nearly a million copies. Some of the leading supplements are *El País Semanal, Blanco y Negro (ABC)* and *La Revista de El Mundo*.

We will end our discussion of newspapers by mentioning that many Spanish dailies now have an online version, readily accessible to readers thoughout the world. *El País Digital, El Mundo, Marca Digital* and *ABC* are the four leading websites. Another is *La Estrella Digital*, the country's only newspaper that is exclusively online.

A list of the top twenty magazines in Spain, with their headquarters and average circulation, will reveal new surprises:[9]

Top Twenty Spanish Magazines

Canal + Revista (Madrid)	1,555,232
Pronto (Madrid)	807,232
¡Hola! (Madrid)	627,514
Estilo Seguro	362,773
Lecturas (Barcelona)	318,129
National Geographic	288,751
Estrenos Actuales (Madrid)	282,231
Muy Interesante (Madrid)	282,155
Club Rac Catalunya (Barcelona)	280,786
Super Pop (Barcelona)	280,521
Mía (Madrid)	271,480
Quo (Madrid)	270,709
Diez Minutos (Madrid)	268,517
Oro (Madrid)	265,938
Semana (Madrid)	252,014
What's Music?	249,891
Cosas de Casa	247,075
Clara (Barcelona)	240,931
Autoclub (Madrid)	239,580
Mi Casa (Madrid)	222,789

In radical contrast to the top newspapers, not a single one of the leading magazines is devoted to sports. Two are indeed male bastions, the motoring monthlies *Club Rac Catalunya* and *Autoclub*. Others, like the leading *Canal + Revista* and *Estrenos Actuales* (Current Premieres), deal with the entertainment world and are addressed to both men and women. Most of the other magazines target a female audience, who constitute 53 percent of readers of monthlies, 61 percent of weeklies and 79 percent of biweekly publications. Several magazines are domestic, like *Cosas de Casa* (Things about the House) and *Mi Casa* (My House). But by far the biggest group of female journals belongs to the weekly *prensa del corazón*, like *Pronto* (Quick), *¡Hola!* (Hello!), *Lecturas* (Readings), *Diez Minutos* (Ten Minutes) and *Semana* (Week). As their titles suggest, these photo magazines are designed for easy browsing. They are the Spanish versions of *People* magazine, but in general show a much more discreet and respectful attitude toward the rich and famous. One of the reasons for their success is that they have managed to fill the down-market gap left by daily newspapers, whose tone is too serious for many light readers. Spanish dailies do not have personal or gossip columns and the *prensa del corazón* makes up for this lack, although the rumors spread in their pages are usually inoffensive. The implicit code of these magazines is that society's movers and shakers are somehow superior to others, they deserve their privileges and luxuries, and please do not attempt to change the status quo, thank you.

One of these publications, *¡Hola!*, is the founder of the genre and a model for all competitors. Created in 1944, it has flourished under the dictatorship, during the transition and under democracy, stressing the same family values and optimistic approach to life. It is mainly a visual magazine, with glossy color photographs, sometimes touched up for improved effect. *¡Hola!* became so successful that an English-language edition, *Hello!*, was launched in Great Britain in 1988 with the same outmoded design and fawning attitude toward celebrities. Within four years it had reached a weekly circulation of 500,000. *¡Hola!* is also read widely in Latin America and is sold in 108 countries throughout the world.

Who owns Spain's newspapers and magazines? Although the state divested itself of all dailies after the fall of fascism in 1975, it continues to be a major player in the production and consumption of news. It has never ceased to operate Agencia EFE, a news agency founded by Franco in 1938. EFE's editorial line reflects the party in power and functions almost like an office of the state. The government uses EFE at will, exercising the spoils system and manipulating news. When Prime Minister Felipe González decided to oppose Allied bombing of Iraqi cities during the Gulf War, for example, he leaked the story through EFE. The agency is the largest in the Spanish-speaking world with more than one thousand five hundred employees and one thousand terminals around the globe. EFE also offers an impressive range of subscription services in Spain and abroad, including a photo archive and a documentation bank.

The role of the Catholic Church in the media is another legacy of the Franco years. One of the country's first schools of journalism was established at the University of Navarra, a private foundation controlled by the right-wing Catholic group Opus Dei (see Chapter 2, Religion). Several Catholic newspapers survived Francoism but have slowly disappeared. In 1989 the Vatican sold its shares in *El Correo Español-El Pueblo Vasco*; a few years later *Ya* closed its presses in spite of direct infusions of capital from Rome. The Catholic Church still controls several publishing houses and continues to produce a host of bulletins, weeklies, magazines and books.

Although several Spanish dailies belong to the same companies, the concept of newspaper chains is rapidly becoming outdated by the growth of multimedia giants that stretch across print journalism, broadcasting and the Internet. Facts are hard to come by and change constantly; most companies are not listed on the stock exchange and they often conceal information. PRISA (Promotora de Informaciones, S.A.) owns *El País* and has held shares in radio and television stations, film production companies and the book publishing chain Timón. It was the first Spanish group to have spread overseas: it has invested in publications like *Publico* in Portugal, *The Independent* in Great Britain and *La Prensa* in Mexico, as well as radio stations in France.

The only other Spanish giant is ZETA, publisher of *El Periódico de Catalunya*, the nation's sixth leading daily. The company started with the controversial magazine *Interviú* during the transition to democracy and later expanded to become a regional press chain with a series of general and special interest magazines, comic books, pornographic monthlies, a production and distribution company for erotic films, partial holdings in a television network and investments in a vast range of economic sectors from construction to tourism and food. Initially in partnership with the infamous Robert Murdoch, ZETA has also collaborated with Banesto, one of the nation's largest banks. In fact the wealthiest banks—Banesto, Banco de Bilbao and Banco de Santander Central Hispano—have huge investments in the press, radio and television.

Spain has also been an attractive target for the acquisition and expansion strategies of foreign multimedia groups. While the market in northern Europe had become nearly saturated by the mid-1980s, Spain and other Mediterranean countries retained more possibilities for growth. Two years after *El Mundo* was launched in 1989, the Italian giant Rizzoli-Corriere della Sera owned 45 percent of the paper. Two of Spain's five largest book publishers came under foreign control (Bertelsmann and Springer); Hachette and Haymarket also had large holdings in the industry. This process will surely accelerate as the nation becomes further integrated with the European Union. The new media in Spain will resemble the new media in other Western countries, with a handful of giant conglomerates controlling more and more information.

RADIO

"Radio in Spain is something more than just radio." This is how the well-known writer Manuel Vázquez Montalbán describes his favorite medium, which is also the one preferred by many other Spaniards. Radio is the most spontaneous of all media, can be listened to in public and private, and lends itself perfectly to the country's oral culture. It satisfies the Spaniards' hunger for conversation and their interest in other people, in things local and familiar.

Spain is a country in love with radio. It is third on the globe in the number of stations per capita, has the largest audience in Europe and one of the largest in the world. More than half of the adult population tunes in every day.

Like the press, radio served as a propaganda tool during the Civil War (1936–39) and the dictatorship. The state-owned network, RNE (Radio Nacional de España), dominated the airwaves and controlled the licensing of private stations. After Franco's death, the medium played an especially vital role in the transition to democracy. It reached its highest moment on the night of February 23, 1981, when an attempted coup d'etat nearly overturned the fledgling constitutional democracy. People all over the country huddled around their radios to learn that the rebel soldiers had surrendered to the legal authorities. That evening was known forever after as the "night of the transistors."

The main legacy of fascism is the continued role of the state in broadcasting. The government runs RNE and may slant the news in its favor, just as it does with the press through Agencia EFE. The great difference between the two media is that public radio does not have a virtual monopoly on news, and loses more listeners to private stations every year. It had 3.5 million listeners in 1988 and only 2.6 million in 1997, a decline of 25 percent.

The shift to democracy was not accompanied by radical change in Radio Nacional's structure and mission. Unlike the BBC, it has never had a concept of public service broadcasting; it has failed to establish a higher standard to be imitated by commercial stations. In fact the private networks have forced RNE to improve its programming in order to hold its market share. In an effort to distinguish itself from its competitors, public radio finally banned advertising.

Since the Constitution of 1978, the semiautonomous regions have created their own stations. They broadcast in Catalan, Galician and Basque. Catalunya Radio has the largest audience share in its area, Canal Nou transmits in Catalan to the Valencian Community, while Galician and Basque Radio transmit exclusively in their regional languages. These stations reach 20–25 percent of the listening audience in their respective areas. They have helped to consolidate a sense of identity in those autonomous communities with distinctive cultural traditions. The Castilian-speaking areas of the country also have stations run by their regional governments.

The Catholic Church plays an active role in broadcasting. The ideology of its COPE network (Cadena de Ondas Populares) is predictably conservative, but most of its programming is secular. It captured 31 percent of listeners in 1996 when the Socialist government was in crisis, but its share has dropped slightly in recent years.

The other major networks in Spain are SER (Sociedad Española de Radiodifusión), also with 31 percent of listeners, and Onda 0 with 21 percent. SER's ideology is center-left and is the preferred wavelength of listeners under the age of forty-five. It owns four of the country's five most popular stations, including Cadena Dial, which broadcasts Latin American and U.S. Latin music around the clock, and Radiolé, which plays only Spanish songs. Onda 0, owned by the powerful national organization for the blind (ONCE), is farther to the right in its politics and has an older listening audience. There are also many independent radio stations in Spain; some broadcast without a license. These mavericks have become so common and loved by listeners that the government has stopped policing them, even granting them financial aid in some cases.

What makes Spanish radio so popular and unique? While the medium's style was very stodgy during the Franco years, it has become more lively under democracy. There is greater competition between public and private stations and increased rivalry for listener share. Radio is the medium that feeds the Spanish hunger for conversation. For this reason, talk shows are more popular than music and news, in contrast to most other western countries. Almost two-thirds of listeners have their favorite *tertulias* or talk shows, which tend to concentrate on a particular subject like politics, sports or sex. The *revista de prensa* or newspaper review, discussed with the press above, is an example of a radio (or television) *tertulia*. Slightly different are radio *magacines*, which deal with a greater variety of topics, like talk shows in the United States. These programs are broadcast at all times of day and on many stations. Following the strange Spanish timetable (see Chapter 3), more people listen to the radio between midnight and 1 a.m. than between 7 and 8 in the morning. The peak hours depend on the main meals, like nearly everything else in Spain: after lunch between 3 and 4 p.m., after supper between 10 p.m. and midnight.

Spaniards are naturals in the medium of broadcasting. They love good speaking and demand it from their radio announcers, who are among the highest paid entertainers in the country. Some are national heroes who command immense salaries. Like successful bullfighters, they have their own backup teams on their payroll. Luis del Olmo, Iñaki Gabilondo and Concha García Campoy are household names. While radio announcers in most countries dream of becoming television personalities, the reverse may occur in Spain. After a successful career on Spanish TV, for example, García Campoy decided to move to radio where she could earn more and reach a larger audience.

The greatest threat to the healthy survival of Spanish radio is the increased tendency toward control by multimedia groups. If it can survive this onslaught, its future will be bright. Radio nourishes the country's vibrant oral culture more than any other medium. Speaking for its twenty-one-million fans, Vázquez Montalbán says that they will always be able to close their eyes, tune in their sets, and "see what we cannot see."[10]

TELEVISION

Spain is a country with superb radio and deplorable television. The contrast is all the more striking in a nation where the same government office, Radio Televisión Española (RTVE, Spanish Radio Television), is the largest proprietor in both media (see Photograph 21). Television has never been able to win the people's affection as much as its sister medium. While radio has a brilliant record in the defense of democracy, television has been plagued by partisan politics. If radio tends to be creative and spontaneous, TV is rigid and unimaginative. While radio reflects an image of contemporary Spain at its most vibrant, television portrays an outdated image of a country that existed fifty years ago, if it ever existed at all. One writer gives this sardonic view:

> Television has been and continues to be the obvious negation of all the hopes for modernity and efficiency proclaimed by its chiefs and the coziest refuge for outmoded historical sets and disguises. . . . On the screen appears a constant parade of what no longer exists or matters or is destined to disappear . . . quaint comedies of matters with archaic dialogue that nobody speaks or even understands . . . folkloric or semi-folkloric women who could only be found on an old tin of crackers, Francoist journalists who pontificate when nobody wants to see or hear them if anyone ever did in the first place, old ladies with crooked teeth gossiping around a table, outdated authors who still believe that a writer should be an original or eccentric like a century ago, comedians who are so old-fashioned that they cause depression . . . crude ventriloquists from the immediate postwar period who have not even learned to conceal the movements of their lips, insipid stripteases when the theaters that offer these spectacles are on the verge of collapse for lack of cus-

21. Torrespaña ("Spaintower"), headquarters of TVE (Televisión Española), popularly known as *El Pirulí* (The Lollipop), c. 1995. Photograph reproduced courtesy TVE.

tomers. . . . The effect produced by state television in the viewer (and by the private channels who mimic them) is that of being in a country where time has not passed since 20 November 1975 [the day of Franco's death].[11]

Perhaps the best thing that can be said about national television in Spain is that it uses some of its advertising revenues to support public radio. In this sense the two media have an incestuous relationship. Spanish radio even advertises on TV! The people pay their tribute to their favorite medium by using television sets like radios, listening without watching the screen as they go about their daily business at home, work or play. One critic says, "In our bars, the TV plays while the clients, often indifferent to the multicolored message on the screen, feel themselves irresistibly attracted by the background noise it produces, which allows them to fuse the 'official' world with their own world of wines and pitted olives, paper napkins and greasy mussel shells scattered on the floor."[12]

Viewer polls are probably distorted by the people's habit of using television as background noise. Statistics invariably show Spaniards as television fanatics. Almost 89 percent of the population over fourteen claims to watch the *caja tonta* (idiot box) every day. The average daily viewing in 1997 was an incredible two hours and twenty-nine minutes, higher than any other country in western Europe except Great Britain.[13] Unlike their Anglo-Saxon neighbors, Spaniards do not have the excuse of a bad climate.

Television started in Spain as a government service in 1956, a propaganda tool for the Franco regime. The state monopoly made it more ominous than public radio, which had lower production costs, more local control and a mixture of public and private stations. As in the case of the other media, the dictator's death did not bring an end to government jurisdiction, which continues to this day. The members of Televisión Española's board of governors are elected by the legislature and the director-general is appointed by the executive. Statistics have shown that news coverage tends to be more extensive for the party in power than for its opposition. As if this were not enough to earn the public's mistrust, TVE—the television company within RTVE—has also been a den of financial corruption, malpractice and embezzlement. "The very mention of the word television produces misgivings and reproofs," says Eduardo Haro Tecglen.

The central government has two channels. TVE 1 offers uninterrupted programming for the general public from early morning to late night. TVE 2 has more flexible offerings and pays special attention to sports and cultural events. Both public channels are financed by commercials and subsidies from the government. TVE's huge budget includes funds for its own orchestra and choir, for external broadcasting services, Radio Nacional and the Radio and Television Institute.

It was not until the 1980s that state television began to lose its monopoly. Without permission from Madrid, the autonomous government of the Basque Country created its own channel and began to transmit in 1983. The Catalans countered with their own channel, TV 3, and the Valencians with their Canal Nou. The Galicians followed suit with TVG. These and other channels broadcast in minority languages; like the vernacular radio stations, they have helped to foster a sense of cultural identity among the nation's ethnic minorities. "The Basque, Galician and Catalan regions may be nations without states," said one commentator, "but they have TV networks."[14] Castilian-speaking areas also have their own channels like TeleMadrid in the center and Canal Sur in the south. Together the autonomic channels have a 16 percent share of the viewing audience.

A series of changes rocked the state monopoly of television in the 1990s. Under pressure from the European Union, the government finally agreed to license private channels. Antena 3 was the first to transmit, followed by Tele 5 and Canal +. Antena 3 offers general programming in the style of TVE 1, with a mix of news, sports, drama, sitcoms and game shows. Tele 5— sometimes called "Tele Teta" (Boobs TV) because of its voluptuous host- esses—offers down-market entertainment like game shows and confronta- tional "reality shows." Canal + is a subscription service that specializes in movies, with no commercials. Various multimedia groups control all the private channels, like the radio networks. At the outset Antena 3 was owned largely by Spanish publishing interests, Tele 5 belonged in part to the Italian media magnate Silvio Berlusconi and ONCE, while Canal + was held jointly by PRISA and a French television company. By 2000, foreign control had become even more dominant.

How does Spanish TV differ from the medium in other countries? At its best, it mimics radio in *tertulias* or *magacines* that depend on spontaneous dialogue. A recent example was journalist and novelist Arturo Pérez Reverte's "Código 1"; a current example is Fernando Sánchez Dragó's "Negro sobre blanco," a weekly program of interviews with writers. The *revistas de prensa* or press reviews imitate similar programs on the radio. Much more popular are the *telenovelas* or soap operas imported from Latin America. The only virtue of these maudlin shows is that they eventually reach a conclusion, unlike their counterparts in the United States. Other programs unique to Spain are bullfights broadcast live from around the country, and weekly shows that comment on the world of the *corrida*, like "Tendido Cero" with

Fernando Fernández Román and Federico Arnás. A series on bullfighting titled "Juncal," directed by the film director Jaime de Armiñán and starring the great Spanish actor Francisco Rabal, was a critical and popular success in the late 1980s. Finally, a few sitcoms manage to rise above the prevailing level of mediocrity and may capture a broad national audience, like Antonio Mercero's "Farmacia de guardia," a sort of Spanish "Cheers" that takes place in an all-night pharmacy instead of a bar.

Some programs have been so successful that they have been exported to other countries, especially in Latin America. "Tómbola" pries into the lives of famous people and sometimes includes its own reality show by confronting celebrities and the press. "Gran hermano" (Big Brother) was the "Survivor" of the 2000 season: starting with twelve young men and women who lived in the same house, it eliminated them one by one—through popular vote on the Internet—until the winner took the prize of fifteen million pesetas (some $86,000).

Technologies like cable, satellite and digital television have inaugurated a new era for the medium in Spain. The country has become one of the fastest-growing markets on the continent. Televisión Española Internacional now transmits around the clock to the Americas. Spanish investors, producers and distributors are leading the way in direct broadcast satellite and subscription services in Latin America, Spain's largest potential export market. At the same time, the channels in the country's autonomous regions are becoming more numerous and more competitive. The future of television in Spain, like that of radio and the press, will involve a special combination of regional, national, European and global factors.

SELECTED READINGS

General

Anuario El País 1999. Madrid: Ediciones El País, 1999.

Bustamante, Enrique. "The Mass Media: A Problematic Modernization." In *Spanish Cultural Studies: An Introduction. The Struggle for Modernity*, edited by Helen Graham and Jo Labanyi, 356–361. Oxford: Oxford University Press, 1995.

Deacon, Philip. "The Media in Modern Spanish Culture." In *The Cambridge Companion to Modern Spanish Culture*, edited by David T. Gies, 309–317. Cambridge: Cambridge University Press, 1999.

De Miguel, Amando. *La sociedad española, 1996–97*. Madrid: Editorial Complutense, 1997.

Fernández Sanz, Juan José. *¡Que informen ellos! De cómo el sector español de la comunicación va siendo copiado por los grandes grupos multimedia internacionales.* Madrid: Huerga & Fierro, 1999.

Gibson, Ian. *Fire in the Blood: The New Spaniards.* London: Faber and Faber, 1992.

Hooper, John. *The New Spaniards.* London: Penguin, 1995.

Rodgers, Eamonn, ed. *Encyclopedia of Contemporary Spanish Culture.* London and New York: Routledge, 1999.

The Press

Benn's Guide to Newspapers and Periodicals of the World. London: Benn Brothers, Annual.

Cebrián, Juan Luis. *The Press and Main Street: "El País"—Journalism in Democratic Spain.* Ann Arbor: University of Michigan Press, 1989.

Stanton, Edward F. "The Press." In *Handbook of Spanish Popular Culture,* 191–204. Westport, CT.: Greenwood Press, 1999.

World Press Review. A digest of the international press that reprints articles from Spanish newspapers.

Radio

Díaz, Lorenzo. *La radio en España 1923–1997.* Madrid: Alianza, 1997. Prologue by Manuel Vázquez Montalbán.

Stanton, Edward F. "Radio and Television." In *Handbook of Spanish Popular Culture,* 173–190. Westport, CT: Greenwood Press, 1999.

Television

Díaz, Lorenzo. *Informe sobre la televisión en España.* Barcelona: Ediciones Grupo Zeta, 1999.

———. *La televisión en España 1949–1995.* Madrid: Alianza, 1994. Prologue by Eduardo Haro Tecglen.

Marías, Javier. *Pasiones pasadas.* Barcelona: Anagrama, 1991.

Maxwell, Richard. "Spatial Eruptions, Global Grids: Regionalist TV in Spain and Dialectics of Identity Politics." In *Refiguring Spain: Cinema/Media/Representation,* edited by Marsha Kinder, 260–283. Durham, NC: Duke University Press, 1997.

Rodríguez, Francisco Javier. *La televisión y los españoles. Análisis periodístico de un vicio nacional.* Madrid: Paraninfo, 1993.

OTHER SOURCES

See the website "Sí, Spain" and its special section called "The Media": <http://www.sispain.org>. "Sí, Spain" has a special site on Spanish radio and television: <http://www.elindice.com>. The website "Spain Today" has sections on Spanish press agencies, some fifty digital newspapers and news: <http://www.clark.net/pub/jumpsam/sptoday.shtml>.

5

Cinema

In today's world, just as in former times we spoke of the style of French and Italian cinema, now we can speak, and with good reason, of German and Spanish cinema.

—José Luis Aranguren[1]

How can it be that a small country such as Spain can continuously produce over fifty features a year, 90 percent of which prove to be duds upon release or never even see the light of the screen?

—Peter Besas[2]

The two quotes show the main paradox of contemporary cinema in Spain. On the one hand, the country manages to produce a few brilliant movies every year, which often win important international prizes. On the other, these works may be produced in the most tortuous ways, often lose money, and fail to ensure the continuous production of quality films. In many ways Spanish cinema—like the bullfight and certain other institutions—reflects in miniature the contradictions of a whole society.

If the heyday of Italian film was the late 1940s, the 1950s and 1960s with neorealism and geniuses like Federico Fellini and Michelangelo Antonioni, and the golden age of French movies was the 1960s and 1970s with the New Wave and artists like François Truffault, Jean-Luc Godard and Alain Resnais, the 1980s and 1990s might be seen as the great period of Spanish cinema with directors like Carlos Saura, Vicente Aranda, José Juan Bigas

Luna and Pedro Almodóvar. (Some critics would include the 1970s too, when these directors were already making movies.) Spain has never matched its southern European neighbors in the quantity and class of its production, but the last twenty years have surpassed all others in the nation's past. A sign of the country's new place among film-producing countries is the annual survey of Recent Spanish Cinema, celebrated at the American Cinematheque in Hollywood. Such an event would have been impossible only ten years ago.

The actress Meryl Streep once said, "If the Martians landed and did nothing but go to movies this year, they'd come to the fair conclusion that the chief occupation of women on Earth is hooking. And I don't mean rugs."[3] If the Martians watched only recent Spanish movies, they might come to the conclusion that Spaniards are among the most irreverent, bloodthirsty, sex-hounded people on earth and that the main occupation of both women and men is hooking—as heterosexuals, homosexuals, transsexuals or transvestites. Their conclusions would of course be unfair because film in Spain does not reflect the life of the people any more than it does in other countries. Yet the Martians' impression would not be far from that of most foreigners who have come to expect bizarre, extreme and outrageous works by directors like Almodóvar, Aranda, and Bigas Luna, members of the so-called "Spanish school." Why?

In this chapter we will glance very briefly at the history of Spanish film. Then we will look in greater depth at the major themes and genres of the past twenty years, concentrating on what is unique to Spain. Along the way we will attempt to explain how the nation's contemporary cinema has acquired its outlandish reputation.

Early Spanish cinema was not very different from the new art in other western countries. At least one popular genre soon began to develop without parallels abroad. It consisted of movies set in Andalusia and based on the region's traditional music, *cante jondo* or flamenco. Often called *españoladas*, these films exploited the image of Spain as a backward, rural, exotic country populated by superstitious people, priests and bullfighters—stereotypes created by European Romantics in the nineteenth century and propagated by an endless stream of bad novels, plays and poems both inside and outside the Peninsula. A related genre wove weak plots around the voices of female singers of the *canción española* or *cuplé* (popular Spanish song)—known as *folklóricas*. In these and other guises, the musical *españolada* has continued to fill Spain's silver screens. It may be as hard to kill as the Hollywood melodrama.

Silent movies in Spain rarely caught the attention of foreigners. The most notable exception was Luis Buñuel and Salvador Dalí's *Le chien andalou*

(Andalusian Dog, 1928), filmed in Paris and supposedly based on the director's and the artist's dreams. This surrealist work launched Buñuel's career as his country's most renowned filmmaker. It also initiated the tradition of an "irreverent and mordant" style that would remain a hallmark of Spanish movies until the present time.[4]

Cinema flourished in Spain during the Second Republic (1931–36) until the explosion of the Civil War (1936–39). Documentaries suddenly acquired greater importance on both sides of the front. Some great propaganda movies were filmed by foreigners for the benefit of the Republic, like Joris Ivens' *The Spanish Earth* and André Malraux's *Sierra de Teruel*.

The big sleep in the story of Spanish film started with the victory of General Franco's forces in 1939. The Great Dictator applied rigid rules of censorship that would last for almost forty years. "Anything but sex and politics" was the censors' unwritten rule of thumb, as if filmmaking could follow the rules of polite conversation. Movies in "foreign languages"—including Basque and Catalan—were forbidden. The state dubbed all non-Spanish films in order to impose cultural, political and religious orthodoxy.

By the 1950s some talented young directors were cutting a few chinks in the Franco monolith, shooting films that can still be watched with admiration and pleasure. Luis García Berlanga's *¡Bienvenido, Mr. Marshall!* (Welcome, Mr. Marshall!, 1952) blended foreign and domestic influences to create a new kind of cinematic language for Spain—a process that has characterized artistic change in the country for centuries. The movie has been called the first "Trojan horse" to slip into the fortress of the Franco state.[5] Juan Antonio Bardem's *Muerte de un ciclista* (Death of a Cyclist, 1955) fused elements of Italian neorealism and American film noir in a searing treatment of hypocrisy among the privileged classes. His *Calle Mayor* (Main Street, 1956) continued in a similar vein, presenting an ironic, critical view of Spanish machismo and provincial life. Then the biggest Trojan horse of all slipped into Spain—or rather out. Filmed under Franco's nose, Buñuel's *Viridiana* (1961) won the Golden Palm for the best film at Cannes and was labeled blasphemous by the Vatican, forcing the cagey old director to sneak out of the country with the reels. *Viridiana*, a terse parable of the old and new Spain, was one of the most perfect movies in the history of film. Meanwhile the country's best young directors were learning from Buñuel. A few years later, Carlos Saura pushed the limits of censorship to the breaking point with *La Caza* (The Hunt, 1965), a powerful film that expanded the "language of cinematic violence and its effectiveness for political ends."[6] Víctor Erice's haunting *El espíritu de la colmena* (Spirit of the Beehive, 1973) evoked the postwar period in an original, lyrical style.

All of these works showed Spanish *cine de autor* (auteur cinema) at its best: serious cinema that catered to a small national and international audience in art-house theaters. Following the lead of the state's general director of cinema, José María García Escudero, critics grouped directors like Berlanga, Bardem, Saura, Erice and others—all influenced by Buñuel—in a movement called the New Spanish Cinema. Both the name and the times recalled the French New Wave and the Brazilian Cinema Nôvo, but conditions were radically different in Spain and some historians deny that there was a coherent trend.

"When the rabid dog dies, the rabies dies with him" says a Castilian proverb, but it did not apply to Franco's death. José Luis Borau's *Furtivos* (Poachers, 1975) was delayed for months by censors before its release; the film exposed the violence beneath the surface of Spanish life and became one of the highest grossing movies of the time. Censorship lingered like a bad official habit. Gradually the restrictions withered and the country made up for lost time. Directors openly treated issues of religion, history, politics, ethnicity, regionalism, family and sexuality. The reaction against forty years of repression was often extreme. Many filmmakers confused artistic freedom with female nudity. Some continue to do so but nowadays the nudity can be male as well as female, with large doses of violence and profanity that would be R- or X-rated in the United States. Spain began to acquire its reputation as the home of quirky, outrageous films.

The transition from dictatorship to democracy coincided with the boom of the video market, a phenomenon that made a healthy movie industry even more difficult to achieve. The number of movie houses plummeted from 4,096 in 1980 to 1,773 in 1990, then rose gradually to 2,565 in 1997. With the construction of new multiplexes in shopping malls, the numbers seem to be holding steadier in recent years.

Democracy has not diminished the dominance of foreign movies in Spain. Fifty-one percent of films screened in 1997 were American, followed by French (9 percent), British (8 percent) and German (8 percent); Spanish movies represented only 17 percent of the total. One example suffices: the domestic hit of the year was Santiago Segura's *Torrente, el brazo tonto de la ley* (Torrente, Dumb Arm of the Law), with some 1,800,000 spectators; the biggest foreign splash was of course *Titanic*, seen by 9,000,000.[7] The habit of dubbing foreign films has also continued unabated since the dictatorship: a mere 4 percent of movies imported in Spain have subtitles.[8] Multinational conglomerates like Columbia Tristar, Warner and UIP maintain a stranglehold on distribution and exhibition networks. All of these factors mean that the Spanish movie industry has to play against a stacked deck.

Another legacy from the Franco period is the dreaded film quota. From the 1940s through the 1980s, the government required that a certain proportion of domestic movies be shown in relation to foreign productions. In recent years the quota has been modified to fit the new political reality of Spain in the European Union (EU): Spanish and European films are now grouped together in opposition to all others (primarily American). Theaters must screen at least one Spanish or European work for every three productions from outside the EU.

One important aspect of filmmaking in the Peninsula is not a carryover from the Franco years: the resurgence of cinema in the autonomous regions. We have already seen how democracy revived cultural freedoms in areas like Catalonia, the Basque Country and Galicia. The press, radio, television and the cinema have all benefited from the new atmosphere. More than other regions, Catalonia and Euzkadi have fomented film production within their borders. The two cases offer a fascinating contrast in style. While the Catalans had a cinematic infrastructure before the Civil War, the Basques did not. In spite of this enormous advantage, Catalonia has not been able to develop a viable movie industry. It has placed language above all other criteria, whereas the Basques have sacrificed linguistic purity in favor of common sense. The results have been predictable: most Catalan movies have not managed to break into the Castilian and global markets, while Basque films in Spanish have achieved acclaim at national and international festivals. There has been a "flight of talent" from Catalonia: directors like Vicente Aranda and José Juan Bigas Luna have left the region to make movies in other parts of Spain or abroad. Filmmakers who have not abandoned the region usually shoot works that run for only a few days in theaters, reappear on Catalan TV, and soon fall into oblivion. In contrast, Euzkadi has lured established directors like Pedro Olea, Eloy de la Iglesia, Alfonso Ungría and José Antonio Zorrilla to make films within its tiny borders. It has also nourished the talent of younger directors who have filmed an astonishing number of original movies in the 1980s and especially the 1990s: Montxo Armendáriz's *Tasio* (1984, Grand Prize, Biarritz) and *27 horas* (Twenty-Seven Hours, 1986, Concha de Plata for best film, San Sebastián); Imanol Uribe's *La muerte de Mikel* (Mikel's Death, 1984) and *Días contados* (Just a Few Days, 1994, Concha de Oro for best film, San Sebastián); Juanma Bajo Ulloa's *Alas de mariposa* (Butterfly Wings, 1991, Concha de Oro for best film, San Sebastián), *La madre muerta* (The Dead Mother, 1993, best direction, Montreal Film Festival) and *Airbag* (1997, Goya award for best editing); Alex de la Iglesia's *Acción mutante* (Mutant Action, 1992), *El día de la bestia* (The Day of the Beast, 1995, winner of six Goyas, including best director) and *Perdita Durango* (1997); and Julio Medem's *Vacas* (Cows, 1992, Goya for best new filmmaker), *La ardilla roja* (The Red Squirrel, 1993, young filmmakers award, Cannes), *Tierra* (Earth, 1995) and *Los amantes del Círculo Polar* (Lovers in the Polar Circle, 1998). These films have converted the region into a small cinematic paradise. The Catalan and Basque experiences have relevance far beyond the movie industry, offering two different models for peninsular culture in the twenty-first century.

With the election of the Partido Popular (Conservatives) in 1996, many feared that the protectionist policies of the Socialist period (1983–1996) would be removed. But change has been gradual. Quotas have become more liberal and subsidies have been reduced but not eliminated. In the long run, it appears that government intervention will continue to decrease. Some say that deregulation will be the end of cinema in Spain. Others believe that twenty-five years of protectionism have been a failure and that more creative funding may invigorate the industry. While Televisión Española (TVE) is still the major producer of films in Spain, the public channels in the autonomous regions, as well as the private channels, have begun to compete in recent years. They have the resources to underwrite production and to guarantee transmission. In 1996, for example, the private Canal + televised nearly seventy Spanish movies. In 2000, this channel's cable company Sogecable, in cooperation with its film unit Sogecine, began making larger investments in film production, distribution and exhibition. One of its projects was to produce six twelve-minute shorts to be transmitted on the Internet. Successful directors like Fernando Trueba, Fernando Colomo and Pedro Almodóvar have established their own production companies, both for their works and those of younger artists. Trueba coproduced Bajo Ulloa's *Alas de mariposa* and Chus Gutiérrez's *Sublet* (1992). Colomo supported Mariano Barroso's *Mi hermano del alma* (My Dearest Brother, 1992) and *Éxtasis* (Ecstasy, 1996) and Icíar Bollaín's *¡Hola! ¿Estás sola?* (Hi, Are You Alone?, 1995, winner of a prize at the Festival de Comedia in Peñíscola). The Almodóvar brothers' production company, El Deseo, S.A., backed De la Iglesia's *Acción mutante*, Daniel Calparsoro's *Pasajes* (Passages, 1996), Mónica Laguna's *Tengo una casa* (I Have a House, 1996) and four films by other directors in 1997. For this and other reasons, there has been a real infusion of talent in the 1990s, with a new generation of directors, scriptwriters, actors and technicians who are attempting to revitalize the industry. In 1996, seven out of the ten leading domestic hits were shot by new directors.

Coproduction with other nations has also become more frequent. The government of Prime Minister José María Aznar has encouraged cooperative ventures in order to build a European film industry that will compete with Hollywood. Spain now has coproduction agreements with Portugal, France,

Italy, Germany and Morocco. In 1996 Spain and several Latin American countries formed the Ibermedia Program, whose purpose is to help finance coproduction among its members, and to improve distribution and promotion of films. One writer has called this kind of coproduction "the most up-to-date and vital project in our movie industry."[9] In 2000, two Spanish movies premiered in North America: Mateo Gil's *Nadie conoce a nadie* (Nobody Knows Anybody Else) and José Luis Cuerda's *La lengua de las mariposas* (The Language of Butterflies). Meanwhile, a third feature, Alejandro Amenábar's *Los otros* (The Others), was being shot with Nicole Kidman in another attempt to crack the vast market in the New World.

The most recurrent theme in Spanish cinema after the dictatorship was probably the past. Directors attempted to recuperate the historical past and popular memory from forty years of fascist suppression. Something similar occurred in literature, art, architecture, fashion and design. One critic spoke of a "recuperation" or heritage industry in Spain, with "the refurbishing of museums, restoration of municipal theatres, vogue for local history and reissue of forgotten women writers."[10]

At the time of Franco's illness and death, documentary and semidocumentary films enjoyed a revival as an effort to recover the past. Basilio M. Patino's *Canciones para después de una guerra* (Songs for After a War, 1971, not released until 1976) showed how the fascist regime appropriated popular culture to conceal the misery of everyday life. Pilar Miró's *El crimen de Cuenca* (The Crime in Cuenca, 1979), at first banned for its critical treatment of the Civil Guard, later turned into a box-office smash. In Catalonia, Francesc Bellmunt's *La nova cançó* (The New Catalan Song, 1976) documented and celebrated the songwriters' protest movement of the 1960s and 1970s. In the Basque Country, Fernando Larruquert's *Euskal Herri Musika* (1978) also paid homage to the region's popular music, while Imanol Uribe's *El proceso de Burgos* (The Trial of Burgos, 1979) attacked the Spanish state in defense of Basque separatism and ETA.

After this immediate reaction against the Franco period, there was a gradual shift toward a reimagining of the past in less polemical ways. Carlos Saura's flamenco trilogy—*Bodas de sangre* (Blood Wedding, 1980), *Carmen* (1983) and *El amor brujo* (Love, the Magician, 1986)—dealt partly with problematic historical periods and attempted to recover Andalusian culture from Romantic clichés. His later comeback film, *¡Ay, Carmela!* (1990), was more effective in recuperating the *canción española* or *cuplé* as an expression of political freedom. In Erice's *El sur* (The South, 1982), Manuel Gutiérrez Aragón's *Demonios en el jardín* (Devils in the Garden, 1982) and Jaime Chávarri's *Las bicicletas son para el verano* (Bicycles Are for Summer, 1984), the perspective of the past was filtered through the eyes of children. All of these directors had grown up during the Civil War or the 1940s. They have been called "children of Franco," whose growth and vision were stunted but also galvanized by repression and resistance. Their works often contain Oedipal narratives whose main figure is a powerful male, but who may be substituted by a dominant female who assumes the lost patriarchal power; a violent struggle ensues involving sacrifice, massacre and other forms of bloodshed related to the war and its aftermath.[11]

By the mid-1980s, radical politics and resistance had given way to films that framed the past in terms of individuals more than groups, often within an atmosphere of nostalgia. Chávarri's *Las cosas del querer* (The Things of Love, 1989) evoked the music, costume and décor of the 1930s and 1940s while representing the sexual and social dynamics of the period. Vicente Aranda's *Amantes* (Lovers, 1990) revealed a disturbing eroticism that did not betray the context of the dark 1950s in which it occurs. In contrast, Fernando Trueba's *Belle Epoque* (1992) converted the prewar period of the First Republic into a kind of contemporary sexual paradise without AIDS. If the past appeared to be colonizing the present in Spanish films of the 1970s and 1980s, in this movie the present occupies the past with no sense of historical context. "Trueba's version of 1930s Spain has clearly been transfigured by social and moral revolutions that have come afterwards and this rural arcadia is a composite mixture of 1960s hippy culture, the cult of 'make love not war,' plus generous helpings of 1970s and 1980s feminism as well as gender-bending and a postmodern taste for blurring political, moral, and sexual boundaries."[12] With this kind of winning formula, it is no wonder that *Belle Epoque* became a box-office hit, swept the Spanish Goya awards, and won the Oscar for the year's best foreign film. Trueba made a second sweep in 1998 with *La niña de tus ojos* (The Girl of Your Dreams), a story of a group of Spaniards who travel to Nazi Germany to make a musical based on Andalusian folklore. The film showed the enduring attraction of historical cinema and the *españolada* tradition. We may be seeing a retro-vogue in historical cinema that exploits an internal market of older, nostalgic spectators and an external audience of viewers with an anachronistic vision of Spain.[13]

Trueba is one of the filmmakers who has been loosely associated with *la movida* ("movement"), a complex subculture in the early years of Spanish democracy, centered in Madrid. In contrast to the brooding, introspective "children of Franco," this younger generation of directors, musicians, painters, photographers and designers had not suffered the direct experience of the war and its immediate aftermath. Fatigued by perpetual debates about the past and future of Spain, they developed a consciously lighter style with a glossy contemporary look. Like their predecessors, they favored rebellion against traditional social mores but without a political agenda. "Any act of transgression was acceptable, as long as it was destructive, absurd, blasphemous and ironic."[14] They laughed at the pieties of the new Left as well as the old Right.

The leading exponent of the movement was Pedro Almodóvar. Some critics called him a flash-in-the-pan who would disappear with the *movida* and the Socialist Spain of the 1980s. Yet he has survived to become the most famous Spaniard in the world with the possible exception of King Juan Carlos and Antonio Banderas, an actor who made his reputation in Almodóvar's films. Although he was snubbed for years by the Spanish academy, his movies continue to win awards and popular acclaim. One of his best works, *Todo sobre mi madre* (All About My Mother, 1999), took the Golden Globe and the Oscar for best foreign film.

Almodóvar's movies have an unmistakable look and feel. In other words, they have style, whether you like it or not. The adjective "Almodóvarian" has come to mean wacky, outlandish, zany and melodramatic. His films have been called kitsch, camp, pastiche, postmodern. Colors, costumes, makeup and mise-en-scène involve every one of the senses, including nonsense. The normal in everyday life becomes abnormal and vice versa. Marginal characters claim center stage: a porno queen, a punk-rock musician, a lesbian or pregnant nun, a serial killer, a homicidal bullfighter, a homosexual filmmaker, a sex-changed actress, a drag-artist magistrate. The world is turned upside down and inside out. The Spain of his films is more feminine than patriarchal, more motherly than machista.

Pedro Almodóvar is the first Spanish director since Buñuel to crack the global market without going to Hollywood. Yet he has influenced tinsel town in his own way. In several of his 1980s films, Almodóvar used Antonio Banderas as a consistently weak, sexually ambiguous protagonist: *Matador* (1986), *La ley del deseo* (The Law of Desire, 1987), *Mujeres al borde de un ataque de nervios* (Women on the Verge of a Nervous Breakdown, 1988) and *¡Atame!* (Tie Me Up! Tie Me Down!, 1989). After the director had guaranteed Banderas' international renown, the actor went to Hollywood to make a series of movies in which he became the latest embodiment of the Latin lover: *Mambo Kings* (1992), *The House of Spirits* (1993) and Trueba's *Two Much* (1995). But in at least two other American films—*Philadelphia* (1993) and *Interview with the Vampire* (1994)—he played sexual shifters who recalled his earlier Spanish films. Banderas still carries the trace of his Almodóvarian roles, a character who transgresses the borders of gender and sexuality while exercising an erotic appeal for all spectators, male or female, straight or gay. In this way the actor and the director, with their global star power, have remade the image of the Hispanic male in Hollywood.[15]

We could speak of the "Almodóvar effect" that has allowed other directors to reach an international audience as members of the "Spanish school." Trueba's *Belle Epoque* is a notable example, as is the recent work of the Catalan designer-artist turned director, Bigas Luna. If Almodóvar converted the male body into the object of the homosexual gaze, Bigas Luna did the same from the female perspective in his *Las edades de Lulú* (The Ages of Lulu, 1991). His "Iberian trilogy"—*Jamón, jamón* (Ham, Ham, 1992), *Huevos de oro* (Golden Balls, 1993) and *La teta y la luna* (The Tit and the Moon, 1994)—probably could not have been exported successfully without Almodóvar's precedent. These movies are daring and erotic in their treatment of Spanish men who find themselves torn between a traditional culture and a new world in which women hold increasing power. With the director's typical emphasis on color and close-ups, sex and food seem to hold as much importance in these films as they do in Spanish life.

If directors like Almodóvar and Bigas Luna have created a new Spanish male in their films, they and others have also portrayed a new Spanish woman. A whole generation of actresses, born between the mid-1940s and the early 1960s, has been cast in leading roles that would have been unthinkable in earlier years. Carmen Maura, Marisa Paredes, Ana Belén, Assumpta Serna and Victoria Abril "consistently represent women as complex, multidimensional, thinking subjects in their negotiation of the social, professional, emotional and sexual changes which have characterized post-Franco Spain."[16] It is not by chance that these artists have figured prominently in movies by directors like Saura, Aranda, Gutiérrez Aragón and Almodóvar, who have often transgressed social and sexual norms in their work. As they have reached their forties and fifties, these women have played parts for middle-aged characters that would have been unlikely in previous movies dominated by the iconographic power of the young female body. Following these well-established stars, a younger generation of actresses has also been involved in the remaking of gender. Emma Suárez, Maribel Verdú, Ariadna Gil and Penélope Cruz—born in the 1960s and 1970s—represent the experience and concerns of young women raised in the period of the transition and democracy. Although their good looks have not remained unexploited, they also display a more spontaneous, natural style of acting, very different from the heavy, tragic roles of the older generation.

Most surprising of all, women filmmakers have broken the sexual barrier in the patriarchal world of Spanish cinema. Pilar Miró and Josefina Molina—practically the only female directors of the 1970s and 1980s—have made recent movies that show strong women characters in a variety of historical contexts. Miró's *Tu nombre envenena mis sueños* (Your Name Poisons My Dreams, 1996) focused on female revenge in the oppressive atmosphere of the 1940s. Molina's remake of the 1940s classic, *La Lola se va a los Puertos* (Lola Goes to the Sea, 1993), renewed the tired genre of the *españolada* and portrayed the female protagonist as desiring subject rather than object of the male gaze.

Younger women filmmakers have followed Miró and Molina's example. Chus Gutiérrez's *Alma gitana* (Gypsy Soul, 1995) drew on the Spanish musical and dance tradition, altering it to examine racial intolerance and the oppression of women in gypsy society. Arantxa Lazcano's *Años oscuros* (Dark Years, 1993) dealt with the experience of a young girl growing up in the Basque Country in the 1950s, while Azucena Rodríguez's *Entre rojas* (Among Reds, 1995) treated the political wing of a women's prison in the 1970s. Rodríguez has also followed the recurrent comic trend in Spanish cinema in her *Puede ser divertido* (It Can Be Fun, 1995), but she undermined the genre by filming from a female point of view. Icíar Bollaín's *¡Hola! ¿Estás sola?*, Isabel Coixet's *Cosas que nunca te dije* (Things I Never Told You, 1995) and Eva Lesmes' *Pon un hombre en tu vida* (Put a Man in Your Life, 1996) all used female protagonists to show the contradictions of Spanish machismo.

Other women directors have attempted to reach an international audience. Rosa Vergés' debut *Boom boom* (1990), set in Barcelona, placed Catalan culture in a global context. It is a sign of the times that some of the filmmakers mentioned here have studied in the United States. Chus Gutiérrez's work is closely connected to independent American cinema. Her debut film *Sublet*, significantly titled in English, concerned the experiences of a young Spanish woman living in New York. Marta Balletbó-Coll shot her first feature, *Costa Brava* (Family Album, 1994), in Spain with a Catalan cast performing in English so that she could gain access to a global market. This film broke new ground in peninsular cinema by treating a lesbian romance as "something taken for granted . . . no longer a social problem or a psychic anomaly."[17]

Women filmmakers have not exploited violence as much as their male counterparts. The 1990s saw a new trend that exceeded all other periods of Spanish cinema—already one of the bloodiest in the world. At the age of twenty-six, Alex de la Iglesia convinced Almodóvar's production company, El Deseo, S.A., to finance his first major, full-length feature film, *Acción mutante*, a hybrid spoof of sci-fi, the kidnap/hijack movie and the shoot-out western. The young director parodied the trash movie in an orgy of blood, murder and gore. His next work, *El día de la bestia*, cruelly satirized films of "demonic possession" like *The Exorcist* and *The Omen*. A still younger director at twenty-three, Alejandro Amenábar took on a more problematical genre in *Tesis* (Thesis, 1996), winner of seven Goya awards. While rejecting the male violence of the degenerate snuff movie, this film undeniably owed some of its success to the prurient appeal of criminal dismemberment and mutilation. Leave it to the Spaniards to push screen violence as far as it can go without transgressing the law. Amenábar's second feature, *Abre los ojos* (Open Your Eyes, 1998), is a suspense film that proved his talent does not depend only on sensationalism.

We will end our chapter on Spanish cinema by looking at three movies from the 1999 season. Carlos Saura's *Goya en Burdeos* (Goya in Bordeaux) shows that the old child of Franco still has a few more reels in his pocket. This work evokes the final years of the great Spanish painter Francisco de Goya, exiled in southern France after the Peninsular Campaign of 1808–1814 (Spain's War of Independence). Employing some of the best talent in the world—Vittorio Storaro's beautiful cinematography, Francisco Rabal's superb acting in the role of the eighty-two-year-old Goya—Saura recalls through flashbacks the artist's past loves and tragedies, including his affair with the powerful Duquesa de Alba. After the colossal disaster of his *El Dorado* (1987), the director should have learned that historical epics are not his strong suit. (That movie was the greatest money-loser in the history of film in Spain, a country where cinematic bombs are a national institution.) But the new film is a visual knockout that is much closer to the director's heart: through Goya's life and personality he conflates some of the deepest concerns of his own art and times. The movie followed Almodóvar's *Todo sobre mi madre* with five Goya awards.

It would be hard to imagine a film more different from *Goya en Burdeos* than Benito Zambrano's *Solas* (Women Alone). Saura's movie is his thirtieth, Zambrano's his first. The veteran director's film is an expensive historical epic, *Solas* a low-budget movie with a cast of mostly unknown actors. *Goya en Burdeos* sees history from the perspective of its male protagonist, while Zambrano focuses on the present from the point of view of two women. When her father is hospitalized, a young woman is forced to live temporarily with her mother. One of their neighbors is an old man who lives alone with his dog. With affection and stubbornness, the mother manages to break her daughter's hardness and the old man's solitude. *Solas* follows the trend of recent films, discussed above, of placing women center stage. Winner of two prizes at the Berlin Festival and five Goyas, including those for best original screenplay and new director, the movie shows the abundance of fresh talent in recent Spanish cinema. Benito Zambrano is thirty-four and one of the most promising filmmakers in Spain.

The 1999 season was the year of motherhood in Spanish movies. Pedro Almodóvar's *Todo sobre mi madre* ended up as the biggest commercial and critical success, sweeping seven Goyas as well as a Golden Globe and Oscar. This movie is another vehicle for actresses by the director from La Mancha: six of the seven leading roles belong to women. Manuela, a thirty-eight-year-old woman living in Madrid, loses her teenage son in a car accident and decides to go to Barcelona in search of the boy's father. The Catalan city has never looked so attractive as it does through Almodóvar's lens, with its art nouveau and art deco buildings, its intimate plazas with palm trees, its Mediterranean light and color. Here Manuela meets an old friend who makes a living as a transvestite hooker (no surprise), and a young HIV-positive nun who has just learned that she is pregnant (ho hum). The three characters, along with a lesbian, drug-addicted actress, develop a female bond among themselves. They show that womanhood can be either born or made in Almodóvar's world: "authenticity is when you most resemble the person you dreamed you'd be," says one character. The nun gives birth to a son and dies of AIDS. At the funeral Manuela meets her former husband, the father of her dead son who has become a transvestite hooker (there are no more surprises by now). She decides to adopt the baby and returns to Madrid to raise the child, having overcome grief through female compassion and solidarity. The beauty of the film does not lie in the arbitrary plot but in the winning characters who transcend the melodrama, in their hilarious dialogue, in the rapid rhythm and flawless cutting, in the glorious colors and textures, in the sheer cinematic energy and style.

The three movies from the 1999 season give a fairly representative sampler of current Spanish film. Still obsessed with the past, the surviving "children of Franco," like Saura, continue to make thoughtful, ambitious *cine de autor* favored by small audiences in art-house theaters in Spain and abroad. The next generation of directors, embodied by Almodóvar, have focused their lens on the present and created films as beautiful as their predecessors' but less introspective and aimed at a larger, global public. Finally, younger directors like Benito Zambrano—some of them women—seem to come out of nowhere and create a few brilliant movies each year.

All three of the new works show the continued vitality of Spanish cinema in spite of the economic problems that plague the industry. Spain resembles the other European countries in that it must compete with the American juggernaut. Yet in some ways Spanish cinema enjoys a privileged situation. It continues to receive generous infusions of official aid, both from the national and regional governments. Unlike France, Italy or Germany, it has built-in cultural and linguistic appeal to hundreds of millions of Spanish-speaking spectators in Latin America and the United States. Via the company Ibermedia, it has increased coproductions with Cuba, Mexico and Argentina. If Spain learns to tap this immense market in the western hemisphere, it could have one of the most influential cinemas in the world.

SELECTED READINGS

Anuario El País 1999. Madrid: Ediciones El País, 1999.

Bermúdez, Xavier. *Buñuel. Espejo y sueño.* Valencia: Mirada, 2000.

Besas, Peter. "The Financial Structure of Spanish Cinema." In *Refiguring Spain: Cinema/Media/Representation,* edited by Marsha Kinder, 241–259. Durham, NC: Duke University Press, 1997.

D'Lugo, Marvin. *The Films of Carlos Saura: The Practice of Seeing.* Princeton, NJ: Princeton University Press, 1991.

———, ed. *Guide to the Cinema of Spain.* Westport, CT: Greenwood Press, 1997.

———. "Introduction." *Post-Script.* Special issue dedicated to Spanish film after 1992. I am indebted to Prof. D'Lugo for allowing me to consult this essay before its publication.

Evans, Peter. "Back to the Future: Cinema and Democracy." In *Spanish Cultural Studies. An Introduction. The Struggle for Modernity,* edited by Helen Graham and Jo Labanyi, 326–331. Oxford: Oxford University Press, 1995.

———. "Culture and Cinema, 1975–1996." In *The Cambridge Companion to Modern Spanish Culture,* edited by David T. Gies, 267–277. Cambridge: Cambridge University Press, 1999.

Heredero, Carlos F. *20 nuevos directores del cine español.* Madrid: Alianza, 1999.

Hopewell, John. *Out of the Past: Spanish Cinema after Franco.* London: British Film Institute, 1986.

Jordan, Barry, and Rikki Morgan-Tamosunas. *Contemporary Spanish Cinema.* Manchester: Manchester University Press, 1998.

Kinder, Marsha. *Blood Cinema: The Reconstruction of National Identity in Spain.* Berkeley: University of California Press, 1993.

———, ed. *Refiguring Spain: Cinema/Media/Representation.* Durham, NC: Duke University Press, 1997.

Otero, José María. "El horizonte de las coproducciones." In *Los límites de la frontera: la coproducción en el cine español,* 17–27. VII Congreso de la AEHC (Asociación Española de Historiadores del Cine). Madrid: Academia de las Artes y las Ciencias Cinematográficas de España, 1999.

Rodgers, Eamonn, ed. *Encyclopedia of Contemporary Spanish Culture.* London and New York: Routledge, 1999.

Torres, Augusto M., ed. *Diccionario del cine español.* Madrid: Espasa Calpe, 1994.

Vernon, Kathleen M. "Culture and Cinema to 1975." In *The Cambridge Companion to Modern Spanish Culture,* edited by Gies, 248–266. Cambridge: Cambridge University Press, 1999.

OTHER SOURCES

The best resource for the study of Spanish film in the United States is the Instituto Cervantes, 122 East 42nd Street, Suite #807, New York, NY 10168; telephone (212) 689–4232, fax (212) 545-8837, e-mail <cervanny@class.org>. For a reasonable annual membership fee, you can borrow videos by mail from a large catalogue of Spanish feature films, documentaries and television programs. Spanish and other European movies can be rented or purchased from Facets Video, 1517 West Fullerton Avenue, Chicago, IL 60614.

For the student in Spain, the Filmoteca Española has the world's most complete collection of Spanish films and related documents: Carretera Dehesa de la Villa, 28040 Madrid, Spain. The Filmoteca also has its own theater, the Cine Doré, which runs constant film cycles and festivals: Calle Santa Isabel 3, 28012 Madrid. The Center for Cinematic Research FILM-HISTORIA is based at the University of Barcelona. For information, you can write José M. Caparrós-Lera c/o FILM HISTORIA, Centre for Cinematic Research, P.O. Box 12109, 08080 Barcelona, Spain; e-mail <filmhist@trivium.gh.ub.es/>.

Several sites on the World Wide Web can be helpful to students of Spanish film. One of the best is Cinema Studies at the University of Barcelona: <http://www.swcp.com/~cmora/cine.html/>. Another is <http://www.todocine.com>.

6

Literature

A literature where tragedy is never far below the surface, where life and death go hand in glove and where the East and the West meet.
—Gerald Brenan, *The Literature of the Spanish People*[1]

Walking through Madrid's Retiro Park in late May and early June, along the graveled paths lined with flowering chestnut trees, one will see more than four hundred stands offering books for sale, from cheap paperbacks to leather-bound encyclopedias. Authors sign copies of their books and puppeteers put on shows for children. There are braille, multimedia and other special productions. The Madrid Book Fair attracts some 2.5 million visitors every year and sales reach 500,000 copies.[2]

Literature in Spain is visible and exciting as in few other countries. We have seen in Chapter 4 (Media) how colorful street kiosks display books in addition to newspapers and magazines. Publication parties (*presentaciones*) are often lavish events where authors, publishers, journalists and intellectuals gather. Writers hold forth at *tertulias* or informal discussions in restaurants and bars like the famous Café Gijón in downtown Madrid. Literary prizes abound, some of them very lucrative; Catalonia alone has more than three hundred. In contrast to the situation in the United States or the United Kingdom, writers and intellectuals have the media's ear; people actually listen to them. Membership elections and speeches by poets, playwrights and novelists at the Real Academia Española (Royal Spanish Academy) can be important news events. In more than fifty cities throughout the world, the

Instituto Cervantes—Spain's version of the Alliance Française, the Goethe Institut or the British Council—promotes Spanish language, letters and culture.

Judging by these and other facts, one would think that literature and publishing are thriving in Spain. Yet by this time we have learned to be suspicious of appearances in a country where truths often lie deep below the surface. The literature of Spain is one of the richest anywhere, but always seems to be in crisis. The nation ranks fifth in publishing in the world yet it has the lowest level of readership in Europe (50 percent). If the publishing industry in Spanish America had not collapsed in the 1970s, allowing Spain to penetrate markets in its former colonies, the situation would be much worse. Out of thirty-three hundred publishing houses, only seven hundred produce more than ten books a year, and five or six conglomerates print more than half of all titles. Corporate takeovers have become the rule of the day, as in the rest of Europe and North America. The medium-sized fish eat the small fry and they are in turn swallowed by the big fish: Anaya purchased Siruela; Santillana bought Alfaguara; Planeta acquired Seix Barral, Espasa Calpe and Destino; Plaza y Janés took over Lumen only to be absorbed by the German media giant, Bertelsmann. Publishing in Spain, like the media and cinema, runs the risk of being colonized by international giants with little concern for local people or conditions.

When we discuss literature in Spain, we need to remember that books are published in four languages. Titles in Castilian (Spanish) account for 77 percent of production; those in Catalan for 12 percent; those in Basque and Galician for 2.5 percent each.[3] All these languages have their own literatures, unique in their origins and traditions. At the end of this chapter we will refer briefly to the minority literatures.

Our emphasis will be on the present, as in all other parts of this book. From the past we will only mention those writers and works that remain living parts of the tradition; some fine old authors must be sacrificed for lack of space. Even so we will not be able to mention all the superb writers of the twentieth century. Nor will we have room to discuss the vibrant Spanish-language literatures of Latin America.

THE PAST (1000–1975)

Some literary chauvinists boast that the literature of Spain began with the Romans, claiming Seneca, Martial and others as national treasures. This is tantamount to calling Julius Caesar an Italian writer because he lived in what would one day become Italy. Greeks, Romans and Arabs all lived in the

Iberian Peninsula, but their writings in their own languages do not belong to the history of Spanish literature.

The earliest literary expressions in a Romance dialect grew out of the contacts between the three peoples of the Bible—Christians, Muslims and Jews. Short lyrical poems were sung or written around 1050 A.D. in a dialect called Mozarabic—related to early Spanish—spoken by Christians who lived in Andalusia under Moorish rule. These sensuous little jewels, known as *kharjas*, were tacked onto longer poems in Arabic or Hebrew. They tell the plight of girls who yearn for their absent lovers:

> Little mouth of pearls,
> sweet as honey,
> come, kiss me.
> My master, come to me!
> Join with me in love,
> you who fled me.[4]

Spanish literature begins with a handful of erotic miniatures where "the East and the West meet" (Brenan). This hybrid quality prevails in many other works written during the Middle Ages in the Peninsula.

All literatures are born in verse, but in few cultures has poetry flourished as in Spain. This is especially true of anonymous folk-poetry, similar to the *kharjas*. As the great poet Antonio Machado would say centuries later, "In our literature everything that is not folklore is pedantry. . . . True poetry is created by the people."[5] In the early Middle Ages, largely unknown Galician poets created *cantigas de amigo*, "the most beautiful song poetry of the Middle Ages,"[6] while nameless poets in Castile and Andalusia sang *villancicos* for every occasion—harvests, weddings, funerals, pilgrimages—or ballads of love, religion, legend and war. This abundant traditional verse flows like a river—now above ground, now below—through a thousand years of Spanish life. At times it has been ignored and almost lost, but it has always surfaced to freshen and nourish. During the early euphoria of the Renaissance, for example, when the fashion of elegant Italian verse-forms threatened to dominate the field, some poets rediscovered the traditional lyric, absorbing it in their poems and plays. Mystic writers like St. Teresa and St. John of the Cross, playwrights like Lope de Vega and Tirso de Molina, Baroque poets like Francisco de Quevedo and Luis de Góngora felt the pull of folk-poetry. All moved gracefully between the two styles, high and low, Italianate and Spanish. Among the major writers of the early modern period—also known as the Golden Age (c. 1500–1675)—only Garcilaso de la Vega, Luis de León,

Fernando de Herrera and Pedro Calderón de la Barca failed to immerse themselves in this mighty river of anonymous poetry. It went underground in the dry period of the Enlightenment, only to erupt like a geyser under the Romantics. Nineteenth-century poets like Gustavo Adolfo Bécquer and Rosalía de Castro renewed the stale rhetoric of Spanish verse with infusions of popular songs and ballads. They passed on their legacy to Antonio Machado, Juan Ramón Jiménez and the constellation of brilliant poets who turned the twentieth century into a second golden age of poetry in Spain: Jorge Guillén, Pedro Salinas, Federico García Lorca, Vicente Aleixandre, Rafael Alberti, Luis Cernuda, Miguel Hernández. In the following verses by Lorca we see a fusion of traditional verse with a modern sensibility; these lines recall the erotic quality of the *kharjas*, written almost a thousand years earlier in the poet's native Andalusia:

> Nobody understood the perfume
> of the dark magnolia in your womb.
> Nobody knew that you tormented
> a hummingbird of love in your teeth.[7]

After poetry, drama has been one of the peaks of Spanish literature. In fact the two are closely entwined: poetic drama has flourished in the Peninsula more than any other western country. Only Great Britain has a theatrical tradition as rich as Spain's, but prose drama has prevailed there after the Elizabethan period. Like nearly everything in Spain, theater started late, but soon made up for lost ground. By the early sixteenth century, playwrights had begun to realize the dramatic potential of the Spanish language. By the seventeenth century, the whole nation was swept up in a theatrical passion. The Church saw this fervor as a threat to religion and public morals; in spite of bans and threats of excommunication, people continued to fill the playhouses. Dramatists could not produce plays fast enough to satisfy the public's hunger for new works. The most famous dramatist, Lope de Veda, could turn out two full plays in a week. He wrote an estimated fifteen hundred *comedias* (plays), not to mention his novels and poetry. No wonder Cervantes called him, with a pinch of envy and malice, a *monstruo de la naturaleza*, a portent of nature. Unlike Shakespeare, Lope did not create masterpieces that are read and performed around the world. The power of his works is in the sum, in the prodigious life, action and love he poured into them. The same could be said of Tirso de Molina and Pedro Calderón de la Barca, the other major dramatists of the period. Tirso wrote *El Burlador de Sevilla* (The Mocker of Sevilla, 1630), the debut of that irresistible sinner, Don Juan. The

Andalusian lover, Don Juan, and the Castilian knight, Don Quixote, are the two mythical figures given to the world by Spain. Among the many works inspired by Tirso's character are Wolfgang Mozart's *Don Giovanni*, Lord Byron's *Don Juan* and George Bernard Shaw's *Man and Superman*. Like Tirso, Calderón de la Barca was a man of the cloth. His *La vida es sueño* (Life Is a Dream, 1635) showed the sacred side of Spanish life much more than *El Burlador*. The play has some good poetry, but today reads like a theological treatise in verse. It was the agony of a tradition that had endured for centuries, a literature "where tragedy is never far below the surface, where life and death go hand in hand" (Brenan). It was also the end of a marriage between art and religion that had created an unprecedented flowering of verse, drama and prose.

Like poetry, theater enjoyed a revival in the nineteenth century. José de Zorrilla wrote *Don Juan Tenorio* (1844), a Romantic version of *El Burlador de Sevilla*. While Tirso de Molina sent his Don Juan to hell for breaking the laws of God and man, Zorrilla saved the sinner through a woman's love. *Don Juan Tenorio* is still performed in Spanish-speaking cities throughout the world around November 2, All Souls' Day, to celebrate the triumph of love over death.

The members of the so-called "Generation of 1898" wrote drama as well as fiction and poetry. Jacinto Benavente penned moralistic dramas that quickly fell out of favor. Ramón del Valle-Inclán wrote experimental dramas that are still performed today. But the renewal of Spanish drama was carried out above all by a brilliant member of the next generation, García Lorca. Combining the tradition of the Golden Age *comedia*, the linguistic innovations of Valle-Inclán and other modern writers with his own unbelievable poetic gift, he wrote a string of plays in both verse and prose that are the most frequently performed works on the Spanish stage. The summit of Lorca's drama was his trilogy of rural tragedies—*Bodas de Sangre* (Blood Wedding, 1933), *Yerma* (Barren, 1934) and *La casa de Bernarda Alba* (The House of Bernarda Alba, 1936). He also wrote some of the most original poetry of the twentieth century. There was almost no limit to what Lorca might have done—if he had not been assassinated in the early days of the Civil War (1936–1939). In addition to being a poet and playwright, he was also a talented painter and musician. No other artist in any country could match the variety and depth of his talent.

In general Spanish literature is somewhat less fertile in prose than in drama and poetry. It has been especially poor in speculative works, due in part to the oppressive influence of kings, clerics and generals. Or it could be that Spaniards are so "obsessed by the problems of their own country that they have not much to give, in the way of ideas, to the rest of Europe."[8] Nor until quite recently has the nation produced a respectable body of letters, diaries, memoirs and autobiographies. If we were to judge by published works, we might believe that Spaniards did not have private lives until the late twentieth century.

The one exception to the relative weakness of prose is an important one, the novel. Fernando de Rojas' unclassifiable *Celestina* (1499) has been called the first European novel, as well as one of the greatest—in spite of the fact that it was published as a play. It was followed half a century later by a slim, anonymous masterpiece that created a whole new kind of fiction. *Lazarillo de Tormes* was the first picaresque novel and remains the best, a compelling story about a young boy who goes from one master to another in search of food and shelter, exposing a mordant, ironic cross section of Spanish society. The work was imitated for centuries in all the major European languages. The picaresque became one of the most original contributions of Spain to world literature.

Miguel de Cervantes, often known as the Spanish Shakespeare, absorbed the influences of the picaresque and other forms to create his *Don Quixote* (1605–1615), the most widely read book in the Castilian language. What began as a parody of novels of chivalry—the pulp fiction of the time—ended as a mature synthesis of every major genre of writing. The work also owed a special debt to popular literature: "Without novels of chivalry and ancient ballads to parody, Cervantes might not have written his *Quixote*. . . . Without his assimilation and mastery of a language ripe with wisdom and popular consciousness, neither the immortal work nor anything like it could have been written."[9] Cervantes presents the Spanish world of his time, from picaresque thieves and prostitutes to priests and nobles. His protagonists and foils, the visionary gentleman Don Quixote and the pragmatic peasant Sancho Panza, are two of the most memorable characters in fiction. Thanks to his subtle, ironic mind, Cervantes was able to rise above the religious and political fanaticism of the period to anticipate the modern sense of freedom.

After the seventeenth century, the novel passed through a drought until its rebirth in the mid-1800s. The third great Spanish novelist, after Rojas and Cervantes, was Benito Pérez Galdós. Unlike his predecessors, he did not concentrate his vision into a single great work, but spread it across a lifetime of production. He has been called the Spanish Balzac and Dickens, although he never equaled them in mastery of plot or style. Hemingway told a Spanish friend that Galdós' work reminded him of "an old man's stale urine."[10]

The novel was one of the preferred forms of the well-known Generation of 1898, named for the disastrous Spanish-American War that drove Spain from its last colonies and forced the country to reevaluate its place in the world. Pío Baroja was a Basque doctor who preferred writing to practicing medicine; he was not so much a novelist as a talkative misanthrope armed with a typewriter. Yet the loose nature of his writing sometimes managed to give a spontaneous sense of life. His contemporary Miguel de Unamuno, the most well-known Spanish philosopher of the twentieth century, was a better thinker than novelist. His fiction always seemed to be moved by ideas more than plot or character. Valle-Inclán was the purest writer of the time, an eccentric Galician whose works have outlasted those of everyone else in his generation. His sense of the grotesque (*esperpento*) still has an oddly contemporary ring.

On the eve of the Civil War, Spain was in the forefront of world literature for the first time since the seventeenth century. The poets Machado and Jiménez (Nobel Prize, 1956), the playwrights Valle-Inclán and Benavente (Nobel Prize, 1922) and the novelists Baroja and Valle-Inclán were still alive. Unamuno and José Ortega y Gasset gave the country its two best philosophers in centuries. Better still, younger writers like Guillén, Salinas, Lorca, Aleixandre, and Cernuda were approaching the height of their powers. The situation in the other arts was nearly as brilliant. In painting, Pablo Picasso, Joan Miró and Salvador Dalí had conquered Paris. In music, Manuel de Falla combined the best influences of the country's popular tradition with those of the European vanguard. In film, Luis Buñuel blended Spanish themes with surrealism. In short, Spain was an artistic superpower unsurpassed by any other country in the world.

The Civil War killed some of these artists and drove others into exile. Spanish art passed from the limelight into the shadows. For half a century a brain-drain would deplete the ranks of the nation's artists, intellectuals and scientists. Referring to the years of Franco's dictatorship (1939–1975), historians speak of "two Spains": one at home, languishing under tyranny and censorship; the other abroad, "*la España peregrina*" (pilgrim Spain), yearning for the homeland.

In retrospect, it is surprising that literature managed to survive as well as it did. First of all, censorship was never as efficient as it was in Germany under the Nazis. By nature, bureaucrats are not literary critics; they often failed to catch the subtlety of passages in poems, plays, short stories and novels. Poetry suffered less than the other genres because it tends to be more elliptical and because it normally does not reach a large public. Moreover, the censors could be manipulated by personal contacts and influences, as in every other area of Spanish life. Second, translations of foreign works allowed writers to keep abreast of currents abroad. Third, beginning in the 1950s, the tourist invasion brought other foreign influences to the country. Finally, the boom of Latin American literature, with the residence of writers like Gabriel García Márquez and Mario Vargas Llosa in Spain, led to the creation of a pan-Hispanic literature that would break down the barriers between the mother country and its former colonies.

A glance at the literature of the dictatorship might make us wonder who were the victors and who the defeated. If the fascists won the Civil War, they lost the cultural battle. Leading poets like Aleixandre, Blas de Otero, Jaime Gil de Biedma, Gloria Fuertes and Angel González were either neutral in politics or connected to the leftist underground. The one dramatist who consistently wrote plays worthy of Spain's powerful theatrical tradition, Antonio Buero Vallejo, had been a combatant for the Spanish Republic and had suffered years of prison. Novelists like Camilo José Cela, Miguel Delibes, Carmen Laforet, Luis Martín Santos and Ana María Matute revealed a critical and ironic vision of Spain in their works. These and other writers kept Spanish literature alive during the darkest times of tyranny, poverty and isolation. For this reason it has been said that Francoism really ended before the Generalissimo died in 1975. The irrationality, informality, irony and complexity of many works already reflected writing in other countries, as well as anticipating the literature of post-Franco democracy. Poets, dramatists and novelists had steadily criticized, parodied and undermined the fascist monolith. In the eyes of many Spaniards and most foreigners, writers, artists and intellectuals had won the moral battle. When the Generalissimo finally died in November 1975, Spain had already entered the modern and the postmodern world.

THE PRESENT (1975–2000)

After the brief euphoria that followed Franco's death, the country fell into a period of disenchantment (*desencanto*). Some writers found it hard to recover their inspiration. Novelist Juan Goytisolo, for example, had based most of his novels on a cynical view of Francoist Spain; with the enemy gone, he had little to write *against*.[11] He took years to find a new voice. While fascist diehards chanted "*Con Franco vivíamos mejor*" (We lived better under Franco), the novelist Manuel Vázquez Montalbán spoke for many intellectuals when he punned that "*Contra Franco vivíamos mejor*" (We lived better against Franco). Speaking for both sides, others added ironically, "*Bajo Franco éramos más jóvenes*" (We were younger under Franco).

The best example of literary success in contemporary Spain is Camilo José Cela. Rare among Spanish writers, he managed to live from his pen for some thirty years under the fascists; later he won the Nobel Prize for literature (1989) and the Cervantes Prize (1995) under the Socialists. Only a protean figure like Cela could have pulled off such a trick. Although he was a combatant on the winning side in the Civil War, like so many Spaniards he changed his political tune and became a curmudgeonly defender of democratic Spain. Cela has carried out a kind of personal campaign in favor of freedom of speech, especially the freedom to cuss, swear and write scatology. His two-volume *Diccionario secreto* (Secret Dictionary) and four-volume *Enciclopedia del erotismo* (Encyclopedia of Eroticism) have added to his reputation as the Spanish writer with the most salacious tongue since Quevedo. His ingenious *Rol de cornudos* (Rollcall of Cuckolds) is an anthology of quotations by Spanish writers from the Middle Ages to the modern period, along with many of his own words, to describe no less than 364 varieties of men whose wives deceive them. But the main reason for Cela's success is his mastery of the Spanish language in all registers, from classical rhetoric to contemporary slang. He has assimilated major influences from the past—the *Celestina*, the picaresque, Cervantes, Quevedo, Goya, Galdós and the realists, Valle-Inclán and the modernists, surrealism and the vanguard—mixed them with his own sardonic vision and created a series of powerful, violent novels stretching from *La familia de Pascual Duarte* (The Family of Pascual Duarte, 1942) through *La colmena* (The Hive, 1951), *San Camilo, 1936* (1969), *Oficio de tinieblas 5* (Tenebrae, 1973), *Mazurca para dos muertos* (Mazurca for Two Cadavers, 1983) to *Madera de boj* (Boxwood, 1999). The bloodshed, degrading sexuality and incest, pessimism, despair and obsession with death, all expressed in a rich, vast range of language, make Cela a writer who could hardly be from any other country but Spain.[12]

Almost the antithesis of the flamboyant Cela is the Castilian novelist Miguel Delibes, who for fifty years has quietly and steadily created a body of fiction from his home in Valladolid (Old Castile). Several generations of Spanish readers have remained loyal to this writer, born like them into the provincial bourgeoisie, who has expressed the wistfulness of lost ambitions, the truths that reside in nature, the need for tolerance and solidarity to heal the country's wounds. Like other novelists of his generation, Delibes has seen the Civil War and its aftermath as the prime sources of tension in Spanish society. *Mi idolatrado hijo Sisí* (My Beloved Son Sisí, 1953) and *Cinco horas con Mario* (Five Hours with Mario, 1966) attempt to surpass the divisiveness of the conflict through a kind of stoic resignation and understanding. Later novels like *El disputado voto del señor Cayo* (The Fight for Señor Cayo's Vote, 1978), *Los santos inocentes* (The Holy Innocents, 1981), *377A, Madera de héroe* (The Stuff of Heroes, 1987), and *El hereje* (The

Heretic, 1998) refine the author's vision and make him one of the most sensible voices in Spanish letters. The author has also published several volumes of memoirs, in particular on his favorite pastimes of hunting and fishing. After winning the National Prize for Literature for his last novel, Miguel Delibes declared that "I will not write again, although other miracles have occurred."[13]

Carmen Martín Gaite, slightly younger than Delibes, also had her origins in Old Castile, but at a young age she moved to Madrid. There she joined a group of writers who shared a critical view of the Franco regime and a desire to regenerate Spanish fiction. Unlike most male novelists, she preferred to describe the lives of women, as in her *El cuarto de atrás* (The Back Room, 1978), *Nubosidad variable* (Partly Cloudy, 1992) and *Irse de casa* (Leaving Home, 1998). Like Cela and Delibes, she mastered many registers of colloquial Spanish, especially the language of intimacy, popular culture and the media. Martín Gaite often blended her fiction with autobiographical elements and reflections on the act of writing. In addition to her novels, she published theater, poetry, essays and memoirs. Several of her works have been adapted for television and the cinema; she also wrote scripts for TV. Until her death in 2000, Carmen Martín Gaite was an example of the writer as a semipublic figure in Spain: several of her works were adapted for cinema, she wrote scripts for television, participated in literary events organized by the Juan March Foundation, and was a popular figure at the Madrid Book Fair.

A much younger novelist, Juan Marsé, bases his novels in Catalonia but has opted for writing in Castilian rather than Catalan. In this way he has reached an audience both within and outside his native region. His works bear emotional and sarcastic witness to the pain of life in postwar Barcelona. *Ultimas tardes con Teresa* (Last Evenings with Teresa, 1966) exposes the class barriers in Catalan society during the Franco period. *Si te dicen que caí* (The Fallen, 1973) explores the potential for self-deception among children who attempt to reconstruct their past through memories, imagination, rumors and films. In *La muchacha de las bragas de oro* (The Girl with the Golden Panties, 1978), a fascist historian tries to justify his past by writing an autobiography, only to discover that the fiction he creates is closer to truth than the memories he attempts to deny. In *El amante bilingüe* (The Bilingual Lover, 1990), Marsé creates a protagonist with a name curiously similar to his own—Juan Marés—a *charnego* (immigrant in Catalonia) whose masculine identity is destroyed by his wealthy wife and the discrimination against outsiders in a nationalistic society. At the end of the novel, the character's personality disintegrates, his bilingualism lapses into meaningless babble, and the narration grinds to a halt. In his most recent novel, *Rabos de lagartija*

(Lizard Tails, 2000), an unborn fetus tells the story of his brother in the postwar years, with the freshness and awe of someone whose sensibility has not been deadened by the world. For reasons hard to fathom, several of Juan Marsé's novels have been turned into movies, mostly by the Catalan director Vicente Aranda. Some of these films have been successful, but cinema can hardly capture the linguistic and stylistic density of the author's voice.

Rosa Montero is one of a new breed of women authors with a devoted readership. Unlike most American and British writers who tend to teach for a living, Montero and other Spanish authors work as journalists. She started to write for the newspaper *El País* at the age of eighteen and has not ceased contributing to its pages, participating in an estimated two thousand interviews over a span of thirty years. She has won several awards for her reporting. Montero's career as a novelist began with an editor's request for a collection of interviews with women. Wishing to depart from a purely journalistic style, she wrote a narrative documentary titled *Crónica de desamor* (Absent Love: A Chronicle, 1979), containing the stories of four women who express their opinions about divorce, sexuality, birth control, abortion, homosexuality and other topics that had been forbidden during the dictatorship. Montero eased into fiction with *La función Delta* (The Delta Function, 1981), focusing on a woman who recalls her life in the 1980s as she dies in the year 2010. After the success of these works, the author tried her hand at various fictional genres and styles: *Te trataré como a una reina* (I'll Treat You Like a Queen, 1983) is a murder mystery that reveals the inequality of the sexes; *Temblor* (Trembling, 1990) is an allegory of a post-holocaust world of the future; *El nido de los sueños* (The Nest of Dreams, 1991) is a children's novel; *Bella y oscura* (Beautiful and Dark, 1993) shows the influence of magic realism in its fusion of fantasy and reportage. Montero's latest novel, *La hija del caníbal* (Daughter of the Cannibal, 1998), may be her most balanced work of fiction, with male characters who are as complex and fascinating as the women. Rosa Montero's critics consider her creative work to be too journalistic. She defends herself by saying that journalism does not necessarily run contrary to fiction, and that it may be considered a new genre of literature.

Antonio Muñoz Molina is another contemporary novelist who shifts nimbly between fiction and journalism. In his occasional return to the period of the Spanish Republic and Civil War, he resembles the novelists of earlier generations but without an ideological axe to grind and with a more lyrical, sensuous style. He is one of those writers who burst on the scene with a language and a vision that already seemed complete: critics speak of the "initial maturity" of Muñoz Molina's work.[14] From the beginning he showed a predilection for rhythmic language that sometimes seems closer to verse than prose; for the unexpected adjective in phrases like "light and cruel music"; for synesthesia or blending of sensorial impressions as in "fragrance of shadows"; for striking images like "cafés so sad that they are frequented only by the dead." Muñoz Molina's first novel, *Beatus ille* (1986), evoked the artistic generation of the 1930s in Spain. After experiments with the thriller—*Invierno en Lisboa* (Winter in Lisbon, 1987)—and the spy novel—*Beltenebros* (1989)—he wrote another brilliant evocation of the Civil War in *El jinete polaco* (The Polish Horseman, 1992). His latest novel, *Plenilunio* (Full Moon, 1997), is a murder mystery written in the author's signature poetic style. Muñoz Molina's novels have been best-sellers and some have been turned into films. In addition to fiction he has published collections of essays drawn from his newspaper columns.

The last novelist we will discuss here is Javier Marías, who could be seen as representative of some recent trends in Spanish fiction. While most of the writers mentioned above have shown an obsession with recent Spanish history, he has made a conscious effort to escape the ghosts of the Republic and Civil War. Most of his novels resist the nostalgic pull of the past and are set in a kind of dateless present. Marías' protagonists are typically bourgeois, selfish and lonely; in the end they may discover nothing more than a hint of their possible maturity. These characters often have nothing peculiarly Spanish about them and they could be from any western country, especially Great Britain, for which the novelist shows a particular attraction. Marías is the most Anglophile of novelists in Spain, a country whose writers have normally received their influences from France, Italy or Germany. His novels include *Todas las almas* (All the Souls, 1989), *Corazón tan blanco* (A Heart So White, 1992) and *Mañana en la batalla piensa en mí* (Remember Me Tomorrow in the Battle, 1994). He has also published short stories—*Cuando fui mortal* (When I Was Mortal, 1996)—collected articles, travel writings, biographies and translations.

Authors like Javier Marías and Antonio Muñoz Molina represent the generation of Spanish novelists who have lived most of their lives since Franco's death. We have seen that Muñoz Molina sets some of his works in the past, but overall he too favors the present. Unlike older writers such as Delibes, Martín Gaite and Marsé, who experienced the Civil War and lived most of their lives under the dictatorship, the younger novelists do not feel compelled to dwell on recent Spanish history. For this and other reasons their books often contain more humor, irony and parody, and may resemble works by foreign writers more than those of their Spanish predecessors. Tragedy does not always threaten and life is far more interesting than death. These books often have a cosmopolitan tone and setting. One critic has noted that "out of a choice that can only be significant, the protagonists of *Jinete polaco* by Muñoz Molina and *Corazón tan blanco* by Marías work as translators and live out their conflicts in airports and between foreign sheets."[15] The novels of both authors are translated into major languages and have won literary prizes abroad. Antonio Muñoz Molina and Javier Marías represent the coming of age of Spanish writing, the trend toward a more European or global literature.

Another important trend is the flourishing of autobiographical writing. Cela has said, "the pirouettes of memory against the backdrop of time . . . would be, without any doubt, a wonderful ingredient for cooking literature."[16] As we have seen earlier, memoirs and letters were scarce before Franco's death. After the public nature of so much writing during the years of resistance, we are now seeing a more private kind of communication based on immediate experience and direct emotion. Precedents include Carlos Barral's *Años de penitencia* (Years of Penitence, 1975), *Años sin excusa* (Years without Forgiveness, 1978), and *Cuando las horas veloces* (The Swift Hours, 1986) and Rosa Chacel's *Alcancía, Ida* (Piggy Bank, Departure) and *Alcancía, Vuelta* (Piggy Bank, Return), both published in 1982. It is no coincidence that these works did not appear until the dictatorship had crumbled. The current trend owes a lot to the Catalan poet Pere Gimferrer's delicate *Dietaris* (Diaries), written in the late 1970s and translated into Spanish in 1982, and to journalist Francisco Umbral's popular column, "Diario de un snob" (Diary of a Snob), published in *El País* throughout the 1980s. Most of the other writers in this genre have also been linked to major newspapers. Miguel Sánchez Ostiz's *La negra provincia de Flaubert* (Flaubert's Black Province, 1986) is a personal journey through French literature, music and memories as seen from the city of Pamplona. The title of Rafael Sánchez Ferlosio's diaries reveals his somber desperation—*Vendrán más años malos y nos harán más ciegos* (More Bad Years Will Come and Make Us Blinder, 1993). Following Barral's ironic model, the poet Antonio Martínez Sarrión has come out with both the first volume of his memoirs, *Infancia y corrupciones* (Infancy and Corruption, 1993) and a diary, *Cargar la suerte* (untranslatable, 1995). Manuel Vicent has used his terse prose to evoke his native Levante in *Contra paraíso* (Against Paradise, 1993) and *Tranvía a la Malvarrosa* (Streetcar to Malvarrosa, 1994), works that lie midway between the novel and imaginary memoirs. Finally, poet, novelist and journalist Andrés Trapiello has produced an apparently endless series of reminiscences under the title of "Salón de los pasos perdidos" (The Hall of Forgotten Steps), which also combines memory and fiction: *El gato encerrado* (The Caged Cat, 1990), *Locuras sin fundamento* (Madness without Reason, 1992), *El tejado de vidrio* (The Glass Roof, 1994) and *Las nubes por dentro* (The Clouds Inside, 1996). These books are all quite different but overlap in their use of private voices to comment on recent events. This may be the newest form of participation by writers in public life, in a society that is "fluid, forgetful and permissive."[17]

Not by chance have we considered prose before poetry and the theater in the contemporary period. While these two genres were often the peaks of Spanish literature from the beginnings through the mid-twentieth century, they have now been displaced by fiction. The same has occurred in other countries. One critic says "the novel has eclipsed poetry, both as what writers write and what readers read and, since the 1960s, narrative has come to dominate literary education as well."[18] The change is partly related to the commercialization of publishing and the commodification of the book—two terms as ugly as the phenomena they describe. If best-selling novelists now become media figures who command huge advances, they tend to write fiction instead of poetry or drama, two genres known to be risky investments. Many of the best-selling memoirs cited above were in fact written by poets in search of a larger audience: Gimferrer and Martínez Sarrión have written primarily in verse, while Chacel and Trapiello have also published poetry. Some critics have spoken of a "flight from poetry" and we might say something similar of contemporary theater, as we will see in the next chapter (Chapter 7, Performing Arts).

Spanish verse is heir to one of the richest poetic traditions in modern Europe. However, the death or exile of many members of the pre-Civil War generation left a vacuum during the dictatorship. Poets like Aleixandre, Otero and Gil de Biedma wrote social, existential work that often fell under the censor's knife. In search of different themes, younger writers sought a more personal tone. Claudio Rodríguez wrote dense visionary poetry, José Angel Valente created a minimalist style, Francisco Brines published dark metaphysical verse. In 1970, a selection of talented young poets appeared in a famous anthology compiled by José María Castellet, *Nueve novísimos poetas españoles* (Nine Very New Spanish Poets, 1970), that fell like a bomb in Spain's closed literary world. These artists, all in their twenties or early thirties, suddenly brought Spanish writing into the contemporary world of popular culture, kitsch and camp. They rejected the loose form of the social poets and returned to the crafted verse of the prewar masters, while seeking new subject matter. They had cosmopolitan influences that ranged from the Spanish classics to Arthur Rimbaud, Rubén Darío, surrealism and the vanguard, Ezra Pound, T. S. Eliot and contemporary writers in Europe, America and Asia. Here are some lines from Pere Gimferrer's long poem *La muerte en Beverly Hills* (Death in Beverly Hills, 1967), included in Castellet's famous anthology:

Jean Harlow's smiles! The bungalow at dawn and the glittering
   sea . . .
I know your fingernails painted red, the bewitching oval of your
   face, your nymphette's smile, pasty and moist . . .
When the dawn arrives they will find me dead and call Charlie
   Chan.[19]

These poets fused personal stories with the collective myths of popular culture—usually American: the movies, television, jazz, rock and roll. Poets like
Gimferrer, Guillermo Carnero, Leopoldo María Panero and Ana María Moix
possess a vast knowledge of both the high and the low traditions, the old and
the new. Their poetry has been associated with "culturalism" for its constant
references to literature, film, art, music and the media.

Some poets of this generation have continued writing in a similar vein,
while others have changed with the times. Moving from Spanish to Catalan
in 1970, Gimferrer has not swerved in his search for poetic perfection. (We
will discuss his later work under the minority literatures below.) Carnero has
also continued to create highly intellectual poetry, but has moved back and
forth from free verse to structured forms like the sonnet. Panero evolved
toward a more narrative poetry. Moix turned to the short story and the novel.
Another poet, Luis Antonio de Villena, started in the mode of the *novísimos*
but later denounced the excesses of culturalism. He made his reputation as
a poet with a sensual, luxurious style, often with erotic themes and word
play:

because there is nothing like placing the hand
of love on the youthful plane of a body,
and setting fire to that artful text.[20]

Although he continues publishing poetry, Villena has made a second reputation as a novelist, short-story writer, biographer and chronicler of the contemporary cultural situation, especially the gay scene and nightlife of Madrid.
In this too he is an example of the flight from verse into more popular genres.

Spanish poetry in the 1980s has followed two general trends. First, some
poets have continued in the line of the *novísimos* or the minimalists, showing
extreme care for sound and form and a continued sympathy for vanguardist
experimentation. Jaime Siles is a professor of ancient literature who writes
understated verse with classic and baroque echoes. María Victoria Atencia
creates poems that are usually short, subtle and intimate. Andrés Sánchez

Robayna has published many volumes of verse with a metaphysical bent. Finally, Amparo Amorós often develops the theme of poetry and life; here a flight of seagulls recalls art's power to stop time:

> In their perfect moment
> the seagulls
> do not fly
> they fall into the air
> delivered to the wind.[21]

The second major group in the last two decades comprises the "poets of experience" or "the new sentimentality," who disdain the experiments of the *novísimos* in favor of a more accessible poetry, returning in some ways to the social poets of the 1960s. Luis García Montero has become a spokesman for this group; he believes that poetry should steer a middle course between the irrationalism of the vanguard and the pragmatism of the neocapitalist world.[22] Jon Juarísti, the best poet from the Basque Country, writes in an impressive range of voices, tones and registers. Lastly, Felipe Benítez Reyes also has a varied style; here he evokes the nostalgia for lost youth:

> The girls give themselves as always
> and young boys drink from the same cup
> that we emptied in our time
> when the world belonged to us.[23]

Perhaps the most significant trend in both poetry and prose is the explosion of female writing. This has been made possible by the improved social status of women, the expansion of the publishing industry and the emergence of subgenres, like erotic literature, to which many female authors have contributed. In the novel we saw the names of Martín Gaite and Montero; we could have mentioned many more—Esther Tusquets, Marina Mayoral, Lourdes Ortiz, Soledad Puértolas, Almudena Grandes, Lucía Etxebarria. In poetry, Ana Rossetti and Blanca Andreu are examples of women who challenge accepted attitudes about gender and sexuality. In brilliantly polished lines, Rossetti reverses traditional gender roles by granting desire and the erotic gaze to the woman:

> To wander
> along the double avenue of your legs,

to travel along the smooth burning honey,
take my time, and on the promiscuous edge,
where the enigma conceals its portent,
to restrain myself . . . [24]

Like so many male poets, Rossetti has also fled to other genres like the novel and has even written an opera libretto. Once the *enfant terrible* of Spanish letters, Andreu has now passed her fortieth birthday without abandoning poetry. There are many other fine female poets in Spain today: Margarita Merino, Almudena Guzmán, Luisa Castro and Ana Merino, to mention only a few.

The regional literatures of Spain are usually not translated into Castilian and are therefore unaccessible to most foreigners. Catalonia has a venerable literary tradition going back to the Middle Ages. Poets Ausias March, Jacinto Verdaguer, Joan Maragall, Josep Carner, Carles Riba, J. V. Foix and Salvador Espriu left a powerful medium for their descendants, as did prose writers like Josep Pla, Pere Calders, Joan Fuster and Llorenç Villalonga. Although Catalan literature suffered from brutal prohibition and censorship during the Franco years, it has recovered and remains a vital part of the region's culture. As we have seen above, some writers from the region have published only in Castilian, like Goytisolo, Marsé and Vázquez Montalbán. Others have preferred their native language, like Mercè Rodoreda, Joan Brossa and Montserrat Roig. Here we will look at two contemporary authors who have cast their lot with Catalan.

Terençi Moix's debut on the literary scene of the 1960s was regarded as a minor Copernican revolution. While other writers were still struggling to come to terms with the Civil War and its aftermath, Moix leaped into the new world of pop, mass and gay cultures. He is the author of many novels as well as essays and dramas. Moix's fiction falls into two distinct groups. Some works, like *La increada consciència de la raça* (The Uncreated Conscience of the Race, 1974), adopt a realistic style to narrate events from Catalonian history and the author's homosexual past. Others, like *La caiguda de l'imperi sodomita* (The Fall of the Sodomite Empire, 1974), combine fantasies and myths from popular culture. Although he began his career in Catalan, Moix switched to Castilian in 1983 and soon became the country's best-selling author. After proving himself on the national stage, Moix returned to Catalan in 1992 with his novel *El sexe dels àngels* (The Sex of the Angels). All his works are now translated immediately into Castilian in order to capture both markets. Although he has been a great popular success, many critics consider Moix to be a lightweight and either disparage his writing or ignore it altogether.[25] In any case, his works contrast sharply with those of earlier novelists and place him squarely in a postmodern world.

Catalonia is proud to have the most prestigious poet in all of Spain, Pere Gimferrer. His works are translated into Castilian and are always major literary events. Gimferrer is an example of the complete *hombre de letras* or man of letters, equally at home in prose and verse but always centering his work in poetry. Besides many volumes of verse, he has published his diaries (mentioned above), criticism, essays and a novel. Gimferrer is also a fanatical lover of film, has written on the movies, and incorporates cinematic techniques in his verse—abrupt cuts, montage and flashbacks. His early collections of poetry stressed the search for identity. Like other *novísimos*, he has written erotic poetry that sees sexuality—even coprophilia, for example—as a path to higher perception. His later works deal more with the process of creation itself, turning into a kind of meta-poetry whose subject is the failure of language to capture life. The formal perfection of Gimferrer's verse makes his pessimism easier to swallow.

The literature of Galicia is written in *galego* or Galician (see Chapter 1, Context). Like Catalan, it has an ancient tradition and suffered terribly under the dictatorship. With only half the population of Catalonia and a less prosperous economy, however, its literature and other cultural forms are more precarious. The Xunta de Galicia, the semiautonomous regional government, has probably been more successful in preserving the cultural legacy than in stimulating new creativity. Galician writers have followed in the footsteps of their famous predecessors like Rosalía de Castro and Celso Emilio Ferreiro in poetry and Edward Blanco Amor and Alvaro Cunqueiro in the novel. Carlos Casares is a post–Civil War poet, novelist and critic who has opened his work to international and experimental influences. Younger writers like Ramiro Fonte, Manuel Rivas and Xohana Torres revisit old Galician themes of poverty, migration and loss with new ideas and imagery, confronting the region's traditional past with the technology and consumerism of the postmodern world. As always, the musicality of *galego* makes poetry an especially beautiful genre in this region.

Finally, the Basque Country has an even smaller population and a less venerable tradition than either Galicia or Catalonia. While in these two regions literature has always been a primary cultural expression, in Euzkadi it has been overshadowed by popular music and dance. Nevertheless, the modest expansion of *euskera* in the last quarter of the twentieth century, plus generous assistance from the semiautonomous government, has encouraged publication in the regional language. Arantxa Urretabizkaia is a successful woman author who writes in Basque. Bernardo Atxaga is the first writer whose work in *euskera* has achieved local, national and international success. His remarkable collection of short stories, *Obabakoak* (The People of Obaba, 1988), abandons the portrayal of regional life in favor of pastiche and collage. As the author says in the postscript, "Today, nothing is uniquely characteristic. The world is everywhere."[26] His words could be a motto for all writing in Spain today, whether in Basque, Galician, Catalan or Castilian.

Literature in the Iberian Peninsula has changed dramatically since Gerald Brenan described its classic emphasis on death and tragedy with a fusion of western and eastern influences. In many writers today, in both prose and poetry, the tragic sense of life is alleviated by a postmodern sense of irony and humor, and influences from the non-Western world are no more prevalent than in France. Yet in other ways, the situation is not so different. Most Spanish writers still have a pessimistic vision, as do most of their compatriots. A happy ending to a Spanish novel or short story is when the protagonist learns the reason for his misery.[27] Low readership, the removal of literary works from school curricula and the dominance of the electronic media have made many writers skeptical about the future of their medium. Some believe that Spanish literature is hanging on the edge of an abyss, that its present flourishing may be like the last days of Pompeii.[28] Others respond by saying that there are more good young writers in Spain than at any time in its history.

SELECTING READINGS

Alborg, J. L. *Historia de la literatura española*. 5 vols. Madrid: Gredos, 1966–1995.

Alvar, Carlos, José-Carlos Mainer and Rosa Navarro. *Breve historia de la literatura española*. Madrid: Alianza, 1998. The best one-volume history of Spanish literature.

Brenan, Gerald. *The Literature of the Spanish People*. Cambridge: Cambridge University Press, 1962.

García de la Concha, Víctor, ed. *Historia de la literatura española*. 9 vols. Madrid: Espasa Calpe, 1995–present.

Gies, David T., ed. *The Cambridge Companion to Modern Spanish Culture*. Cambridge: Cambridge University Press, 1999.

Graham, Helen, and Jo Labanyi, eds. *Spanish Cultural Studies: An Introduction*. Oxford: Oxford University Press, 1995.

Gullón, Ricardo, ed. *Diccionario de la literatura española e hispanoamericana*. 2 vols. Madrid: Alianza, 1993.

Mayhew, Jonathan. "Poetry." In *Encyclopedia of Contemporary Spanish Culture*, edited by Eamonn Rodgers, 403–405. London and New York: Routledge, 1999.

Pozuelo Yvancos, José María, and Rosa María Aradra Sánchez. *Teoría del canon y literatura española*. Madrid: Cátedra, 2000.

Pritchett, V. S. *The Spanish Temper*. New York: Knopf, 1955.

Rodgers, Eamonn. "Publishing." In *Encyclopedia of Contemporary Spanish Culture*, edited by Eamonn Rodgers, 427–428. London: Routledge, 1999.

Smith, Paul J. *Laws of Desire: Questions of Homosexuality in Spanish Writing and Film, 1960–1990*. Oxford: Oxford University Press, 1992.

Soldevila Durante, Ignacio. "Novel." In *Encyclopedia of Contemporary Spanish Culture*, edited by Eamonn Rodgers, 369–373.

OTHER SOURCES

See the information on the Instituto Cervantes under "Other Sources" in Chapter 1 (Context).

The Biblioteca Nacional (National Library) can be reached online at <http://www.bne.es>.

The Real Academia Española (Royal Spanish Academy) can be reached by mail at Calle Felipe IV 4, 28014 Madrid, Spain; telephone 011–34–91–420–1614; telefax 011–34–91–420–1478.

The academies of the minority languages can be reached by mail. For Basque: Academia de la Lengua Vasca (Euskaltzaindia), Plaza Barria 15, 48005 Bilbao, Spain. For Catalan: Secció Filológica, Institut d'Estudis Catalans, Calle del Carme, 08002 Barcelona, Spain. For Galician: Real Academia Galega, Calle Alfredo Brasas 10, 15701 Santiago de Compostela (La Coruña), Spain.

There are many websites on Spanish literature. The search engine "Olé" is a good place to start: <http://www.ole.es>. The online magazine *Melibea* has articles on both Spanish literature and language: <http://www.abaforum.es/is/melibea>.

A website on Basque literature is <http://www.bizkaia.net/Bizkaia/castellano/Informacion_general/Cultura/C2LITERA.HTM>. For Catalan literature consult <http://www.uv.es/filcat/docencia/oca/catalana/4489.htm>. For Galician literature see <http://www.crtvg.es/espanol/libros/inicio.html>.

7

Performing Arts

Theater has always been an art of criticism, persecuted by the state; now that it has money and protection and is covered by the sacred mantle of culture, we must ask ourselves if this is a new form of censorship.
—Eduardo Haro Tecglen[1]

Quien canta, sus males espanta (Whoever sings has a heart that rings).
—Spanish proverb

Spain is a country of dancers.
—Laura Kumin, "To Live Is to Dance"[2]

The Olympics had never seen anything like it. In the opening ceremony, a cast of ten thousand and a crew of seven hundred turned the floor of Montjuic Stadium into a symbolic Mediterranean Sea where gods and monsters grappled in the mythical foundation of Barcelona. Two weeks later, the closing ceremonies were even more sensational in an allegory of the creation, with a magnificent dance of the stars, the sun, moon and planets. Both events re-created ancient myths through the movement of the human body and the most sophisticated technology. The result was a pyrotechnical tour de force that set a new conceptual and artistic precedent—still unmatched—for Olympic ceremonies.

The 1992 Barcelona games were a showcase for the performing arts in Spain overall, and Catalonia in particular. This small, Maryland-sized region has more than five hundred amateur and professional groups who act in theaters and especially in the streets, following the Mediterranean tradition of performing in public spaces. To a somewhat lesser extent, all the world's a stage in the rest of the Peninsula, too. We have seen that Spain has an enduring theater equaled only by England.

Music and dance also thrive, with problems of infrastructure similar to those we have noted in the cinema (Chapter 5). Perhaps no other country has projected a clearer artistic profile. Everyone recognizes "Spanish" songs and dances, although their recognition often depends on cultural stereotypes that reduce the country to a sun-drenched land of wine, women, gypsies, toreros and siestas. Or as the nineteenth-century traveler Richard Ford said, "Bull-fights, bandits, and black eyes."[3]

Like film and literature, the performing arts suffered terribly during the Civil War (1936–1939) and the forty years of Franco's dictatorship. Many playwrights, musicians and performers died in the conflict, escaped into exile or languished in prison. Notable examples were the dramatists Federico García Lorca and Antonio Buero Vallejo, the actor Josep Maria Flotats and the composer Manuel de Falla. Those who remained were subjected to censorship and isolated from foreign influences. Yet Franco's claim to represent the purest Spanish tradition made it impossible for the regime to suppress popular forms like folk music and dance. After all, they could also be exploited as tourist attractions. For this and other reasons, they prospered more than classical music and dance.

As in cinema and literature, the regeneration of the performing arts did not wait for the aging dictator to give up his last breath. Playwrights, performance theater groups and singer-songwriters resisted the government with humor, irony and satire. By the time Franco died in 1975, the country's cultural lag had already narrowed. Then the cork popped out of the bottle and Spain saw its greatest artistic explosion since the early 1930s. The world's eyes turned on the Peninsula and liked what it saw. Instead of imitating foreign fashions, Spain leapt into the artistic vanguard in a period of great fervor and experimentation. *La movida*, a trendy movement centered in Madrid, energized pop music and rock, performance theater, dance, cinema and the visual arts. Other cities like Barcelona, Valencia and Vigo created their own versions of the *movida*. In 1982 the Socialists took power and promoted an *estado cultural*, a state that supports culture rather than suppressing it. The idea was to preserve the national heritage and to put Spain on the world's artistic map again. In the first seven years of Socialist rule, expenditures for the arts increased by some 70 percent. In keeping with the decentralization of power under democracy, the state granted a generous portion of the new funds to the autonomous regions. This devolution has continued to the present day. Catalonia recently won a lawsuit against the national government, assuring that monies for the performing arts be administered directly by the regions. The conservative government, elected in 1996, has not reversed this trend in spite of its centralist policies. On the other hand, the state has encouraged privatization in the arts as in other fields, making public subsidies more scarce. Private foundations, banks and large businesses have taken up some of the slack, but the performing arts, like the cinema (Chapter 5) and the visual arts (Chapter 8), continue to endure a chronic shortage of funds.

We will see how these general forces have influenced the theater, music and dance in Spain. As in all other chapters, our emphasis will be on the contemporary scene.

THEATER

We saw earlier that Spain is heir to one of the world's great dramatic traditions (Chapter 6, Literature). Because of its necessarily public nature, the theater suffered even more persecution and censorship than other arts under the Franco dictatorship (1939–1975). The stage was dominated by light, domestic comedies, psychological melodramas, musical revues and other examples of the "culture of evasion." Alejandro Casona wrote popular, well-crafted plays whose happy endings hardly reflected the lives of his public. It was Buero Vallejo, an ex-Republican soldier, condemned to death after the Civil War and fresh out of prison, who changed the direction of Spanish theater. His *Historia de una escalera* (Story of a Stairway, 1949) was not escapist drama, but a work about normal people with everyday problems, in which an apartment building's stairway represented the mediocrity of the place and times. During the next forty years, Buero continued writing plays about solitary rebellion, authenticity and the dignity of the oppressed. His near-contemporary Alfonso Sastre, even more daring and radical, was involved in a movement known as the Theater of Social Agitation. His intense drama *Escuadra hacia la muerte* (Death Squadron, 1953) was one of more than fifty plays that he would write during the next half-century, many of them banned or censored. Joaquín Calvo Sotelo's *La muralla* (The Wall, 1954) was the most successful of all the "plays of denunciation." Along the same lines, Lauro Olmo's *La camisa* (The Shirt, 1961) vividly portrayed the plight and aspirations of the country's working class. Independent theater groups, often associated with the universities, also staged new works. The pages of the journal *Primer Acto* (First Act) offered a forum for new ideas.

Not all change derived from the opposition. In 1954 the state had sponsored the creation of the Teatro Nacional de Cámara y Ensayo (National Chamber Theater). Classical drama—less dangerous than new theater—underwent a revival. The director José Tamayo renewed the tradition of the medieval and early-modern *autos sacramentales* (morality plays) and brought drama to a wider public by staging performances in open-air venues like the bullring in Sevilla, the Roman theater in Mérida and the Retiro Park in Madrid. He also introduced hungry Spanish audiences to foreign dramatists like Luigi Pirandello, Eugene Ionesco and Arthur Miller. Tamayo summed up his career by saying that he tried to achieve three goals in his theater: uneasiness, immensity and wonder.[4]

Director Adolfo Marsillach carried out a similar mission, revitalizing the classic Spanish theater as well as staging works by outstanding foreign dramatists. He was one of the forces behind the Corral de Comedias of Almagro, where the month-long International Festival draws theatrical talent from all over Spain as well as other countries. It has become the Spanish equivalent of England's Globe Theater, where audiences can see sixteenth- and seventeenth-century plays performed in a period playhouse. In 1998 Marsillach wrote and directed a dance version of the classical play *La Celestina*, with original music and choreography.

After Franco's death, the censorship laws were repealed and Spanish audiences were treated to the forbidden fruits of the previous forty years. Experimental drama, theater of the absurd and in the nude were all signs of the new freedom. In the 1980s, the dictates of the *estado cultural* called for increased public support of drama and other performing arts. The Instituto Nacional de las Artes Escénicas y de la Música (National Institute for the Performing Arts and Music, or INAEM) was established with four branches, later reduced to three—one for classic works, one for contemporary dramas and one for *zarzuelas* or light operas (see below under Music). INAEM in turn created the Red Nacional de Teatros y Auditorios (National Network of Theaters and Auditoriums) with the purpose of making public theaters available to drama companies. With the reorganization of the country into autonomous communities, many regional centers for theatrical production and study have sprung up, with new companies and festivals. Old hands like Tamayo and Marsillach have held important positions, continuing to direct plays along with younger artists like Miguel Narros and Lluís Pasqual.

The large public theaters have tended to give official support to the leading Spanish playwrights of the 1920s and the 1930s, as part of the Socialists' effort to revive the culture of the pre–Civil War period. Works by Ramón del Valle-Inclán, Rafael Alberti and especially Federico García Lorca have been performed repeatedly. Several Catalan dramatists have also enjoyed revivals, such as Josep Pla and Santiago Rusiñol. In addition, the public theaters have staged works by some of the best contemporary Spanish playwrights, many of whom had been censored or banned under the dictatorship: Fernando Arrabal, Antonio Gala, Francisco Nieva, Rodolf Sirera. Younger dramatists like Sergi Belbel and Paloma Pedrero have also enjoyed success in recent years.

Advances in the contemporary Spanish theater have been in representation more than composition. One critic has complained that "theater has almost disappeared as a literary genre."[5] Indeed it has become a performing art as much as a literary expression. The popularity of visual culture has led to innovations in staging and design. In both large and small theaters, cinematic projections and the imaginative use of lighting are now employed as a matter of course. Even conservative audiences have come to accept the new visual techniques with their power to suggest space, time and emotion. Designers have also been making more conscious use of color. Nieva, for example, has used color and fabric for visual and acoustic effects both in his own works and in those he creates for other playwrights. Some scenographers have played with the expressive potential of the human body: Carlos Cytrynowski, for example, has used actors as rugs, trees and tables.

The increased emphasis on visual elements has led some designers to use nontraditional spaces, such as markets, train stations, subway platforms, garages, factories and warehouses. The architect Andre d'Odorico, for one, employs bare spaces to evoke the relationship between mass and emptiness, often with chiaroscuro lighting. Performance-theater companies also prefer innovative venues, both indoors and outdoors. In this and many other ways, these groups have been the most daring and creative on the Spanish stage.

Like so many other contemporary arts, performance theater in the Peninsula had its origins under the dictatorship. Both then and now it has flourished in Catalonia more than in other regions, perhaps because of the city's strong Mediterranean traditions of mime, circus, carnival and open-air spectacle. The first of these companies, Els Joglars (The Minstrels), founded in 1962, took a radically anti-Franco stance from the beginning. Even after the dictator's death, the group continued to suffer censorship, imprisonment and forced exile. Under the leadership of the dynamic Albert Boadella, Els Joglars confronted the chief bugaboos of Spanish culture—the Church, the State and the Army—offending many citizens along the way. The troupe has been in the vanguard of technical innovation as well as political satire, collaborating with experimental set designers from Catalonia like Iago Pericot and Fabià Puigserver. It has been influenced by both European and American performance theater. Like Jerzy Grotowsky and others, Boadella places many physical demands on his actors, exploiting gesture and movement. Music has been an important part of his stagings too, as in the controversial *Mary d'Ous* (Egg Mary), structured like a church canon. Els Joglars has crossed the boundary between high and low cultures, starring in popular series on both Catalan and Spanish television.

Another ensemble from Catalonia, Els Comediants (The Actors or Comedians), has done more than any other troupe to incorporate carnivalesque traditions into performance theater. Carnival had been banned under Franco as a pagan, "non-Spanish" celebration. Its recovery, along with other local festivals, formed part of the revival of popular culture in Catalonia and other regions under the new democracy. Like Els Joglars, Els Comediants blends local traditions with experimental theater. Their *Dimonis* (Devils, 1982), for example, is structured like the *via crucis* (Way of the Cross) in the Catholic Church, but with carnival techniques like satire, grotesque and the inversion of values. The show is usually performed in the open air, preferably in the streets, where observers may be jostled by the members of the troupe amidst fireworks and music. "The experience for the spectator who has not previously encountered this sort of theatre is memorable, if hazardous, as the sparks from the fireworks land on the crowds."[6] The group could never get away with this kind of activity in most northern European countries or the United States, and has even been forbidden from performing in some Spanish towns, where safety regulations tend to be more lax. Els Comediants has also been involved in musical production and film. Their most spectacular work took place at the XXV Olympic Games in Barcelona, where they mobilized 850 people in the unforgettable closing ceremonies.

A third company, La Fura dels Baus (Rats in the Sewer), could be described as a bad-boy shock troupe or a performance group of the rock age. Its members are the authors, directors, designers, musicians, choreographers, actors and ushers at their own performances. Spectators at their shows also have to be careful: "If the sky does not fall on viewers' heads, they may have to detour to avoid a 'meteorite' of meat or flower, water or paint."[7] The meteorites are one of the *fureros'* tactics for keeping their audience on the move, in a living, changing choreography of actors and spectators. "One does not watch a performance of La Fura. One participates."[8] In the fall of 2000, the ensemble staged an operatic work titled *Don Quixote en Barcelona*, in which both a Spanish and a Catalan flag were supposed to be burned on stage, and the spectators would be sprinkled with rain. The general director of the famous Liceu Theater requested that La Fura omit both scenes. The incident reveals why the ensemble prefers nontraditional spaces where it can get away with such mischief, like markets, train stations and abandoned factories. Its *Suz/o/Suz* (untranslatable) has been performed in a Madrid morgue and a Sydney garage. Under the influence of Antonin Artaud's primitive ritualism, the actors may enact destructive violence, as when they demolish a car with sledgehammers in *Accions* (Actions). The company's most recent project surpassed anything it or any other performance group has attempted so far. *Big Opera Mundi* (*BOM*) started at midnight on the first day of the year 2000, and took place in twenty-four cities of the world, each with a specific theme. The first act in Wellington, New Zealand dealt with the Big Bang; the final act in Samoa, twenty-three midnights later, dealt with *BOM* itself. The event was "a multinational rave, or a theatrical Rio or Kyoto summit, or . . . just another megalomaniac bluff."[9] Besides producing drama and opera, the *fureros* have developed digital theater, organized exhibitions and public events like the opening ceremonies of the 1992 Olympics, participated in videos and films, released CDs and created advertisements for multinational companies.

Although these three companies have brought Catalan theater to the world, the region has many other groups who continue to seek new theatrical experiences. Some of these include La Cubana (The Cuban Woman) and the Teatre Lliure (Free Theater) that performs from written scripts under directors like Lluís Pasqual; Dagoll Dagom, whose musicals can rival the best of Broadway or London's West End; and the comedy team El Tricicle (The Tricycle), which combines gymnastics with impressive stage machinery and special effects. Many smaller ensembles stage performances in fringe theaters, discos and bars. Finally, there are hundreds of amateur groups who participate in local events like La Passió (passion plays during Easter Week) and Els Pastorets (nativity plays).

Theater in Spain will probably always be in crisis. In the past it suffered from neglect or censorship. Since the advent of the *estado cultural* in the 1980s, it has received more funding and protection from the national, regional, provincial and local governments. Some believe that protectionism can also be dangerous. During their decade-and-a-half in power, the Socialists tended to support liberal producers, directors and playwrights. Since winning the elections in 1996, the conservatives have attempted to correct the balance. The autonomous regions also have their own agendas, sometimes preferring mediocre dramas in the minority languages (especially Catalan) to superior works in Castilian. (The same occurs in the cinema: see Chapter 5.) The prestige of international festivals and homages or anniversaries sometimes absorbs so much public money that little remains for the dramatists who could write about what is really happening in the country. In 1998, for example, there were centenary homages to the playwrights of the famous Generation of 1898 (especially Valle-Inclán) and García Lorca, as well as Bertolt Brecht. One critic summed up the year by saying "it brought nothing unforgettable, but neither did it take away our hopes."[10]

MUSIC

In a classic study, Gilbert Chase speaks of "the Spanish idiom" in music.[11] It is easy to recognize but hard to define. One can hear it in traditional or folk music, including flamenco; in the *cuplé* or *canción española* (Spanish song); in *zarzuela* or light opera; and in some pop and classical music. The idiom is characterized by the chromatic scale, melisma (multiple notes sung on a single syllable), irregular rhythm and asymmetric structure. It is especially common in the southern and central parts of the Peninsula. Composers from other regions—Pablo Sarasate, Isaac Albéniz, Enrique Granados—have assimilated this style and made it the "national" idiom of Spain. Foreign composers, especially French, have interpreted it as the only Spanish music (Georges Bizet, Claude Debussy, Maurice Ravel).

A more general quality of the Spanish idiom is emotiveness. One writer notes: "To white Anglo-Saxon Protestants it seems sappy, shameless and in bad taste to reveal the depths of the soul,"[12] which is precisely what many Spanish singers do in traditional music and pop. For them, the notion of "cool" is completely foreign. A typical first impression of *cante jondo* or "deep" flamenco is that "it is a combination of singing and weeping," not to say screaming, hiccuping or worse.[13] The contrast between Hispanic effusion and Anglo-Saxon restraint will help us understand the different genres of music discussed below.

Some fifty years ago, Chase called Spanish folk music "the richest in the world."[14] This is no longer the case, as the country has become modernized and exposed to foreign influences. One critic says:

In the information age, Spanish folkmusic is fast disappearing since children no longer play in the streets making up games and singing songs, but instead stay inside, watch television and play with video games. . . . Fewer children know the words to traditional songs and young people no longer memorize poetry. Rock music, particularly American, has largely displaced folk music, and fewer young people learn folkdances.[15]

The same critic goes on to say that the current emphasis on political and cultural autonomy has caused a renaissance of regional music that is often artificial, overfueled by local funding.

Yet folk music remains more alive in Spain than in most Western countries. The Spanish people have songs (and dances) for almost any occasion: for childbirth, rocking babies to sleep (lullabies), children's games, patronal feasts (fiestas), courtship, weddings, funerals, work in the field or town. Spaniards sing at New Years', Carnival, Easter, Pentecost, May rituals, St. John's or Midsummer Day, Christmas. They will even sing without a special occasion, after a meal in a restaurant, for example. Foreigners are always surprised to see that everyone seems to know the words by heart, from the oldsters to the children. This kind of collective singing is most common in the northern half of the Peninsula.

Folk music also includes instrumental pieces played alone or to accompany dances in various regional styles (see Dance, below). The most common stringed instruments are the guitar, the lute and their many relatives, like the four-stringed *guitarrillo* and the mandolin-like *bandurria*. Wind instruments include the *dulzaina* and *chirimía*, similar to wooden clarinets or oboes, and the *gaita* or bagpipe with its air bag, drones and melody pipes, heard in the Celtic regions of Asturias and Galicia (see Photograph 22). *Gaitas* are quite different from the pipes of Great Britain and Ireland, as can be appreciated in the increasingly popular jams between pipers from different countries in the current Celtic revival. Another popular wind instrument is the plaintive *txistu*, the reedy flute of the Basque Country and Navarre, where it has become an icon of traditional music.

Flamenco is a composite art form that involves dance and guitar in addition to singing, often called *cante jondo* (deep song). It was "interactive" long before the term became fashionable: the public often participates with complicated snapping of fingers (*pitos*), clapping of palms (*palmadas*) and stamping of heels (*taconeo*). True *jondos* (devotees) scorn castanets, which are employed only in the most frivolous flamenco styles, such as danceable *alegrías* and *bulerías*. The deepest, most sacred forms are *siguiriyas* and *soleares*.

Cante jondo originated in Andalusia and spread gradually to parts of Extremadura, New Castile, Murcia, Alicante and Valencia. It used to be as extraneous to northern Spain as the blues to New England. Nevertheless, in the nineteenth century flamenco became synonymous with "Spanish" music for most foreigners. Curiously, changing patterns of migration have made this stereotype less false in the last twenty-five years, as immigrants from the poor, rural south have moved north to Madrid, Bilbao and Barcelona, not to mention France (home of Tino de Geraldo, José el Francés and the Gipsy

22. Asturian *gaitas* or bagpipes, Moreda de Aller (Asturias), 1988. Photograph by Cristina García Rodero, Getty Research Institute, Research Library, 90.R.34.

Kings, all of Spanish origin). In this way the cliché of flamenco as the "typical" music of Spain has become partly true.

Intensity and emotiveness are the hallmarks of *cante jondo*. Singers (*cantaores* or *cantaoras*) do not make mellifluous, beautiful melodies but express their emotion in the most direct and powerful way possible. They strive to produce the feeling of ecstasy that may have been the object of all early music. One writer says that flamenco and the bullfight offer "the only true catharsis in Western culture."[16]

Cante jondo started as folk song, performed by anonymous singers who sang music by unknown composers. As it acquired its modern form in the late eighteenth century, some *cantaores* and *cantaoras* became well known for interpreting certain genres. A few even established dynasties in which the elders passed on their skills like holy secrets to the young. Many of these figures and their successors had quirky nicknames like "Mad Matthew," "The Boy of Jerez," "Frasco the Colored One," "The Child of the Combs." Some dynasties continue to the present day. Although nicknames have become less popular in the electronic age, contemporary performers have sported monikers like Camarón de la Isla (Shrimp of San Fernando), José el Francés (Joseph the Frenchman) and Caño Roto (Broken Pipe).

Flamenco has shown more resilience and capacity for change than any other folk music in the Peninsula. Unlike all other forms discussed above, it has thrived in the new world of mass culture. Yet many purists still abhor change of any sort. Here is how one critic excoriates the popular term *nuevo flamenco* (new flamenco): "Flamenco is flamenco, and adjectives are superfluous. Those who are incapable of singing in the right way insist on calling it new, seeking refuge in little flamenquified ditties which, moreover, earn them a pile of money."[17] In spite of carping criticism by purists, *cante jondo* is unique in its ability to evolve without abandoning its ancestral roots. A form like *bulerías*, for example, has absorbed genres as diverse as *cuplés* (see below) and *rancheras* (Mexican country). Other international genres—jazz, blues, salsa, bossa nova, rock, Peruvian, Moroccan and other ethnic styles—have also blended with Andalusian sounds. Two brilliant performers, the guitarist Paco de Lucía and the singer Enrique Morente, were the first to mix flamenco with foreign music. Others like Camarón de la Isla, Lolé y Manuel, Caño Roto, Pata Negra, Ketama and Barbería del Sur followed their lead. Still younger artists have gone even further in crossover or *mestizaje* (mixing). In this way flamenco has changed more in the last twenty years than in the previous twenty decades. It will never be the same. It has become a highly exportable commodity with almost unlimited possibilities for evolution and success. The international hit "La Macarena" shows how this music—even in diluted form—can become an international sensation.

Related to folk music but lacking its anonymity, the *cuplé*—sometimes known as *tonadilla* or *canción española*—has undergone a revival in recent years. It is a light, short piece that uses some typical forms of peninsular poetry and music. The *cuplé* is a hybrid that combines the techniques of the

"Spanish idiom" of Andalusia—melisma and ornamentation—with the symmetrical form and refrain of folk songs in Old Castile and León. Born in the turbid atmosphere of the late nineteenth-century *café cantante* or music hall, it achieved so much popularity in the first half of the twentieth century that people began to call it "the Spanish song" or even the *canción nacional* (national song). Artists like Raquel Meller, Pastora Imperio, Concha Piquer, Lola Flores and Sara Montiel enjoyed fabulously successful careers on stage and screen. With its sentimental, patriotic tone, the *cuplé* was promoted by the Franco regime as an embodiment of Spanish values. Several scholars have revindicated this music as a channel for releasing emotion during the miserable years of the dictatorship, when it was sung for survival. Although the lyrics are melodramatic and trite, the music is almost irresistible. One critic says of the famous *cuplé* "El Relicario": "I can lament the ineptitude of the lyrics . . . grind my teeth at the voice and affectations of Raquel Meller [the singer], and still accept without the slightest guilt that I like this song, that it gives me pleasure, that I know the words by heart and that I can sing it whenever I feel like it."[18] In the neoconservative 1990s, the *cuplé* enjoyed a revival and flourished. It is featured on radio and television programs. Pedro Almodóvar, the most popular Spanish film director in history, has used it in his movies and in his stage appearances. The style has also absorbed influences of jazz and pop music. One critic says: "The *cuplé* is a compendium of the contradictions that make up Spanish modernity, harnessing tradition and innovation."[19]

The history of pop music in Spain reflects the social and political transformation of the country in the last fifty years. Until the 1960s, it consisted mainly of songs with folk roots, like flamenco and *cuplés*, both favored by the Francoist regime as expressions of the "national" spirit. The tourist boom of the 1960s, plus the American presence at military bases throughout the Peninsula, brought the latest foreign music into Spain. Singers like Raphael and Julio Iglesias made their reputation as Spanish versions of international stars. Music festivals were another conduit of foreign influence. The 1970s were the decade of *cantautores* or singer-songwriters like Raimon and Joan Manuel Serrat, who combined catchy melodies with political protest, often paying the price in the form of banning, censorship and jail. This trend coalesced as the *nova cançó* in Catalonia, where resistance to the regime was stronger than in other areas. After the death of Franco in 1975, prejudice against non-Spanish music almost disappeared. Progressive rock and the "new wave" revolutionized the pop scene with powerful lyrics and electric guitars. Under the influence of the *movida* in the 1980s, new bands with improbable names sprang up overnight, most of them playing punk: Gabinete Caligari

(Dr. Caligari's Cabinet), Caca de Luxe (Doo-Doo Deluxe), Derribos Arias (Arias Demolition), Parálisis Permanente (Permanent Paralysis), Radio Futura (Future Radio), El Ultimo de la Fila (The Last in Line) and Loquillo y los Trogloditas (Crazy Guy and the Troglodytes). This was also the heyday of independent record companies. Although many of them disappeared or were bought out by multinationals, Spain is still estimated to have more independent labels than any country in Europe, nearly a thousand at last count.[20] Barcelona is the capital of this alternative culture, with a host of small labels, clubs, DJs, stores, magazines and a yearly festival called SONAR (SOUND).[21] Recordings usually reflect international trends like grunge, ska, light rave, house, techno-pop, Eurotrance. Foreign songs continue to dominate the charts: in 1998, thirteen out of the top twenty albums belonged to non-Spanish singers or groups, and only four of the top twenty songs were by Spaniards.

Rock music will probably never take root in Spain as it has in the United States and northern Europe. This may be explained by the nature of Hispanic society. One commentator says:

Rock is the product of a youth culture which is in turn the result of a rejection of established social values. In societies where family ties are still strong, it is impossible to create such a youth culture. The problem with Spanish rock musicians—even the most talented of them—is that they look and sound like (and indeed are) nice kids with well-scrubbed faces who would not recognize a generation gap if they fell into one.[22]

Flamenco fusion is the exception that proves the rule: it manages to combine the anger of rock music with the anguish of *cante jondo*. It could be the country's biggest contribution to international youth culture.

Pop music in Spain always seems to be at a disadvantage. Until recently, there was no national mainstream press (like *Rolling Stone*) or television station (like MTV). News and talk shows are much more popular on Spanish radio than music programs. The situation may be changing as the country becomes further integrated with western Europe and continues to penetrate markets in its former colonies. For the first time since the 1980s, Spanish singers and groups are again topping the charts in Latin America. Rosana and Pedro Guerra (both singer-songwriters from the Canary Islands), rocker Rosario and soft-rock duo Ella Baila Sola (She Dances Alone) have done major tours in Latin America. Pop diva Mónica Naranjo made inroads in the domestic market only after initial success in Mexico. The latest superstar, Alejandro Sanz, has demonstrated the potential of the country's pop music in both North and South America. His fourth Warner album "Más" has sold more than any Spanish recording in history, over five million copies. Some critics believe he has paved the way for other artists to ride the global wave of Latino music. Whether or not they are right, the future of pop music in the Spanish language will necessarily involve mutual influences between Spain and Latin America. In 1999, the National Academy of Recording Arts and Sciences announced the creation of its first international extension (LARAS), which will collaborate with the Spanish author-rights society SGAE (Sociedad General de Autores Españoles) to sponsor Latin Grammy Awards. The event will honor artists from Latin America, the United States, Spain and Portugal, a global market with enormous potential.

We will begin our discussion of classical music with *zarzuela*, the Spanish light opera; it has one foot in the palace and the other in the street. The genre takes its name from the Palacio de la Zarzuela north of Madrid, in an area surrounded by *zarzas* (brambles); the Spanish royal family now resides in the palace. The origins of *zarzuela* were courtly but its subject matter, staging, dance and music all feature signs of popular culture. The genre has been compared to operetta, *Singspiel* or Broadway musical, but is really unique to Spain. It is theater that alternates music and spoken dialogue. It has two styles: the *género chico* or one-act comic operettas, and *zarzuela grande*, normally in three acts and more serious, resembling romantic opera. The writer Manuel Vázquez Montalbán has defined *zarzuela* as "a total music spectacle, spoken and sung, much closer to the popular reality and the real sentimentality of the people than the opera, in which tenors are unable to request a glass of water because they would have to do it by singing."[23]

The genre acquired its current form in the eighteenth century, along with the bullfight, flamenco and other expressions of popular culture. *Zarzuelas* flourished in the following century when no less than fifteen hundred were composed—most of them deservedly forgotten. The standard repertoire, like that of classical opera, comes chiefly from the second half of the 1800s: Francisco Barbieri with *Pan y toros* (Bread and Bullfights, 1864) and *El barberillo de Lavapiés* (The Little Barber of Lavapiés, 1874); Federico Chueca with *La Gran Vía* (Main Street, 1886); Tomás Bretón with *La Verbena de la Paloma* (The Feast of Our Lady of the Dove, 1893); and Ruperto Chapí with *La Revoltosa* (The Unruly Lass, 1897). The *zarzuela* survived during the dictatorship when it was nurtured as another expression of picturesque, folkloric Spain, the country with the most beautiful women and the most dashing *caballeros*, the best wine, the sunniest climate and the best life anywhere. As the country opened up to the world, people abandoned this music as a symbol of a past they wanted to forget. But *zarzuela* had a small renaissance in the neoconservative atmosphere of the 1990s, and nowadays performances at the Teatro de la Zarzuela in Madrid are often sold out. Spain's famous tenor, Plácido Domingo, has launched a personal campaign to redeem the genre and incorporate it in the worldwide operatic repertoire. His father was the founder of a *zarzuela* company in Mexico and young Plácido had his unofficial debut in its performances. He has said: "*Zarzuela* today is at the threshold of international recognition . . . I would like to see *zarzuela* accepted as a valid genre, together with opera, operetta and musicals."[24] Domingo's desire is to form a company based in both Miami and Mexico City. The genre has in fact retained footholds in Mexico, Cuba, Puerto Rico, Colombia and Argentina as well as Spain. The New York City Opera and the Washington Opera have staged complete *zarzuelas*. The University of Texas at El Paso houses the only resident company in the United States.

Classical opera in Spain has not thrived as much as native *zarzuela*. Few countries have more internationally recognized singers, yet the nation lacks a company where they could work on a regular basis. Plácido Domingo, Montserrat Caballé, José Carreras, Teresa Berganza, Victoria de los Ángeles and others have been forced to base their careers outside of Spain. The restoration and reopening of two beautiful nineteenth-century buildings—the Liceu Theater in Barcelona (gutted by fire in 1994) and the Royal Theater in Madrid (racked by corruption throughout the 1990s) gives the country two of the best opera houses in the world. They are also used for concerts, ballets, conferences and other public events. While some optimists claim that these venues automatically make the country a part of the international musical scene, others are more skeptical. One critic says, "To think that by reopening the Royal Theater or . . . the Liceu . . . we now have a passport to enter the European musical world, seems an error or a vain illusion when we still have so many problems, beginning with musical education."[25]

The problems could be summarized as lack of funds. The Franco regime ignored classical music even more than the other arts, probably because it had little propaganda value for the regime. With typical Spanish exaggeration, Jesús López Cobos remarked that being a conductor in Spain was like being a bullfighter in Finland. He has spent much of his career leading German, British and American orchestras. After the Socialists' ascension to power in 1982, López Cobos was invited to conduct the Orquesta Nacional de España (ONE, National Orchestra of Spain). He set out to inculcate "musical discipline" in his players, but resigned just five years later. A commentator explains:

Like France and Italy, Spain is not a country with a great orchestral tradition. Perhaps it has something to do with Latin society, which values spontaneity more than discipline and rewards individuals rather than collective achievement. At all events, the conservatories of southern Europe are designed to turn out soloists rather than rank-and-file players. A former member of the ONE once said that the problem with tuning up for a Spanish orchestra is that "everyone has his or her own conception of *la* [A]."[26]

If we think of how few of the country's orchestras travel outside of Spain, and how many brilliant soloists follow the international concert circuit, we may conclude that this writer is correct. In addition to the opera *divos* and *divas* cited above, we could recall brilliant artists like Pablo Casals (cello), Alicia de Larrocha and José Iturbi (piano), Nicanor Zabaleta (harp), Andrés Segovia and Narciso Yepes (guitar).

The only Spanish composer since Manuel de Falla to reach an international audience has been Joaquín Rodrigo (1901–1999), author of the well-known "Concierto de Aranjuez" for guitar and orchestra. This piece was intended to evoke the nation's glorious past (the town of Aranjuez was the monarchy's summer resort), and made Rodrigo the leading exponent of the Nationalist movement. It could serve as a modern example of the "Spanish idiom." Rodrigo achieved another success in "Fantasía para un gentilhombre" (Fantasy for a Gentleman), also for guitar and orchestra. His other works include ballet, opera, chamber music and compositions for piano, guitar, voice and orchestra. Joaquín Rodrigo was the first composer to be awarded the Prince of Asturias Prize for the Arts (1996).

Younger composers have often rejected the "Spanish idiom" in favor of international trends. We have seen the same occur in Spain's literature and film. The distinguished composer and director Cristóbal Halffter asserted that there has been greater musical activity in the country since 1985 than ever before, but that it is hampered by "ill-prepared bureaucrats, inadequate funding, political machinations, and autonomous rivalry."[27] In 1995 one critic acclaimed the awakening of the country's music from a "pronounced forty-year lethargy."[28] At the same time, the president of the National Association of Symphony Orchestras noticed the increased amount of musical activity and the growing number of professional orchestras (more than twenty). Yet in the same year, only 5 percent of Spaniards attended a classical musical event, and this audience was limited chiefly to middle-class people between the ages of twenty to forty-five. These figures remind us ominously of statistics on reading (Chapter 6, Literature). Once more we see immense artistic talent hindered by indifference from the state and the public.

Seasonal festivals help to compensate for the neglect suffered by classical music during most of the year. The Bach Festival in San Sebastián and those in Granada and Santander have been celebrated for a half-century; the Contemporary Musical Festival in Alicante has been in existence for some fifteen years. Other annual celebrations include the Mozart Festival in Madrid, the La Coruña Opera Festival, the Week of Chamber Music in Oviedo and the Festival of Religious Music in Cuenca. The province of Barcelona alone has some forty-eight music festivals, ranging from classic to rock. *Festivales de flamenco* are held in Sevilla (*Bienal*), Córdoba, Jerez de la Frontera, Almería, Valencia and many smaller towns, like La Unión and Marchena. Jazz events are celebrated annually in Barcelona, Valencia, Madrid, Salamanca, and Málaga.

DANCE

Folk dancing in Spain is as rich as the country's traditional music. Although far less famous than flamenco, the *jota* is the closest thing to a national dance. It belongs first and foremost to the region of Aragón, but is also seen in Navarre, Castile, Andalusia and Valencia. Nobody knows when it originated. Unlike flamenco the *jota* is never solitary, featuring at least two performers like so many folk dances in northern Spain. It represents the perennial theme of courtship but lacks the erotic energy of flamenco.

The *fandango* is also performed in many parts of the country. Its origins are even more mysterious than the *jota's*. It too varies greatly according to regions. The Andalusian styles—*fandanguillos, granadinas, malagueñas* and *murcianas*—constitute part of the flamenco repertoire and are very different from the northern variants.

The *bolero* is another dance seen in diverse regions of Spain. It must be distinguished from the sentimental Latin American song which it resembles in name only. Here is how Chase describes the *bolero*: "The dancers merely walk around—but what beauty and fascination there is in the mere walk of a good Spanish dancer! Pride and nobility of bearing are united to the utmost gracefulness of carriage."[29] These words could refer to many traditional dances in Spain.

Some musicologists consider the *bolero* to be an offshoot of the *seguidilla*, a dance and song found all over Spain with the usual variants. It has been performed continuously in La Mancha (New Castile) since the sixteenth century. The best-known variety are *sevillanas*, which have become a national craze in the last ten years. Spaniards from all walks of life study this lively style as Americans might take lessons in ballroom dancing or aerobics.

The most typical dance of Galicia is the *muiñeira* (from *muiño*, mill), sung and danced to the accompaniment of the *gaita gallega*, the region's bagpipe, along with drum and tambourine. In the Basque Country, the principal dance is the eight-part *aurresku*, of which the *zortzico* is the most well known. None of these styles rivals Catalonia's *sardana* in importance. This graceful, lilting dance, performed in a circle by people of all ages, is a symbol of Catalan identity and regional pride (see Photograph 23).

Like *cante jondo*, flamenco dance has undergone a rebirth in the last twenty years. It has absorbed influences of other genres like jazz, salsa, rock and modern dance. From the traditional *tablao* (improvised stage), artists have moved to large-scale concert halls. Sara Baras directs a flamenco troupe composed of women only. Dancer-choreographers like Antonio Canales, Carmen Cortés and Joaquín Cortés have expanded the limits of the form beyond the imagination of purists. A former member of Spain's National Ballet, Joaquín Cortés uses the term "flamenco fusion" to describe his original choreography. His company includes some fourteen dancers, five singers and nine musicians who play violin, double bass, flute and bongo drums in addition to the usual guitars. Cortés' shows are extravaganzas with all the high-tech paraphernalia of rock concerts—computers, spotlights and lasers. His 1999 tour, "Soul (Alma)," combined traditional flamenco with Cuban rhythms, soul and gospel.

Traditional dancing is taught in the conservatories under the name of *escuela bolera* (bolero school), along with ballet and modern. Ballet has flourished less than other styles. Classical dance companies "are still treated as step-children when it comes to government subsidies."[30] The country's restored showcases, the Teatre del Liceu in Barcelona and the Teatro Real in Madrid, once had resident companies but now have none. The Ballet Nacional de España, which recently celebrated its twentieth anniversary, has been racked by rivalries and frequent changes in management. The Compañía Nacional de Danza leans toward modern styles and techniques. Its director, dancer-choreographer Nacho Duato, did his training at the Rambert School in London, Maurice Béjart's Ballet of the Twentieth Century in Brussels, and the Alvin Ailey American Dance Center in New York City; he then worked for ten years with the Netherlands Dance Theater in The Hague. His international education is typical of a new generation of Spanish performers, in stark contrast to their sedentary predecessors. Combining ballet and modern dance, Duato's repertory has a particularly Mediterranean flair.

23. Catalans perform their national dance, the *sardana*, Barcelona, 1988. Photograph by Cristina García Rodero, Getty Research Institute, Research Library, 90.R.34.

The company performs pieces by Duato himself, Jiri Kylian, William Forsythe and other names in contemporary ballet with occasional opportunities for Spanish choreographers. Duato's charisma and energy have brought dance to the attention of the general public. In 1998 he was awarded the Medalla de Oro de las Bellas Artes (Gold Medal for the Fine Arts). The following year he helped found the Compañía Dos (Company Two), a school for young dancers based on a similar ensemble in The Hague.

Some artists have preferred to make their careers in other European countries or the United States. María Giménez has been prima ballerina of the Zurich Opera. Ángel Corella dances for the American Ballet Theater in New York City. Winner of the Concours International de Dance de Paris, he is considered one of the greatest ballet dancers in the world.

Since the National Dance Company no longer performs pure classical ballet, other groups have attempted to fill the gap. Víctor Ullate's Ballet de la Comunidad de Madrid is probably the country's most prestigious ensemble. It receives more government subsidies than any other group. Another major company is the Ballet de Zaragoza.

Modern dance has thrived much more than classical in Spain. Since Franco's death, it has been seen as the appropriate expression for a young democracy seeking to make up for half a century of artistic stagnation. It has followed a path similar to flamenco's. Sometimes it may be hard to draw a line between modern dance and performance theater: groups like Els Joglars, Els Comediants and La Fura dels Baus depend on body movement and choreography as much as plot and dialogue. It is not surprising that Catalonia has been the region where contemporary dance has flourished more than anywhere else in the Peninsula. Barcelona still has the country's largest concentration of contemporary ensembles. In 1980 the Institut de Teatre created the only ongoing conservatory program in the field. La Fábrica has also been a training ground for young dancers and choreographers. The Gelabert/Azzopardi Companyia de Dansa became the first group of its kind to receive subsidies from the national government. Lanónima Imperial, Danat Dansa, Mudances and Mal Pelo are other Catalan ensembles that have made themselves well known in Spain and the rest of Europe.

Valencia is the country's second capital of modern dance and the seat of a national choreography center. The city's most famous company, Ananda Dansa, places dance in a narrative context, crossing the boundaries between spectacle and theater. One of its most popular productions, "Crónica civil V-36/9" (Civilian Chronicle, Valencia 1936–39), portrays the city during the Civil War through the eyes of its children. In 1998 the group premiered its "Vivo en tiempos sombríos" (I Live in Somber Times) and a work based on the theater of Brecht, with music by Kurt Weill. Ananda Dansa has traveled to more than fifteen countries.

The dance scene in Madrid is almost as lively as in the Catalan-speaking regions of the country. The core group of 10 & 10 Danza began its career under the tutelage of Carmen Senra, one of the pioneers of modern dance in the nation's capital. The ensemble recently celebrated its tenth anniversary—a rare achievement in the ephemeral world of modern dance in Spain—and has staged more than twenty original works, many dealing with the complexities of sexual relationships and identity.

Dance festivals occur throughout the year in Spain. Since 1988 Valencia has hosted Dansa a Valencia, a showcase for presenters, dancers and choreographers. San Sebastián holds its annual Maiatza Dantzan, Valladolid its Muestra Internacional de Danza and Madrid its Veranos de la Villa (Summers in the Capital) and Festival de Otoño (Autumn Festival), major events that embrace all the performing arts. Barcelona's Festival Grec features a three-day dance marathon in the streets.

SELECTED READINGS

General

Anuario El País 1999, 2000, 2001, 2002. Madrid: El País. Summarizes the year in the arts and many other fields.

Hooper, John. *The New Spaniards*. London: Penguin, 1995.

Rodgers, Eamonn. "Performing Arts." In *Encyclopedia of Contemporary Spanish Culture*, edited by Eamonn Rodgers, 393–395. London: Routledge, 1999.

Theater

George, David. "Els Comediants," "Els Joglars," "La Fura dels Baus." In *Encyclopedia of Contemporary Spanish Culture*, edited by Eamonn Rodgers, 117, 210–211, 277–278.

Vilches de Frutos, María Francisca. "Theatre." In *Encyclopedia of Contemporary Spanish Culture*, edited by Eamonn Rodgers, 513–516.

Zatlin, Phyllis. "Theater and Culture, 1936–1996." In *The Cambridge Companion to Modern Spanish Culture*, edited by David T. Gies, 222–236. Cambridge: Cambridge University Press, 1999.

Music

Barce, Ramón, ed. *Actualidad y futuro de la zarzuela*. Madrid: Alpuerto, 1994.

Berne, Terry. "Spain and Portugal." *Billboard* 111, no. 47 (November 20, 1999): 91.

Blas Vega, José. *La canción española. (De la caramba a Isabel Pantoja)*. Madrid: Calambur, 1996.

Chase, Gilbert. *The Music of Spain*. 2nd ed. New York: Dover, 1959.

Dolz i Ferrer, Enric. "Music." In *Encyclopedia of Contemporary Spanish Culture*, edited by Eamonn Rodgers, 355–357.

Mitchell, Timothy. *Flamenco Deep Song*. New Haven, CT: Yale University Press, 1994.

Regidor Arribas, Ramón. *Aquellas zarzuelas*. Madrid: Alianza, 1996.

Stanton, Edward F. "Music." In *Handbook of Spanish Popular Culture*, 127–152. Westport, CT: Greenwood Press, 1999.

Tinnell, Roger D. "Spanish Music and Cultural Identity." In *The Cambridge Companion to Modern Spanish Culture*, edited by David T. Gies, 287–297.

Zinger, Pablo. "The Spanish Songbook." *Opera News* 62, no. 1 (July 1997): 12–17.

Dance

Blanco Lou, Carlos. "Dance." In *Encyclopedia of Contemporary Spanish Culture*, edited by Eamonn Rodgers, 136–138.

Kumin, Laura. "Letter from Spain." *Dance Magazine* 72, no. 10 (October 1998): 34–35.

———. "To Live Is to Dance." In *The Cambridge Companion to Modern Spanish Culture*, edited by David T. Gies, 298–306.

Matteo. *The Language of Spanish Dance*. Norman: University of Oklahoma Press, 1993.

OTHER SOURCES

For information on the theater, music and dance, see the website "infoEscena 2002" at <http://www.infoescena.es>. For music, see the website "Olé" and its special section "Música": <http://www.terra.es>. There are innumerable sites for flamenco, based both in Spain and in other countries. One is <http://www.flamenco-world.com/>. For *zarzuela*, see <http://www.ciudadfutura.com/madrid>. *Billboard* magazine prints the pop charts in Spain and occasional feature articles on Spanish pop music.

8

Visual Arts

Museums have . . . emerged as one of the emblems and engines driving
Spain into democracy.

—Selma Reuben Holo[1]

Walking down the beautiful Paseo del Prado in Madrid, with its trees, gardens, fountains and statues along the wide avenue, one is only a stone's throw from three of Europe's finest museums. First, the venerable Prado in an eighteenth-century building that is home to many old masters from Spain and other countries. Second, the elegant Thyssen-Bornemisza, also in a neoclassical building, with a privately acquired collection matched only by the British royal family's. Third, the brilliant Reina Sofía, located in another eighteenth-century edifice that was once Madrid's General Hospital, with an unparalleled assembly of modern and contemporary works from Spain and other countries (see Photograph 24). The Casón del Buen Retiro (the Prado's annex), the National Museum of Decorative Arts, the Army Museum and the National Museum of Archaeology are also nearby. Finally, there are dozens of excellent private galleries within walking distance. For all these reasons, the Paseo del Prado has become known as the "Avenue of the Arts," and its neighborhood may have the highest density of fine painting and sculpture in the world. Madrid is both the national and artistic capital of Spain.

Other cities can also boast of important collections. As we have seen earlier (Chapter 7, Performing Arts), the decentralization of power, with greater dispersal of funds to the autonomous regions and municipalities, has

24. Museo Nacional Centro de Arte Reina Sofía, Madrid, 2001. Photograph by Museo Nacional Centro de Arte Reina Sofía.

strengthened the arts throughout the Peninsula. Many museums, both old and new, are more than mere repositories of artifacts; they are important makers of local, provincial and regional identity. Other collections reveal the evolving culture of the new, democratic Spain. We will begin our survey of the visual arts by looking at some of the notable spaces where they are housed.

Spain's most sensational new museum is the Guggenheim in Bilbao, a rhapsody in titanium and limestone created by the American architect Frank Gehry. In its first year of operation, more than a million people passed through its doors. "Not since Richard Rogers and Renzo Piano's Centre Pompidou regenerated the Marais district of Paris, a quarter of a century ago, has a museum been such an engine for urban renewal."[2] The Guggenheim alone has put Bilbao on the map again, restored its confidence and become a model for other cities throughout the world.[3] It is also a dramatic symbol of a nationalistic region "jumping" over the central Spanish tradition in favor of global culture.

Catalonia has also asserted its independence from Madrid; it resembles a "nation within a nation" in its funding and display of the arts. Some two hundred of Spain's approximately one thousand museums and collections are located in the city of Barcelona alone, capital of the Catalan autonomous region. The most famous is probably the Pablo Picasso, located in the city's Gothic Quarter. Although the artist had always been a symbol of resistance to General Franco, the dictator allowed the collection to open in 1963. Picasso himself donated pieces from his personal holdings, as did his widow Jacqueline after the artist's death. Joan Miró, the most famous Catalan painter of the century, also donated many of his creations to the foundation named after him. It opened in Barcelona in 1975, six months before Franco's death. The well-known architect Josep Lluís Sert, a longtime friend of the artist, designed the building in a contemporary style that represented a controversial rupture with the past. The collection itself was no less controversial, with contemporary works by Miró and the likes of Eduardo Chillida, Julio González, Antonio Saura, Marcel Duchamp, Max Ernst, Henri Matisse, Henry Moore and Robert Rauschenberg. The Joan Miró Foundation Museum rapidly became a civic institution of Catalan identity and symbolic resistance to the dictatorship. Barcelona's most famous living artist, Antoni Tàpies, also has a foundation named after him, dramatically housed in a renovated building designed by one of the Catalan modernist architects of the late nineteenth century, Pere Domènech i Montaner. (The most famous member of this school was Antoni Gaudí.) A few years later, the National Museum of Catalan Art (MNAC) consolidated numerous smaller collections into a "national" institution. It is located in the imposing Palau Nacional (National Palace), built in 1929 for the International Exposition and renovated by the Italian architect Gae Aulenti.

> Like the Pinakotheks of Germany, the Louvre of France, and the national galleries in England, Canada, and the United States, Catalonia wanted MNAC to be a museum that symbolized a country, that country being in this case a region within a nation-state. The objective was thus intrinsically political. . . . In this context MNAC is an expensive and expansive affirmation of the marriage of museums and politics. The spectacular quality of its core collections, along with its intriguing site and architectural presence, make it a compelling affirmation of Catalonia and its creative spirit.[4]

The 1992 Olympic Games in Barcelona gave more impetus to the artistic revolution in the area; the city sponsored a vast sculptural project, an outdoor museum composed of seventy large pieces scattered throughout the metropolis. Half of the commissioned sculptors were Catalan or Spanish, the remainder from other countries in Europe and the Americas. The Barcelona Public Sculpture Project showed how local and regional identity could be promoted in an international context. Three years after the Olympics, the Barcelona Museum of Contemporary Art (MACBA) opened its doors to the public. Designed by American Richard Meier, who is also the architect of the Getty Center in Los Angeles, MACBA has been a wasps' nest from the beginning. The institution did not possess a substantial collection when it began its operations. Even if it had, the building does not have enough wall space for hanging a sizeable selection of paintings, and its glass walls do not permit control of the blinding sunlight that floods the galleries. MACBA is a good example of how signature museums can be colossal failures if they emphasize architecture to the detriment of the artwork.

Before leaving Catalonia to discuss other regional museums, we should examine the powerful La Caixa Foundation, named after a savings and pension bank that has been in existence for more than a century. The most ambitious of all Spanish foundations, it has always dedicated a large part of its ample budget to the arts and humanities. Although it specializes in Catalan art, La Caixa has been much less closed-minded than some institutions in the region, which have purposely ignored works from other parts of Spain and the world. Although it had no permanent building until very recently, the Caixa has become a de facto museum, developing original projects that reach hundreds of thousands of people every year. In 1999 it announced plans to adopt the Casaramona factory, another icon of Barcelona's modernist movement, as a permanent space to exhibit the foundation's superb collection of painting, sculpture and other artwork.

The Valencian Community is another Catalan-speaking region that has encouraged the construction of new museums. Its capital of Valencia, a city of 750,000 people, has more than seventy alone: archaeological, maritime, ethnological, fine arts, ecclesiastical, scientific, medical, military, agricultural, historic and monographic collections have sprouted all over the city, with more on the way. One writer says:

> It sometimes strikes the visitor to Valencia that there are more museums than necessary. They seem to have sprung up without planning and, sometimes (as in the case of the new science museum), without collections. Even the former director of the Cultural Patrimony of Valencia, the official whose business included museums, wrote that this growth could be described as a "veritable museological bulimia."[5]

The city's signature museum, the Institut Valencià d'Art Modern (IVAM), will help us understand other institutions in Spain. Like the Museum of Modern Art (MOMA) in New York City, this institution has become so famous that it is simply called by its acronym. The original site is a gorgeous seven-hundred-year-old convent now called the Centre del Carmé, whose chapel houses the museum's changing exhibitions. It is "recognized as one of the most striking examples of adaptive reuse of ancient buildings in Europe."[6] Across the street and down the block from the Carmé is IVAM's second building, the Centre Julio González, named for the Catalan artist whose iron sculptures make up the museum's core collection (see Photograph 25). Designed by a team of five Valencian architects, this structure is everything the Carmé is not: new rather than old, simple rather than complex, unpretentious rather than ornate. Yet it too is tied deeply to the past. In one of the basement galleries, visitors can see the remains of Valencia's ancient city walls. The new built on the foundations of the old: this is the key to IVAM's appeal and to the city's, the region's and the country's attempts to save the past and create new structures for the future. IVAM is also typical of new institutions in Spain and other countries in its attempt to create a museum without walls (or at least external walls). Not content merely to showcase fine works of art, the Institute has undertaken public education and outreach programs in order to involve citizens at large. Interactive workshops draw children and adults into the creative process, teaching them the excitement of making artistic discoveries. IVAM also organizes conferences

25. Centre Julio González, Institut Valencià d'Art Modern (IVAM), 2001. Photograph courtesy IVAM, Generalitat Valenciana.

and symposia and produces publications both for scholars and the general public. It was so successful in its first years that the new Museo Nacional Centro de Arte Reina Sofía, the national museum of modern and contemporary art in Madrid, followed its example in many ways. The fact that the state was inspired by a regional institution is a sign of how much old centralist attitudes have changed in democratic Spain.

Andalusia has also carried out ambitious projects in the visual arts. Since millions of foreigners flock to this sunny area every year, the autonomous government has vigorously supported cultural tourism throughout its large territory. The region's General Plan for Cultural Properties (1985) was the first document of its kind in Spain. It states that the cultural patrimony is the country's principal contribution to world civilization and should be protected, enriched and transmitted to all citizens as an essential ingredient of a dignified quality of life. The 1992 Universal Exposition (Expo '92), held in Andalusia's capital of Sevilla, was a perfect opportunity for the city and the region to promote its culture, just as the Olympic Games had been for Barcelona and Catalonia the same year. The enormous monastery of La Cartuja (Santa María de las Cuevas), located across the River Guadalquivir from the city, was chosen as the site for the event. Five architects drew up designs for the immediate purpose of creating a Royal Pavilion for Expo '92, as well as a nontraditional museum that would function permanently as a gallery, library, archive, conference center, painting and sculpture conservation workshop, architectural complex and garden. The collection of painting, sculpture and other works was intentionally reduced to a bare minimum in order to foreground the buildings themselves. At first La Cartuja appeared to thrive. After a few years, however, crowds began to diminish; visitors felt that the collection was too sparse. Soon the site was not attracting enough people to justify its continuation. The country's political shift from a socialist to a conservative government in 1996 put the old monastery in limbo. The following year La Cartuja became the Andalusian Center for Contemporary Art (CAAC). Since then it has absorbed other collections and realized that a successful museum must display sufficient works to attract a wide range of visitors. Unlike some institutions located in Catalonia and the Basque Country, CAAC focuses on regional art without prejudice against "Spanish" or international works.

One regional collection with great symbolic importance is the Sephardic Museum in Toledo (New Castile). Situated in the former capital of the Spanish Empire, close to Madrid, this institution poses key questions about national identity. Housed in the beautiful Synagogue Samuel Ha-Levy (Sinagoga del Tránsito), it was restored and reopened in 1994 with abundant support from local, regional and national governments. Since then, some 250,000 people a year have visited the Sephardic Museum. Built in the elaborate Mudéjar style of the fourteenth century, the interior has delicate friezes that fuse Islamic, Hebrew and Christian motifs below a coffered ceiling of larchwood inlaid with ivory. In collaboration with the local university in the Castilla-La Mancha region, courses on the history and culture of the Sephardim have been offered at the museum. The institution's purpose is to recover the historical memory of the Jews who lived in the Iberian Peninsula for a thousand years before their expulsion in 1492 (see Chapter 1, Context). It could be seen as a metaphor of democratic Spain, a country that rejects the Francoist ideology portraying its history and identity as exclusively Catholic and European.

The Iberian Peninsula has rich and ancient traditions in the visual arts, from the cave paintings of Altamira to pre-classical sculptures like the queenly Dama de Elche, Roman mosaics, Visigothic goldwork, Islamic, Jewish and Christian architecture, decorative arts, painting and sculpture since the birth of the modern country to the present. As in previous chapters, our emphasis here will be on the present. In fact it has only been in the last twenty years that we can observe a significant increase in public awareness and funding for the arts. During the Franco dictatorship (1939–1975), "artistic innovation took place in spite of, not because of, government attitudes."[7] With the establishment of democracy, the new Ministry of Culture increased spending for the arts dramatically while offering tax incentives to individual and corporate collectors. A 1985 law made it illegal to alter, sell or export without permission sites or objects listed on the General Register of the nation's cultural patrimony, much of which belongs to the Catholic Church. Existing private foundations spent more on the arts while new ones came into existence. Banks and *cajas de ahorros* (savings banks) were required by the state to expend a specified portion of their profits on community works, including the arts. The larger universities also played a more important role by building galleries and organizing exhibits. During the heady years of the *movida* in the 1980s (see Chapter 7), art became a symbol of Spanish youth, energy, experimentation, creativity, diversification and tolerance. Waiters and cabbies argued for and against the government's policies in the arts.

Every Spanish who read a newspaper or watched television seemed to have an opinion about Picasso's *Guernica* once it had come home: should it be moved from the venerable Prado to the upstart Reina Sofía? should it retain its protective glass shield? should it be allowed to leave

Madrid for loan to exhibitions as close as the Guggenheim Museum
Bilbao or as far as Paris?[8]

By the 1990s, large companies were jumping on the cultural bandwagon,
seeing painting, sculpture and photography as vehicles for investment and
public relations. Art had become big business in Spain. Museums and foundations also began to purchase and display more and better works from other
countries, making a wider range of art accessible to Spaniards and foreigners.
In spite of all these changes, the visual arts always seem to be underfunded,
like the cinema (Chapter 5) and the performing arts (Chapter 7).

We will look at the current situation in architecture, painting, sculpture
and photography. In the postmodern world of Spain, it may be difficult to
draw boundaries between these different fields in the visual arts. The flourishing of painting and sculpture, for example, has enabled Spanish architects
to upgrade old institutions or design new ones. In our discussion of the
Institut Valencià d'Art Modern (IVAM), we have seen how that museum
has joined the two enterprises of assembling works of art and providing a
striking space for their exhibition. In the case of the Barcelona Museum of
Contemporary Art and Sevilla's La Cartuja, we have seen how impressive
buildings can fail as museums if they lose touch with local conditions and
the practical elements of displaying works of art.

ARCHITECTURE

Until the late twentieth century, Spain was known as a country of painters.
For the first time in its history, it is also recognized as a country of major
architects. Franco's death in 1975 released a burst of creativity that affected
the whole range of visual arts, from fashion to interior design, architecture,
painting, sculpture and photography. As the region that had suffered most
under the dictatorship, Catalonia took the lead. By the late 1970s, new
offices, boutiques, discos and bars were more innovative than anything in
the rest of the Peninsula. Fernando Amat, with young artist Javier Mariscal,
created Merbeye, "arguably the first designer bar"[9]: an avant-garde structure
built in a warehouse, characterized by visual jokes and a futuristic treatment
of materials and surfaces. Architect and designer Alfredo Arribas, in collaboration with Mariscal and others, created more original shops, bars and restaurants. He employed the textures and colors of seduction—velvet, suede
and billowing curtains in deep reds, blues and purples. "This was the ultimate
designer experience, with everything—from décor to toilets, menus, logos,
and even the music—designed by Arribas: in short, a totally designed envi-

ronment, offering the youth of Barcelona release from their crowded family apartments and—above all—fun."[10] He became a leading exponent of interiorism, an approach to architecture that featured visual spectacle, humor, parody and surprise. Arribas's designer bar Las Torres de Ávila, created with Mariscal in 1991, represented an elaborate sexual joke: in the "female" tower, patrons looked down through a hole to the bar itself, while in the "male" tower, an enormous piston plunged up and down. Everything turned into parody and play in this totally self-contained, postmodern environment in which there was no "outside." Like so many bold experiments in the post-Franco years, the bar went out of business. Arribas, however, went on to have a successful career both in Spain and abroad, winning several prestigious prizes.

The 1992 Olympiad in Barcelona, with enormous infusions of government and corporate funds, offered a unique opportunity for architects and urban planners. Oriol Bohigas spearheaded the city's renewal program and was chief architect of the Olympic Village. Ricardo Bofill, another Catalan, contributed one of his neo-classical buildings to the main complex. Valencian Santiago Calatrava's graceful communications tower, set beside the Olympic stadium, became the structure most readily identified with the 1992 Games.

Bohigas, Bofill and Calatrava are examples of the new breed of architects in Spain; they are equally at home inside the country or abroad. Bohigas has been an enormous intellectual force in Catalonia, while also designing buildings in other parts of Spain and in foreign countries. As director of Barcelona's School of Architecture, he nourished several generations of students. As we have seen above, he was also the driving force behind the city's ambitious renewal project—highly praised throughout the world—that cleared new green spaces and opened Barcelona to the sea. In addition, Oriol Bohigas is known as an architectural historian and critic. His activities have brought him many distinctions.

Ricardo Bofill who belongs to the next generation of Catalan architects, has enjoyed even more international recognition. At the beginning of his career, he created the Architects' Workshop, a team of designers and intellectuals who believed in a humanistic approach to architecture and town planning. Some of their early creations included El Xanadu (Calp, Alicante, 1968), El Castell (Reus, Tarragona, 1969), and the Muralla Roja (Calp, 1972–1974). These constructions all evoke geometric linearity and labyrinths. The Workshop later grew into an international enterprise with more emphasis on monumental buildings in a neoclassical style. It opened branches in Paris, Montpellier and New York, and completed projects in Barcelona, Bordeaux, Paris, Stockholm, Moscow and Chicago. Two of its more recent projects in Catalonia include the airport (1988–1991) and the Teatre Nacional de Catalunya (1987–1997), both in the capital.

Santiago Calatrava, a member of the next generation, is an architect, engineer and sculptor who specializes in spectacular bridges like the Alamillo gateway for Expo '92 in Sevilla and the sleek white footbridge (Zubi-Zubi) in Bilbao. One of his more recent projects is the Prince of Asturias Science Museum in his native Valencia, with forty-two thousand square meters of floor space and projections for half a million visitors per year. (Unfortunately the collection is not large enough to fill the space.) Like so many famous architects these days, Calatrava has also drawn up plans for a new winery in Spain's La Rioja region, with a distinctive undulating roof.[11]

Rafael Moneo, a native of Tudela (Navarra), is one of the country's few non-Catalan-speaking architects who have achieved international acclaim. Nevertheless, he spent ten formative years at the Barcelona School of Architecture (1970–1980) where he was exposed to the revolution in design that occurred after Franco's death. From 1985–1990 Moneo was dean of the prestigious Graduate School of Design at Harvard. During his tenure there, he worked on the plans for the National Museum of Roman Art in Mérida (Extremadura, 1986), which catapulted him onto the international scene. It is an austere masterpiece where red brick arches stretch over an archaeological excavation. Moneo also supervised the refurbishment of the Villahermosa Palace in Madrid to house the Thyssen Collection (1991). His College of Architects in Tarragona (1992) is another project built over ancient ruins; the construction blends smoothly with the modern city and its daily life. This was an impressive period for Moneo, in which he also completed three ambitious, long-range projects—a new terminal for Sevilla's airport, the Pilar and Joan Miró Museum in Palma de Mallorca and the redesign of Madrid's old Atocha railway station. His latest projects include the Kursaal Conference Center and Concert Hall in San Sebastián (Guipúzcoa, 1999), whose "unstable volumes remind us that the Basques' tribulations have not ended,"[12] and the Julián Chivite winery at Arínzano (Navarra) on the banks of the Ega River, surrounded by mountains (2001). As if these were not enough, Moneo has also completed many buildings abroad, such as the Houston Museum of Fine Arts (1992); the Davis Museum and Cultural Center at Wellesley College (1993); the Potsdamer Platz Hotel and office building in Berlin (1993); the $50 million Our Lady of the Angels in Los Angeles (1996), "the last great cathedral of the millennium"; and the Museum of Modern Art and Architecture on Skeppsholmen Island, Stockholm (1998). Finally, Moneo has won a competition to renew the Prado Museum. The breadth of his interests can be demonstrated by the fact that he is presently supporting a campaign to beatify the great Catalan modernist architect Antoni Gaudí, at the same time as he is undertaking a futuristic project for underground freeways in Madrid. It is not surprising that Rafael Moneo is the first Spaniard to receive the Pritzker Prize, the most coveted international award for achievement in architecture.

Some readers may have noticed that female architects have not been cited in this section. Like most of the visual arts, architecture has been closed to women until very recent times, long after the end of the dictatorship. A recent book on twentieth-century buildings in Madrid, for example, includes 125 projects, only one of which had a female architect—and she belonged to a team that included two men.[13] The situation in painting is hardly better.

PAINTING

Artists like Diego Velázquez, José de Ribera, Francisco de Zurbarán, Bartolomé Esteban Murillo and Francisco de Goya appear in most histories of European painting. In more recent times, one need only cite names like Joaquín Sorolla, Pablo Picasso, Joan Miró, Salvador Dalí and Antoni Tàpies to suggest Spain's contribution to twentieth-century art. Although less well known than these male artists, in the early decades of the twentieth century María Blanchard painted still lifes—destitute women and children in earth colors and muted tones of great beauty and originality. She remains one of the few women who have been able to break into the country's male-dominated art world.

The Civil War (1936–1939) and its aftermath cut off the esthetic richness of the previous decades. The Franco regime strove to erase the vanguard—Picasso, Miró, Dalí—from the nation's memory. Accepted painting tended to be conventional and academic—the work of veteran masters such as Ignacio Zuloaga and José Gutiérrez Solana, landscape artists such as Daniel Vázquez Díaz and Benjamín Palencia. As in architecture, Catalonia was the region that reintegrated the country into the international vanguard. In his famous "matter paintings,"Antoni Tàpies experimented with natural materials like colored earth, sand and marble dust. He also produced collages and sculptures in half a century of creativity that yielded more than seven thousand works. Manuel Millares' monochromatic canvases of torn and shredded sackcloth conveyed a powerful emotional message during the hard years of the dictatorship, as did Antonio Saura's deformed faces of historical figures in grays and blacks, which seemed to exorcise the weight of the past. Painters coalesced in groups like Equipo 57 and Equipo Crónica that became increasingly critical of commercialism in galleries and repression by the state. Crónica's pastiches of iconic paintings from the past—its reworking of the portrait of Phillip II attributed to Alonso Sánchez Coello, or a modernized version of Velázquez's "Las meninas"—linked contemporary art to national tradition, while satirizing the imperial pretensions of the fascist regime and discovering a new pictorial language. Eduardo Arroyo also represented figures of power ironically, earning him the state's hostility.

The death of Franco did not affect Spanish painting as much as it did the public arts like theater and architecture. Greater funding for cultural activities improved the display of the visual arts in new museums and exhibitions, but did not help individual artists immediately. The *movida* tended to highlight painting and sculpture less than music, cinema, fashion and design. The country needed to recover from the trauma of the dictatorship and to recuperate its historical memory. After the definitive return of Picasso's "Guernica"—depicting the brutal bombing of the Basque town by German airplanes, a symbol of Spain's struggle against tyranny—the country hosted a succession of memorable exhibitions, conferences and competitions. "The 1980s were years of euphoria and ephemeral triumphs, but also of serious undertakings and works of undeniable quality; collections were established and museums created to fill old lacunae, and a generation of artists responded eagerly to the challenges."[14]

The public and the media revealed a new appetite for culture and the arts. In 1990 the Prado opened the most comprehensive show of Velázquez's work ever to be displayed. More than half a million people visited the exhibition. On the last day, mobs prevented the museum from closing its doors at the scheduled closing time; irate crowds clashed with members of the Civil Guard. At midnight, people were still gathered in front of the Prado beneath the rain, chanting "We want to come in." Art had become an inalienable right and an object of public consumption. Exhibits of Ribera in 1992 and Goya in 1996 (the 250th anniversary of his birth) also attracted huge numbers of visitors, as did a centenary celebration of the poet and artist Federico García Lorca in 1998.

In the last few decades, many Spanish painters have rediscovered the craft and pleasure of painting, in addition to the narrative potential of the canvas. Guillermo Pérez Villalta's bright works abound in classical architecture and mythology. Ferrán García Sevilla creates images scattered playfully over immense colored surfaces. Miguel Angel Campano paints vigorous landscapes and still lifes. In his large canvases, José María Sicilia combines geometry and coloristic expression. Miquel Barceló, perhaps the contemporary Spanish painter best known outside the country, employs a unique expressionistic style. Antonio López attempts to capture perfect light in his stark, almost photographic work. His painting reached the national spotlight when he withdrew from an exhibition at the Reina Sofía Museum, in protest against the tendency to define modern art in exclusively avant-garde terms, with neglect of realist works.[15]

Spain's biggest annual event for painting is probably Madrid's International Festival of Contemporary Art, sponsored by the ARCO Foundation with generous support from the Spanish government. The organization's mission is to build a collection of recent works—painting, sculpture, photography—from Spain and abroad. It also schedules educational events and counsels large companies on prospective purchases. In 1994, for example, it advised the Coca Cola Foundation on how to spend its twenty-million-peseta budget for the arts. At ARCO 2000 (February 10–15), no less than 234 galleries from twenty-eight countries displayed works. Special shows featured Italian, German, Dutch and Latin American art. Other exhibits related to art books, magazines and CD-Roms. The Spanish Ministry of Education, Culture and Sport organized discussions on acquisition policies in contemporary art museums. With the annual ARCO, the Prado, the Thyssen-Bornemisza, the Reina Sofía, private foundations and commercial galleries, Madrid has become one of the world's leading centers for the visual arts.

SCULPTURE

Sculpture in Spain has never been as well known as painting. Only in the twentieth century have some Spanish sculptors become famous on the international scene. During the Franco years, official sculpture was predictably behind the times. One great artist from the Basque region, Eduardo Chillida, kept the flame of originality alive and helped connect Spain to the international vanguard, much as Tàpies did for painting. Chillida's lifelong study of stone, steel and wood led to the creation of abstract and complex geometric forms that have no "front" or "back," suggesting different meanings from every side. His sculptures can be enjoyed in open spaces in several Spanish cities, including Madrid. A monographic museum on Chillida's work was dedicated in Zabalaga (Hernani, Guipúzcoa) in 2000, with participation by King Juan Carlos, two European heads of state—Spain's José María Aznar and Germany's Gerhard Schröeder—and the president of Euzkadi, Juan José Ibarretxe.

Another Basque artist, Jorge Oteiza, won international acclaim in the 1950s and 1960s with powerful, minimalist sculptures. An eccentric personality, he refused to sell his work and ceased producing. His reputation faded outside of the Basque Country, but revived when two famous American artists, sculptor Richard Serra and architect Frank Gehry—a hero in Euzkadi because of his Guggenheim Museum—reportedly called Oteiza the greatest abstract sculptor of the twentieth century.

As a more public art, sculpture was liberated by democracy more than painting. Minimalism, conceptualism, land and body art allowed sculptors to overcome the weight of tradition. In the 1980s, many artists concentrated on assemblages and installations rather than traditional statuary. Pepe Espaliú, Pello Irazu, and Miquel Navarro followed this trend. By the 1990s, these spatial experiments had lost some of their novelty and the public seemed to prefer statuary once more. Artists like Ángeles Marco and Adolfo Schlosser worked with skill in their personal idioms. Susana Solano created an original minimalism that has brought her wide recognition. Eva Lootz became well known for her use of new materials like paraffin wax and mercury. A still younger group of artists, born in the 1950s, has carried Spanish sculpture to one of its best moments in recent history. Txomin Badiloa, Cristina Iglesias and Fernando Sinaga belong to this group. However, some critics believe that the "new classicism" of many Spanish sculptors points to a lack of innovation.

One of the country's most interesting projects in recent years is a sculpture park on the river island of Xunqueira in the Galician city of Pontevedra. The project, inspired by Antón Castro and Rosa Olivares, was inaugurated in July 1999, with a dozen pieces by well-known sculptors from Spain and abroad: Fernando Casas, Francisco Leiro, Enrique Velasco, José Pedro Croft, Ian Hamilton Finlay, Richard Long, Robert Morris and Ulrich Rüchriem. Nearly all the works were executed in relation to a specific spot on the island. Together the pieces show a spectrum of trends in contemporary sculpture. With this project the city has recovered an abandoned space and preserved its landscape, while exposing citizens to some of the best outdoor art in Spain.

PHOTOGRAPHY

As in architecture, painting and sculpture, the Spanish Civil War and the dictatorship forced the country to lose several decades in the development of avant-garde photography. Isolation and censorship prevented photographers from free expression of their art. Nevertheless, some managed to keep abreast of international currents. In the 1940s and 1950s, the work of Francesc Català-Roca and Gabriel Cuallado showed the influence of Italian neorealism. Although he was passionately fond of color, Català-Roca became known for his monochrome "snapshots" in which he captured the unusual with a sense of surprise. Cuallado also showed a varied range of greys in his black-

and-white photography, remarkable for its vigorous composition and careful treatment of material objects as well as human subjects. Just before his seventy-fifth birthday, he received two distinctions for a lifetime of work: the Best European Photographer Award (1993) and the National Photography Prize (1994).

After Franco's death, the journal *Nueva Lente* (New Lens) marked the appearance of a more radical vision. A new generation of artists rejected the portrayal of "photogenic" reality. Cristina García Rodero traveled throughout the Peninsula to record religious and profane celebrations in all their cruelty and power (see Chapter 3).[16] She continues to take her camera to all corners of the world in search of collective rituals. García Rodero's work has been exhibited in Spain, the United States and other countries. Rafael Vargas, Carlos Fargas and Juan Urrios also began their careers under the dictatorship and continued to develop in Spain's new democracy. Vargas's photos are often conceived as works of art in their own right. Unlike García Rodero, who prefers black and white, Vargas generally uses color and creates a theatrical setting for his subjects. He is also an experienced architectural photographer. Alfredo Arribas (see Architecture above) has enlarged three of Vargas's photographs depicting the city by night for his "Gran Velvet," composed of images twelve meters in length.

By the 1980s, photography had become a high-art form in Spain. Like the other visual arts, it formed part of the new culture of consumption. In the 1990s and the first years of the new millennium, photographic shows were drawing almost as many visitors as painting and sculpture. Several *bienales* or biannual exhibitions are now celebrated in even years. One of the most established is Barcelona's *Primavera Fotográfica* (Photographic Spring). In 1998 it included 150 expositions in local museums and galleries. A newer event, Madrid's PhotoEspaña International, in its first year (1998) presented seventy-one exhibits in twelve public and private institutions, in addition to films, lectures and workshops. Imago in Salamanca is another new festival; it features both photography and video throughout the summer in this beautiful Castilian city. As in painting and sculpture, more exhibits of foreign photographers are held in Spain than ever before. In 1999, for example, the Reina Sofía Museum presented one of the most complete exhibits to date of the American surrealist Man Ray, while the Calcografía Nacional (Museum of Engraving) displayed a historical reconstruction of the work by *Life* photographer W. Eugene Smith, author of the mythical "Spanish Village" series. In the same year, Madrid's Sala del Canal Isabel II (Canal Isabel II Salon) hosted *Juegos y Simulacros* (Games and Imitations), an itinerant show from the French National Archive of Contemporary Art's collection of sixty-six thousand works, with photographs by artists such as Boltanski, Hanna Collins, Alan Fleischer and Pierre & Gilles. As we can see from these examples, Spain has become a leading center for the exhibition of international photography, as well as the other visual arts.

SELECTED READINGS

Bartolucci, Marisa. "Undiscovered Bilbao." *Atlantic Monthly* (October 2000): 46–53.

Calvo Serraller, Francisco. *Escultura española actual: una generación para un fin de siglo*. Madrid: Fundación Lugar C, 1992.

Chueca Goitia, Fernando, and others. *Arquitectura de Madrid. Siglo XX*. Madrid: Tanais, 1999.

Fernández-Galiano, Luis. "A Century of Spanish Architecture." In *The Cambridge Companion to Modern Spanish Culture*, edited by David T. Gies, 278–286. Cambridge: Cambridge University Press, 1999.

Holo, Selma Reuben. *Beyond the Prado: Museums and Identity in Democratic Spain* Washington, D.C.: Smithsonian Institution Press, 1999.

———. "The Art Museum as a Means of Refiguring Regional Identity in Democratic Spain." In *Refiguring Spain: Cinema/Media/Representation*, edited by Marsha Kinder, 301–326. Durham, NC: Duke University Press, 1997.

Hooper, John. *The New Spaniards*. London: Penguin, 1995. See Chapters 23 ("Art and the Possible: The Politics of Culture") and 24 ("A Journey without Maps").

Martínez, José Martín. "Painting and Sculpture in Modern Spain." In *The Cambridge Companion to Modern Spanish Culture*, edited by David T. Gies, 239–247. Cambridge: Cambridge University Press, 1999.

Pérez Sánchez, Alfonso E., ed. *La pintura española*. 2 vols. Madrid: Electa, 1995.

Rodgers, Eamonn, ed. *Encyclopedia of Contemporary Spanish Culture*. London: Routledge, 1999. See articles on architecture, painting, sculpture and photography, as well as entries on individual artists.

OTHER SOURCES

For the visual arts, see the website "Olé" and its special section on "Arte": <http://www.terra.es>. A good site for information on art galleries, museums, exhibits and artists is <http://3art.es>. The search engine "Yahoo! España" is very useful: <http://es.yahoo.com>. Click on *Arte y cultura*, then *Artes plásticas*, which will take you to links on painting, drawing, silk-screening, sculpture, photography and other arts. Another useful site is "Arte 10," "Doorway to Contemporary Spanish Arts" (in Spanish): <http://www.arte10.com>.

The Spanish Ministry of Education, Culture and Sports publishes regular bulletins on cultural activities. See its website <http://www.mec.es/mec/novedades>.

The Thyssen-Bornemisza Museum has an attractive website: <offcampus.es/museo.thyssen-bornemisza/index.htm>.

Exit. Imagen y Cultura is a new trimonthly magazine published in Spanish and English: <www.exitmedia.net>.

The Art Newspaper (international edition) contains news on the visual arts from around the world. *El Periódico del Arte*, the Spanish edition, is published in Madrid.

Notes

CHAPTER 1

1. Letter to James Gamble (December 12, 1923) in *Ernest Hemingway: Selected Letters 1917–1961*, ed. Carlos Baker (New York: Scribner's, 1981), 107.

2. Website "Transparency International," September 22, 1998, <http://www.transparency.org>.

3. Letter to José Alemany (November 8, 1940), Hemingway Collection, John F. Kennedy Library (Boston).

4. V. S. Pritchett, *The Spanish Temper* (New York: Knopf, 1955), viii.

5. Gerald Brenan, *Thoughts in a Dry Season* (Cambridge: Cambridge University Press, 1978), 152.

6. Salvador de Madariaga, *Spain: A Modern History* (New York: Praeger, 1960), 9–10.

7. Pritchett, *The Spanish Temper*, 85–86.

8. It should be pointed out that the riots were at least partially a reaction to the murder of three Spaniards, apparently by Moroccans.

9. Ernest Hemingway, *Death in the Afternoon* (1932; rpt. New York: Scribner's, 1960), 264.

10. James Michener, *Iberia: Spanish Travels and Reflections* (New York: Random House, 1968), 55–56.

11. Ian Gibson, *Fire in the Blood: The New Spain* (London: Faber and Faber, 1992), 21.

12. Pritchett, *The Spanish Temper*, 6–7.

13. Prof. José Labrador in conversation with author, April 2001.

14. Peter Pierson, *The History of Spain* (Westport, CT: Greenwood Press, 1999), 11.

15. Richard Ford, *Gatherings from Spain* (1846; rpt. London: J. M. Dent & Sons, 1970), 13.

16. For the period 1995–1998, according to the United Nations and the National Center for Health Sciences. The fertility rate in Spain was 107 (lifetime births projected per 100 women of childbearing age). In the United States for 1999, the figure was 208. The number needed for replacement is 211.

17. Antonio Machado, *Juan de Mairena: Sentencias, donaires, apuntes y recuerdos de un profesor apócrifo* (1936; rpt. Madrid: Castalia, 1971), 118.

CHAPTER 2

1. Miguel de Cervantes, *Don Quixote de la Mancha*, ed. John J. Allen, 2 vols. (1605, 1615; rpt. Madrid: Cátedra, 1989), 2:89.

2. Antonio Gala, *La casa sosegada* (Barcelona: Planeta, 1998), 207.

3. Antonio Machado, *Juan de Mairena: Sentencias, donaires, apuntes y recuerdos de un profesor apócrifo* (1936; rpt. Madrid: Castalia, 1971), 142.

4. John Hooper, *The New Spaniards* (London: Penguin, 1995), 126.

5. Hooper, *The New Spaniards*, 133.

6. Rafael Díaz-Salazar and Salvador Giner, "Prefacio," in *Religión y sociedad en España*, eds. Díaz-Salazar and Giner (Madrid: Centro de Investigaciones Sociológicas, 1993), xiii.

7. Hooper, *The New Spaniards*, 141.

8. Hooper, *The New Spaniards*, 135.

9. Audrey Brassloff, "Roman Catholicism," in *Encyclopedia of Contemporary Spanish Culture*, ed. Eamonn Rodgers (London and New York: Routledge, 1999), 456.

10. "En España hay ya más jóvenes no creyentes que católicos practicantes," *El Mundo* (August 3, 1997): 26. This study was conducted by the Fundación para el Análisis y los Estudios Sociales (Foundation for Analysis and Social Studies).

11. "Religión," in *La sociedad española, 1996–1997*, ed. Amando de Miguel (Madrid: Editorial Complutense, 1997), 219–221.

12. "Religión," in *La sociedad española, 1996–1997*, 232.

13. Quoted in Ian Gibson, *Fire in the Blood: The New Spain* (London: Faber and Faber, 1992), 71.

14. Enrique Miret Magdalena, quoted in Gibson, *Fire in the Blood*, 69.

15. "En España hay ya más jóvenes no creyentes que católicos practicantes," *El Mundo* (August 3, 1997): 26.

16. *La sociedad española, 1993–1994*, ed. Amando de Miguel (Madrid: Alianza, 1994), 521.

17. Luis Maldonado, *Religiosidad popular. Nostalgia de lo mágico* (Madrid: Editorial Cristiandad, 1975), 97.

CHAPTER 3

1. C. A. Longhurst, "Social Attitudes," in *Encyclopedia of Contemporary Spanish Culture*, ed. Eamonn Rodgers (London and New York: Routledge, 1999), 486.

2. John Hooper, *The New Spaniards* (London: Penguin, 1995), 196–207.

3. "Lucha contra el narcotráfico," *El Mundo* online (February 6, 2000), <http://www.el-mundo.es>.

4. Longhurst, "Social Attitudes," 485.

5. Juan Luis Cebrián, *The Press and Main Street: "El País"—Journalism in Democratic Spain* (Ann Arbor: University of Michigan Press, 1989), 44.

6. "Sexo y adolescencia," *ABCe* (*ABC* online) (February 3, 2000), <http://www.abc.es>.

7. Hooper, *The New Spaniards*, 161.

8. Paul Theroux, *The Pillars of Hercules: A Grand Tour of the Mediterranean* (New York: G. P. Putnam's Sons, 1995), 61.

9. Theroux, *The Pillars of Hercules*, 62.

10. Carlos A. Malo de Molina, *Los españoles y la sexualidad* (Madrid: Temas de Hoy, 1992), 143.

11. Malo de Molina, *Los españoles y la sexualidad*, 72.

12. Enrique Gil Calvo, "Edad y género (aspectos demográficos, culturales e ideológicos)," in *Sociología de las mujeres españolas*, eds. María Antonia García de León et al. (Madrid: Editorial Complutense, 1996), 29.

13. "La familia, por encima del trabajo, el dinero y los amigos," *El País* (February 5, 1996): 16. This article details the report by the Center of Sociological Research.

14. Miguel de Unamuno, *The Tragic Sense of Life* (1912; rpt. New York: Dover, 1954).

15. Timothy Mitchell, *Blood Sport: A Social History of Bullfighting* (Philadelphia: University of Pennsylvania Press, 1991), 132–133. The title of this otherwise superb book reflects the Anglo-Saxon misconception of the *corrida* as sport; it was imposed on the author by his publisher, who apparently thought it would attract more readers.

16. Paul Theroux, *The Pillars of Hercules*, 56.

17. Manuel Vázquez Montalbán, *Historia y comunicación social* (Madrid: Alianza, 1985), 217.

18. Robert Hughes, *Barcelona* (New York: Knopf, 1992), 21.

19. George Saintsbury, *Notes on a Cellar-Book* (London: Macmillan, 1931), 16.

20. Penelope Casas, *The Foods and Wines of Spain* (New York: Knopf, 1996), xiv.

21. Quoted in Marion Trutter, ed., *Culinaria Spain* (Cologne: Könemann, 1998), 9.

22. *The Foods and Wines of Spain*, xviii.

23. Richard Ford, *Gatherings from Spain* (1846; rpt. London: J. M. Dent & Sons, 1970), 139.

CHAPTER 4

1. Juan Luis Cebrián, *The Press and Main Street: "El País"—Journalism in Democratic Spain* (Ann Arbor: University of Michigan Press, 1989), xxv.

2. Manuel Vázquez Montalbán, Prologue to Lorenzo Díaz, *La radio en España 1923–1997* (Madrid: Alianza, 1993), 28.

3. Eduardo Haro Tecglen, Prologue to Lorenzo Díaz, *La televisión en España 1949–1995* (Madrid: Alianza, 1994), 10.

4. John Hooper, *The New Spaniards* (London: Penguin, 1995), 289.

5. Quoted in Ian Gibson, *Fire in the Blood: The New Spain* (London: Faber & Faber, 1992), 185.

6. Hooper, *The New Spaniards*, 299–300.

7. Hooper, *The New Spaniards*, 292.

8. Figures for 1997 are from *Anuario El País 1999* (Madrid: Ediciones El País, 1999), 216.

9. Figures for 1997 are from *Anuario El País 1999*, 218. The fact that some magazines do not have their headquarters mentioned may indicate that they are based outside of Spain.

10. Vázquez Montalbán, Prologue to Diaz, *La radio en España 1923–1997*, 30.

11. Javier Marías, *Pasiones pasadas* (Barcelona: Anagrama, 1991), 116–118.

12. Francisco Javier Rodríguez, *La televisión y los españoles. Análisis periodístico de un vicio nacional* (Madrid: Paraninfo, 1993), 120.

13. *Anuario El País 1999*, 232.

14. Richard Maxwell, "Spatial Eruptions, Global Grids: Regionalist TV in Spain and Dialectics of Identity Politics," in *Refiguring Spain: Cinema/Media/Representation*, ed. Marsha Kinder (Durham, NC: Duke University Press, 1997), 261.

CHAPTER 5

1. José Luis Aranguren, "Prólogo," in *Cine español 1896–1983*, ed. Augusto M. Torres (Madrid: Ministerio de Cultura, 1984), 12.

2. Peter Besas, "The Financial Structure of the Spanish Cinema," in *Refiguring Spain: Cinema/Media/Representation*, ed. Marsha Kinder (Durham, NC: Duke University Press, 1997), 241.

3. Quoted in "When Women Were in the Movies," in *Gender Images: Readings for Composition*, eds. Melita Schaum & Connie Flanagan (Boston: Houghton Mifflin, 1992), 355.

4. Marvin D'Lugo, "Introduction: Certain Tendencies in Spanish Cinema," in *Guide to the Cinema of Spain*, ed. Marvin D'Lugo (Westport, CT: Greenwood Press, 1997), 4.

5. Fernando Méndez-Leite, *Historia del cine español en 100 películas*, part 9 (Madrid: Jupey, 1975), 134.

6. Marsha Kinder, *Blood Cinema: The Reconstruction of National Identity in Spain* (Berkeley: University of California Press, 1993), 155.

7. These figures and those on the number of movie houses are from *Anuario El País 1999* (Madrid: Ediciones El País, 1999), 277–278.

8. Besas, "The Financial Structure of Spanish Cinema," *Refiguring Spain: Cinema/Media/Representation,* 248.

9. José María Otero, "El horizonte de las coproducciones," in *Los límites de la frontera: la coproducción en el cine español* (Madrid: Academia de las Artes y las Ciencias Cinematográficas de España, 1999), 27.

10. Jo Labanyi, "Conclusion: Modernity and Cultural Pluralism," in *Spanish Cultural Studies: An Introduction. The Struggle for Modernity,* eds. Helen Graham and Jo Labanyi (Oxford: Oxford University Press, 1995), 402–403.

11. Kinder, *Blood Cinema,* 136–275.

12. Barry Jordan and Rikki Morgan-Tamosunas, *Contemporary Spanish Cinema* (Manchester: Manchester University Press, 1998), 58.

13. I owe this insight to Prof. Marvin D'Lugo.

14. Fernando Rodríguez Lafuente, "Cine español: 1939–1990," in *España hoy: Cultura,* ed. Antonio Ramos Gascón, 2 vols. (Madrid: Cátedra, 1991), 1: 265.

15. Marsha Kinder, "Refiguring Socialist Spain: An Introduction," in *Refiguring Spain: Cinema/Media/Representation,* ed. Marsha Kinder (Durham, NC: Duke University Press, 1997), 5–8.

16. Jordan and Morgan-Tamosunas, *Contemporary Spanish Cinema,* 127.

17. Paul J. Smith, review of *Costa Brava* (Family Album), *Sight and Sound* 7 (1997): 43.

CHAPTER 6

1. Gerald Brenan, *The Literature of the Spanish People* (Cambridge: Cambridge University Press, 1962), 465.

2. The Madrid Book Fair is now held on the Paseo de Recoletos instead of the Retiro Park.

3. Eamonn Rodgers, "Publishing," in *Encyclopedia of Contemporary Spanish Culture,* ed. Eamonn Rodgers (London: Routledge, 1999), 427. The author does not account for the remaining 6 percent of production, which may consist of books published in languages like French and English.

4. This and all other translations are mine.

5. *Juan de Mairena,* in Manuel and Antonio Machado, *Obras completas* (Madrid: Biblioteca Nueva, 1984), 1079, 1188.

6. Brenan, *The Literature of the Spanish People,* 457.

7. Federico García Lorca, "Gacela del amor imprevisto," in *Obras completas* (Madrid: Aguilar, 1963), 558.

8. Brenan, *The Literature of the Spanish People,* 464.

9. Antonio Machado, *Juan de Mairena*, in Manuel and Antonio Machado, *Obras completas*, 1078–1079.

10. José Luis Castillo-Puche, *Hemingway entre la vida y la muerte* (Barcelona: Destino, 1968), 342.

11. Unamuno was said to ask when a new literary work appeared, "*Against* whom is that book written?" The anecdote is sometimes cited to demonstrate the polemical nature of literature in Spain.

12. Readers of Chapter 5 (Cinema) will recognize the similarities between Cela's work and many Spanish films of the 1980s and 1990s.

13. Oscar Jara, "No volveré a escribir . . . aunque otros milagros se han dado," *Babab*, No. 3 (July 2000) [website].

14. Pere Gimferrer, Prologue to Antonio Muñoz Molina, *El Robinson urbano* (Barcelona: Seix Barral, 1993), 8. The following examples of the novelist's style are from this Prologue.

15. Carlos Alvar, José-Carlos Mainer and Rosa Navarro, *Breve historia de la literatura española* (Madrid: Alianza, 1998), 673.

16. Camilo José Cela, *A bote pronto* (Barcelona: Seix Barral, 1994), 43.

17. Alvar, Mainer and Navarro, *Breve historia de la literatura española*, 672.

18. Jonathan Culler, *Literary Theory: A Very Short Introduction* (Oxford: Oxford University Press, 1997), 83.

19. Pere Gimferrer, "La muerte en Beverly Hills" [1967], in *Poemas, 1963–1969* (Madrid: Visor, 1979), 55.

20. Luis Antonio de Villena, "El poema es un acto de cuerpo," in *Poesía (1970–1982)* (Madrid: Visor, 1983), 140.

21. Amparo Amorós, "Consentiment," in *Visión y destino: Poesía, 1982–1992* (Madrid: La Palma, 1992), 129.

22. Luis García Montero, "La poesía de la experiencia," in *Complicidades*, ed. Antonio Jiménez Millán (Málaga: Litoral, 1998), 13–21.

23. Felipe Benítez Reyes, "Noche de San Juan," in *La poesía plural*, ed. Luis Antonio de Villena (Madrid: Visor, 1998), 135.

24. Ana Rossetti, "De los pubis angélicos," in *Ellas tienen la palabra. Dos décadas de poesía española*, eds. Noni Benegas and Jesús Munárriz (Madrid: Hiperión, 1997), 102.

25. For example, Moix is not mentioned in the best short history of Spanish literature: Alvar, Mainer and Navarro, *Breve historia de la literatura española*. This omission cannot be wholly attributed to the fact that Moix now writes in Catalan, since he published in Spanish for a period of ten years.

26. Bernardo Atxaga, "A modo de autobiografía," in *Obabakoak* (Barcelona: Ediciones B, 1993), 493.

27. I have adapted this description from Alicia Chudo's delightful *And Quiet Flows the Vodka, or When Pushkin Comes to Shove. The Curmudgeon's Guide to Russian Literature and Culture with The Devil's Dictionary of Received Ideas* (Evanston, IL: Northwestern University Press, 2000), 196–197.

28. Ignacio Soldevila Durante, "Novel," in *Encyclopedia of Contemporary Spanish Culture*, ed. Eamonn Rodgers, 371–372.

CHAPTER 7

1. Eduardo Haro Tecglen, "Teatro. Año de homenajes," in *Anuario El País 1999* (Madrid: El País, 1999), 263.

2. Laura Kumin, "To Live Is to Dance," in *The Cambridge Companion to Modern Spanish Culture*, ed. David T. Gies (Cambridge: Cambridge University Press, 1999), 298.

3. Richard Ford, *Gatherings from Spain* (1846; rpt. London: J. M. Dent & Sons, 1970), 291.

4. Luis Vicente Belmonte Talero, "José Tamayo," in *Encyclopedia of Contemporary Spanish Culture*, ed. Eamonn Rodgers (London: Routledge, 1999), 503.

5. José-Carlos Mainer, in Carlos Alvar, José-Carlos Mainer and Rosa Navarro, *Breve historia de la literatura española* (Madrid: Alianza, 1998), 669.

6. David George, "Els Comediants," in *Encyclopedia of Contemporary Spanish Culture*, ed. Eamonn Rodgers (London: Routledge, 1999), 117.

7. Fernando Antonio Pinheiro Villar de Queiroz, "Will All the World Be a Stage? The *Big Opera Mundi* of La Fura dels Baus," *Romance Quarterly* 46, no. 4 (Fall 1999): 251.

8. María Delgado, quoted in Pinheiro Villar de Queiroz, "Will All the World Be a Stage?": 252.

9. Pinheiro Villar de Queiroz, "Will All the World Be a Stage?": 253.

10. Haro Tecglen, "Teatro. Año de homenajes," 263.

11. Gilbert Chase, *The Music of Spain*, 2nd ed. (New York: Dover, 1959), 131.

12. Antonio Martínez Sarrión, *Cargar la suerte (Diarios 1968–1992)* (Madrid: Alfaguara, 1994), 218–219.

13. Timothy Mitchell, *Flamenco Deep Song* (New Haven, CT: Yale University Press, 1994), 71.

14. Chase, *The Music of Spain*, 222.

15. Roger D. Tinnell, "Spanish Music and Cultural Identity," in *The Cambridge Companion to Modern Spanish Culture*, ed. David T. Gies (Cambridge: Cambridge University Press, 1999), 294.

16. Allen Josephs, *White Wall of Spain: The Mysteries of Andalusian Culture* (Ames: Iowa State University Press, 1983), 20.

17. Ángel Álvarez Caballero, "Flamenco. Punto y aparte en la bienal de Sevilla," in *Anuario El País 1999* (Madrid: El País, 1999), 283.

18. Serge Salaün, *El cuplé* (Madrid: Espasa-Calpe, 1990), 197.

19. Serge Salaün, "The *Cuplé*: Modernity and Mass Culture," in *Spanish Cultural Studies: An Introduction. The Struggle for Modernity*, eds. Helen Graham and Jo Labanyi (Oxford: Oxford University Press, 1995), 90.

20. Terry Berne, "Spain and Portugal," *Billboard* 111, no. 47 (November 20, 1999): 91.

21. Terry Berne, "Barcelona Scene Gains Global Notice," *Billboard* 110, no. 24 (June 13, 1998): 1.

22. John Hooper, *The New Spaniards* (London: Penguin, 1995), 355.

23. Manuel Vázquez Montalbán, *Crónica sentimental de España* (1971; rpt. Madrid: Espasa-Calpe, 1986), 109.

24. Quoted in Pablo Zinger, "The Spanish Songbook," *Opera News* 62, no. 1 (July 1997): 12.

25. Enrique Franco, "Música. Una recuperación necesaria," in *Anuario El País 1999*, 280.

26. Hooper, *The New Spaniards*, 334.

27. Quoted in Tinnell, "Spanish Music and Cultural Identity," 289.

28. Antonio Moral, "Tempus fugit," *Scherzo* 100 (1995): 5.

29. Chase, *The Music of Spain*, 248.

30. Kumin, "Letter from Spain," 34.

CHAPTER 8

1. Selma Reuben Holo, *Beyond the Prado: Museums and Identity in Democratic Spain* (Washington, DC: Smithsonian Institution Press, 1999), 12.

2. Marisa Bartolucci, "Undiscovered Bilbao," *Atlantic Monthly* (October 2000): 48.

3. For example, Gehry has designed a spectacular new Guggenheim along the East River in lower Manhattan; the models for the project bear an obvious resemblance to the museum in Bilbao. The New York Guggenheim is also intended to revitalize a decaying riverscape and to become the city's new cultural icon.

4. Holo, *Beyond the Prado*, 173.

5. Selma Reuben Holo, "The Art Museum as a Means of Refiguring Regional Identity in Democratic Spain," in *Refiguring Spain: Cinema/Media/Representation*, ed. Marsha Kinder (Durham, NC: Duke University Press, 1997), 319. The quotation by the former director of the Cultural Patrimony of Valencia is from Evangelina Rodríguez Cuadros, *Guía de museos de la Comunidad Valenciana* (Valencia: Conselleria de Cultura, Educació i Ciència, 1991), 15.

6. Holo, "The Art Museum as a Means of Refiguring Regional Identity in Democratic Spain," 320.

7. Emma Dent Coad, "Artistic Patronage and Enterprise Culture," in *Spanish Cultural Studies: An Introduction. The Struggle for Modernity*, eds. Helen Graham and Jo Labanyi (Oxford: Oxford University Press, 1995), 373.

8. Holo, *Beyond the Prado*, 12.

9. Emma Dent Coad, "Designer Culture in the 1980s: The Price of Success," in *Spanish Cultural Studies: An Introduction. The Struggle for Modernity*, eds. Graham and Labanyi, 377.

10. Coad, "Designer Culture in the 1980s: The Price of Success," 377–378.

11. See the paragraph on Rafael Moneo below. Frank Gehry & Associates have

designed a futuristic building for the renowned Marqués de Riscal winery in La Rioja.

12. Luis Fernández-Galiano, "Arquitectura. La globalización y sus descontentos," in *Anuario El País 2000* (Madrid: El País, 2000), 301.

13. Fernando Chueca Goitia, Carlos Sambricio, Antón Capitel, Garbriel Ruiz Cabrero and Juan M. Hernández de León, *Arquitectura de Madrid. Siglo XX* (Madrid: Tanais, 1999).

14. José Martín Martínez, "Painting and Sculpture in Modern Spain," in *The Cambridge Companion to Modern Spanish Culture*, ed. David T. Gies (Cambridge: Cambridge University Press, 1999), 246.

15. The incident occurred in 1992. The previous year, director Víctor Erice's prize-winning documentary, *El sol del membrillo*, had filmed López painting a quince tree in his backyard. The title literally means "The Sun of the Quince Tree," but the film was marketed in the United States as "The Dream of Light."

16. Photographs 1 and 3 (Chapter 1), 3–5 (Chapter 2), 7–10, 12–13, 16–17, and 19 (Chapter 3) and 22–23 (Chapter 7) are all by García Rodero and will give the reader a good sampling of her style.

Glossary

bar Much more than a simple bar, it is a café or place where you can have a drink but also breakfast, a light lunch or dinner and almost anything else before, after or in between. A popular saying affirms that there is always a bar on the nearest corner, sometimes two or three.

café, copa y puro Coffee (espresso), a liqueur and a cigar, the classic way to round off a meal in Spain.

cante jondo Deep song, the purest form of traditional music in Andalusia, of which flamenco is a modern and commercial rendition.

churros Deep-fried fritters, the Spanish equivalent of donuts, often eaten for breakfast or with hot chocolate after a night on the town.

Comunidad Autónoma del País Vasco (Autonomous Community of the Basque Country) Corresponding to the Generalitat in Catalonia and the Xunta in Galicia, the autonomous government of the Basque region (Euzkadi). Established in 1979, it comprises the provinces of Alava, Guipúzcoa and Vizcaya.

corrida de toros Literally running of bulls, mistakenly translated as "bullfight." A *corrida* features professional *matadores* and mature bulls, four to five years old. A *novillada* normally features less experienced *toreros* and younger bulls.

encierro Running of fighting bulls or cows through the streets of certain towns, ending in the *plaza de toros* or bullring. The daily *encierro* during the festival of San Fermín in Pamplona is the most widely known.

españolada   Any action or work that exploits the stereotypes of Spain and Spaniards. The *españolada* usually presents the country as an exotic, "different" place full of local color, superstition and picturesque characters like gypsies and bullfighters. Books, films, plays and *zarzuelas* (light operas) based on the *españolada* are usually set in Andalusia; they exploit the flamenco culture of this region, which is mistakenly seen as the most "typical" of Spain.

esperpento   Defined in dictionaries as a scarecrow, nonsense, macabre story or tale, the word was used by the great Spanish writer Ramón del Valle-Inclán (1866–1936) for a series of fictional works characterized by exaggeration, satire, caricature and the grotesque; life "reflected in a concave mirror." In short, black comedy, Spanish style.

fútbol   European football or soccer, known as "the beautiful game." Like many Europeans, some Spaniards suffer from *fútbol* fever.

Generalitat   The Catalan autonomous government, established by statute under the Second Republic in 1932. Abolished by Generalissimo Francisco Franco, the Generalitat was reestablished in 1977 under the presidency of Josep Tarradellas. Catalonia comprises the provinces of Barcelona, Gerona, Lérida and Tarragona.

kiosko   Newsstand or kiosk, found on many sidewalks and corners in Spanish towns, where you can buy newspapers, magazines, books, maps, etc.

leyenda negra (Black Legend)   "The persistent idea that Spaniards are backward, cruel, humorless, and violent, the Spain of the Inquisition, of poverty and ignorance, a 'legend' begun, some authors have it . . . by Protestants in northern Europe to counteract the religious, military, and political power of Spain during the Catholic Monarchs and Philip II in the sixteenth century" (Peter Besas, *Behind the Spanish Lens: Spanish Cinema under Fascism and Democracy* [Denver: Arden Press, 1985], 9).

machismo   A complex term that refers to a man's ability to dominate his surroundings and other people, especially women. The phenomenon is more common in Latin America than in Spain.

merienda   A snack, often a *bocadillo* or Spanish-style sandwich of cheese, ham or chorizo, normally eaten in the late afternoon.

movida   Loosely translatable as "the movement" or "the scene," sometimes called *la movida madrileña* because of its center in Madrid. A complex artistic movement that characterized youth culture in the early period of Spanish democracy from the late 1970s through the mid-1980s. It influenced art forms such as cinema, photography, painting, literature, popular music, fashion and interior design. The director Pedro Almodóvar has been the most successful exponent of the *movida* both in Spain and abroad. The term has also been applied to later expressions of youth culture, like the *movida galega* (Galician *movida*).

paella   A rice and seafood dish that originated in the Levante or eastern coastal region around Valencia, now eaten in all parts of Spain and throughout the world.

paseo   The classic walk or stroll taken by Spaniards in the late afternoon or early evening, usually around a central plaza or square. The *paseo* remains the chief form of exercise for most people in Spain.

patria chica   "Small homeland," a Spaniard's town or local region, in contrast to the *patria grande*, or nation. The loyalty of most Spaniards is first to their family, then to their town or region, lastly to the country as a whole.

pelota   Literally ball, refers to *frontón*, jai alai and all other varieties of handball played in Spain. *Pelota* may be the closest thing to a national sport in the country, but it is played very little in the south.

tapas   The "small foods" or snacks that abound in Spanish bars and cafés in bewildering variety, now imitated throughout the world. It is customary to eat *tapas* with a glass of wine, beer or another beverage, while standing at the counter in bars and cafés.

tertulia   A social gathering in a public place, often on a regular basis, by a group of friends or people with a common interest. Writers, journalists, musicians, artists, lawyers, doctors, bullfight and soccer fans are examples of social groups who gather for *tertulias* in bars, cafés and restaurants. Some of these gatherings have endured for decades and have played an important role in the intellectual history of modern Spain, such as the literary *tertulia* at the famous Café Gijón in Madrid.

tortilla Not to be confused with the corn or flour tortilla of Mexico and Central America, the word in Spain refers to an omelette, particularly the *tortilla española* made with eggs, potatoes and onions.

transición (transition) The period between late 1975 and 1982, from Franco's death to the election of the Socialists. The period includes the legalization of political parties; the first free elections in forty years (1977); referenda approving democratic reforms and a new constitution (1976 and 1978); and two governments of the UCD (Unión de Centro Democrático)—under Adolfo Suárez and Leopoldo Calvo Sotelo—and the general election of 1982, in which Felipe González and his Socialist party swept to power with an overwhelming majority.

Xunta Corresponding to the Generalitat in Catalonia and the Comunidad Autónoma in the Basque Country, the regional government of Galicia. Established in 1981, the Xunta (Galician for junta, or executive) governs the provinces of La Coruña, Lugo, Orense and Pontevedra.

Index

Abortion, 22
Actresses, 118
Agencia EFE, 98
Alcohol, 50, 77–79
Alcoholism, 77
Alfonso the Wise, King, 79
Almodóvar, Pedro, 110, 114, 117–18, 120–21
Altamira, 15, 174
Amat, Fernando, 175
Amenábar, Alejandro, 119–20
Amorós, Amparo, 140
Andalusia, 7; cuisine of, 86; sherry of, 77–78; visual arts in, 173
Andalusian Dog (Buñuel and Dalí), 110–11
Andreu, Blanca, 140–41
Aragón, 5; cuisine of, 84; wine of, 78
Aranda, Vicente, 109, 135
Aranguren, José Luis, 109
Archeology, 14–15
Architecture, 175–78
Armiñán, Jaime de, 106
Arnás, Federico, 106
Arribas, Alfredo, 175–76, 182

Arroyo, Eduardo, 179
Asturias, 4; cuisine of, 82
Atencia, María Victoria, 139
Atheism, and religion, 28
Atxaga, Bernardo, 143
Autobiography, 137–38
Azaña, Manuel, 92

Badajoz, 7
Balaguer, Josemaría Escrivá de, 31, 33
Balearic Islands, 8; cuisine of, 86
Ballesteros, Severiano, 77
Ballet, 164
Balletbó-Coll, Marta, 119
Banderas, Antonio, 117
Barcelona, 6, 7, 22, 30, 31, 53, 157, 159, 161, 162, 165; dance in, 164; museums in, 170; press and, 95, 96; religious sects in, 39; sexuality in, 54, 55; sports in, 73, 76
Barcelona Olympic Games (1992), 145–46, 150, 153, 170
Bardem, Juan Antonio, 111
Baroja, Pío, 131
Basque Country, 4–5; cuisine of, 81,

82, 84, 86–87; dance in, 162; literature of, 140, 142–43; movies of, 113–14; sculpture of, 180–81; traditional sports and games in, 70, 73
Basques, 12; and separatism, 20
Beer, 79
Belief, 34–35
Belle Epoque, 116–18
Benavente, Jacinto, 129
Berasategui, Alberto, 76
Besas, Peter, 109
¡Bienvenido Mr. Marshall! (Welcome, Mr. Marshall!), 111
Big Opera Mundi (BOM), 151
Bigas Luna, José Juan, 109–10, 118
Bilbao, 5, 31, 54, 153; Guggenheim Museum, 169; sexuality and, 54
Birth control, 21–22, 35, 37
Birthrate, 21, 52
Black Legend (*leyenda negra*), 17–18
Blanchard, María, 178
Blasphemy, 39–40
Boadella, Albert, 149–50
Bofill, Ricardo, 176
Bohigas, Oriol, 176
Bolero, 161–62
Borau, José Luis, 112
Brenan, Gerald, 125, 129, 143
Brothels, 51, 56
Bruguera, Sergi, 76
Bullfighting, 12–13, 67–70; and *fiestas*, 57, 70; opposition to, 68, 70
Buñuel, Luis, 28, 110–11

Calatrava, Santiago, 177
Canary Islands, 8; cuisine of, 86
Cantabria, 4; cuisine of, 82
Cante jondo (deep song), 153–55
Carnero, Guillermo, 139
Carnival celebrations, 56, 58, 86
Cartagena, 6
Casas, Penélope, 81

Casona, Alejandro, 147
Castellet, José María, 138
Castile, 3, 6–7; architecture in, 178; cuisine of, 81, 85; dance in, 161–62
Català-Roca, Francesc, 181
Catalonia, 5–6, 147; architecture in, 175–77; cuisine of, 84, 87; dance in, 162; literature of, 141–42; museums in, 169–70; and painting, 178; performing arts of, 145–46, 149–51; wines of, 78–79; work ethic in, 48, 50
Cave paintings, 15
Cebrián, Juan Luis, 91, 94
Cela Camilo José, 132–33, 137
Celestina, La, 130
Censorship, 131, 147–48, 181
Cervantes, Miguel de, 14, 27, 128, 130
Ceuta and Melilla, 8–9
Chase, Gilbert, 152
Cheeses, 82
Chillida, Eduardo, 180
Christianity, 15–17; and correctness, 28; Protestants, 37–38
Church, 17, 21, 30–37; and atheism, 28; and belief, 34–35; and birth control, 21–22, 35, 37; and the Civil War, 29, 31; and education, 31; and *fiestas*, 57; and the media, 30–31, 98–101; and the New World, 27–28; and secularization, 33–34; state support for, 30
Cinema, 109–22; coproduction, 114–15, 122; documentaries, 111, 115; early, 110–11; film quotas, 112–13; foreign, 112; *la movida* ("the movement"), 116–17; regional, 113–14; sex in, 110; and television, 114; violence in, 119–20
Civil War, 18, 28–29, 31; and artists, 131, 146, 178, 181
Classical music, 158–61; festivals, 161; opera, 159; *zarzuela* (light opera), 158–59

Climate, 2–3
Coffee, 50
Colomo, Fernando, 114
Columbus, Christopher, 17
Columnists, 94
Comida (lunch), and siesta, 49
Compañía Nacional de Danza, 162–64
Constitution of 1978, 34, 37; and
    equality, 54; and freedom of
    expression, 94; and radio, 100; and
    sports, 70
Corella, Ángel, 164
Corrida de toros (bullfight), 67–70
Corruption, 1; and bullfighting, 67
Costa Brava (Family Album, film), 119
Crónica, Equipo, 178–79
Cuallado, Gabriel, 181–82
Cuisine, 79–87; of Andalusia, 86; of
    Aragón, 84; of Asturias, 82; of the
    Balearics, 86; of the Basque Country,
    81–82, 84, 86–87; of the Canary
    Islands, 86; of Cantabria, 82; of
    Catalonia, 84; cheeses, 82; of
    Extremadura, 85; of Galicia, 79, 82;
    of La Mancha, 85; of La Rioja, 84;
    misconceptions about, 81; of
    Murcia, 85; of Navarra, 81, 84;
    nouvelle cuisine, 87; pork, 81–82; of
    Valencia, 84–85
Cults and sects, 39
Cuplé, 155–56
Currency, 20
Customs, 47–87
Cycling, 76
Cytrynowski, Carlos, 149

Dalí, Salvador, 110
Dance, 161–65
Dance festivals, 165
Death, 12–14
Death in the Afternoon (Hemingway),
    12–14
Delibes, Miguel, 133–34

De Lucía, Paco, 155
De Miguel, Amando, 34–35, 40
Democracy: and the Church, 34, 37;
    and cinema, 112–13; and the press,
    91; and radio, 100; and the sexual
    revolution, 52; and spending for the
    arts, 174–75; and sports, 70; and
    television, 102
Diet, fresh, 49
Divorce, 54
D'Odorico, Andre, 149
Domingo, Plácido, 159
Dominicans, 31–32
Don Juan, 128–29
Don Juan Tenorio, 129
Don Quixote, 14, 130
Drama, 128–29, 147–52
Drinking habits, 77–79
Drugs, 50–51
Duato, Nacho, 162–64
Ducro River, 6

Ebro River, 5
Education, the Church and, 31
El Burlador de Sevilla, 128–29
El espíritu de la colmena (Spirit of the
    Beehive), 111
El País, 94–95
Els Comediants (The Actors or
    Comedians), 150, 164
Els Joglars (The Minstrels), 149–50,
    164
Emir Mohammed, 38
England, 17
English, 7
Entertainment, 49–50
Erice Víctor, 111, 115
ETA (Basque independence
    movement), 20, 29
European Economic Community, 8,
    20
European Monetary Union, 20
European Union, 49

euskera, 4–5, 12, 142–43
Euzkadi. *See* Basque Country
Expulsion, of Moors and Jews, 17–18, 27, 38
Extremadura, 7; cuisine of, 85

Family, 51; and the birth rate, 52; and divorce, 54; importance of, 56; and marriage, 52–53
Fanaticism, 29–30
Fandango, 161
Fascism, 18
Ferdinand and Isabel, 17
Fernández Román, Fernando, 106
Fidelity, 53
Fiestas, 22, 29, 56–67; carnival celebrations, 58–62; and the Church calendar, 57; "festive escalation," 62; participation in, 57; of San Fermín, 5, 62
Flamenco, 153–55, 162
Flamenco fusion, 157
Folk dancing, 161–62
Folk music, 152–55
Foods, 79–87
Ford, Richard, 20, 146
Franco, Francisco, 18, 29–31, 51
Furtivs (Poachers), 112

Gabilondo, Iñaki, 101
Gala, Antonio, 27
Galdós, Benito Pérez, 130
Galicia, 4; cuisine of, 82; dance in, 162; literature of, 142; music of, 153; wines of, 78
Gambling, 51
García Berlanga, Luis, 111
García Compoy, Concha, 101–2
García Lorca, Federico, 14, 129, 179
García Rodero, Cristina, 57, 70, 182
García, Sergio, 77
Gaudí, Antoni, 178
Gays, 54–55

Germanic tribes, 15
Gibraltar, 7–8
Giménez, Maria, 164
Gimferrer, Pere, 138–39, 142
Golf, 77
Government, 19
Goya en Burdeos (Goya in Bordeaux), 120
Goya, Francisco de, 178–79
Goytisolo, Juan, 132
Guadalquivir River, 7
Guadiana River, 6

Halffter, Cristóbal, 160
Hemingway, Ernest, 1, 12–14, 62, 68, 130
Holo, Selma Reuben, 167
Homosexuality, 54–55

Iglesia, Alex de la, 119
Iglesias, Julio, 156
Illiteracy, 3
Individualism, 13
Indurain, Miguel, 76
Inquisition, 17, 31
Institute of Free Education, 31
Instruments, 153
Ivens, Joris, 111

Jai alai, 73
Jehovah's Witnesses, 37
Jews, 16, 38; expulsion of, 17–18, 27, 38, 174; in *fiestas*, 29; Sephardic Museum, 173–74
Jiménez, Juan Ramón, 128
John Paul II: and "new paganism," 39; and Opus Dei, 33
Juan Carlos, King, 18–19, 38
Juarísti, Jon, 140

Kumin, Laura, 145

La Caixa Foundation, 170–71
La Caza (The Hunt), 111

La Fura dels Baus (Rats in the Sewer), 150–51, 164

La Mancha, 6; cuisine of, 85; dance in, 161–62

La Rioja, 5; cuisine of, 84; wines of, 78

Landscape, 2–9, 21–22

Languages, 1; Asturian, 4; Basque, 4–5, 12, 142–43; Castilian, 6; Catalan, 6, 8; English, 7; Galician, 4

Las Palmas, 8

Latin Americans, 12

Lazarillo de Tormes, 130

Lazcano, Arantxa, 119

Leisure, 48

León, 6–7

Lesbians, 54–55, 119

Levant, 6; cuisine of, 81; wines of, 78

Life expectancy, 19, 52

Liqueurs or spirits, 79

Literature, 125–43; autobiography, 137–38; drama, 128–29, 147–52; future of, 143; novel, 130–31, 132–37; pan-Hispanic, 132; the past, 126–32; poetry, 127–28, 138–41; the present, 132–43; prose, 129–31; publishing houses, 126; regional, 141–43

The Literature of the Spanish People, 125

Logroño, 5

Lope de Vega, 128

López Cobos, Jesús, 159–60

Loyola, Ignacio de, 31

Lunch, and siesta, 49

Machado, Antonio, 23, 28, 127–28

Machismo, 22

Madariaga, Salvador de, 3

Madrid, 6, 7, 14, 16, 20, 22, 30, 31, 38, 105, 125, 134, 153, 159, 161, 162, 167, 178; arts in, 167, 173, 180; cinema and, 116; dance in, 165; food and, 85; International Festival of Contemporary Art, 180; night life in, 14, 139; PhotoEspaña International, 182; press and, 95, 96; religious sects in, 39; sexuality and, 54, 55; sports in, 73, 76

Magazines, 96–98

Malo de Molina, Carlos A., 55

Malraux, André, 111

Manuel Serrat, Joan, 156

Marías, Javier, 136–37

Mariscal, Javier, 175

Marriage: and age, 53; and the birth rate, 52; and divorce, 54; and fidelity, 53

Marsé, Juan, 134–35

Marsillach, Adolfo, 148

Martin Gaite, Carmen, 134

Martinez, Conchita, 76

Meals, 48–49

Media, 91–106; Church and, 30–31, 98, 101; press, 92–99; radio, 99–102; television, 102–6; and totalitarian legacy, 91–92

Men, 22–23; and marriage, 54; and reading, 93

Meseta (plateau), 2–3

Michener, James, 13

Middle class, 19

Military, 21

Millares, Manuel, 178

Minority religions, 37–39

Miró, Joan, 169

Miró, Pilar, 115, 118–19

Modern dance, 164–65

Moix, Ana María, 139

Moix, Terençi, 141–42

Molina, Josefina, 118–19

Molina, Tirso de, 127, 128–29

Moneo, Rafael, 177–78

Montero, Luis García, 140

Montero, Rosa, 135

Moors: expulsion of, 17–18, 27, 38; in

fiestas, 29; invasion of, 15–16. *See also* Muslims

Morente, Enrique, 155

Morocco, 8–9, 12

Motherhood, 120–21

Movida, La, 116–17, 146, 156, 174, 179

Mozarabic, 127

Muerte de un ciclista (Death of a Cyclist), 111

Muñoz Molina, Antonio, 135–37

Murcia, 6; cuisine of, 85

Museums: Barcelona Museum of Contemporary Art, 170; Caixa, 170–71; Guggenheim, 169, 181; IVAM, 171–73; Joan Miró Foundation, 169; Pablo Picasso, 169; photography exhibits, 182–83; Prado, 167; Reina Sofía, 167, 168; sculpture, 180–81; Sephardic, 173–74

Music, 152–61

Muslim Spain, legacy of, 16

Muslims, 8, 12, 15–18, 38. *See also* Moors

National Academy of Recording Arts and Sciences, 158

National Chamber Theater, 148

National Institute for the Performing Arts and Music (INAEM), 148

NATO, 20–21

Navarra, 5, 62; cuisine of, 81, 84, wines of, 78

New Age mysticism, 39

New Castile, 6–7; cuisine of, 85; wine of, 78

Newspapers, 93–96

Newsstands, 92–93, 125

New World, 17, 27–28; contribution to cuisine, 81

Nieva, Francisco, 149

Nocturnal life, 50

Nosotras, 55

Notes on a Cellar-Book, 77

Nueve novísimos poetas españoles, 138–39

Numantia, 15

Obabakoak, 143

Olazábal, José María, 77

Old Castile, 6–7; wines of, 78

Olmo, Lauro, 147

Olmo, Luis del, 101

Olympics, 145–46, 150, 153, 170, 176

Opera, 158–59

Opus Dei, 31–33

Oteiza, Jorge, 180–81

Paella, 84–85

Painting, 175, 178–80

Palma de Mallorca, 8

Pamplona, 31; *fiesta* of San Fermín, 5, 62

Panero, Leopoldo María, 139

Pelota (ball), 73

People, 9–14, 22–23; Arabs, 12; gypsies (Roma), 9–12; inner lives of, 12–14; Latin Americans, 12

Performing arts, 145–65; dance, 161–65; music, 152–61; regeneration of, 146–47; theater, 147–52

Photography, 181–83; bioannual exhibitions, 182

Pilgrimages, 41, 45

Pla, Josep, 79, 149

Poetry, 127–28, 138–41

Political freedom, 20

Pop music, 156–58

Popular religion, 39–45

Pork, 81–82

Pornography, 52

Prado Museum, 167, 177

Press, 92–99; magazines, 96–98; newspapers, 93–96; newsstands, 92–93, 125; online, 96; ownership of, 98–99; primacy of, 93–94; sanctions and censorship, 94; sporting dailies, 96; Sunday editions, 96

Pride, 13–14

Prostitution, 51; decreased importance of, 55–56

Protectionism (cinema), 151

Protestants, 37–38

Publishing houses, 126

Punk music, 156–57

Rabal, Francisco, 106, 120

Radio, 99–102; as propaganda tool, 100; role of state in, 100

Radio Televisión Española (RTVE), 102, 104–5

Raimon, 156

Raphael, 156

Real Academia Española (Royal Spanish Academy), 125–26

"Reconquest," 16–17, 27

Religion, 15–18, 22, 27–45; blasphemy, 39–40; minority, 37–39; popular, 39–45; Protestants, 37–38. *See also* Church

Religious orders, 31–33

Reyes, Felipe Benítez, 140

Ribera, José de, 178–79

Robayna, Andrés Sánchez, 139–40

Rock music, 157

Rodrigo, Joaquín, 160

Rodríguez, Azucena, 119

Rojas, Fernando de, 130

Roman Empire, 15

Rossetti, Ana, 140–41

Sacred festivals and patronal feasts, 40–41, 62

Saffron, 85

Saintsbury, George, 77

Salazar, Antonio, 54

Sánchez Dragó, Fernando, 105

Sánchez Vicario, Arantxa, 76

Sangría, 79

Santander, 4

Santiago de Compostela, 4

Sanz, Alejandro, 157–58

Sastre, Alfonso, 147

Saura, Antonio, 178

Saura, Carlos, 109, 111, 115, 120

Sculpture, 180–81

Secularization, 33–34

Senra, Carmen, 165

Separatism, 3, 20

Sephardic Museum, 173–74

Sert, Josep Lluís, 169

Sevilla, 3, 7, 16, 22, 39, 53, 78, 86, 148, 161, 177; *feria* of, 78; visual arts in, 173, 175

Sex: attitudes toward, 53–54; in the cinema, 110

Sexual revolution, 52

Sherry, 77–78; *solera* system, 78

Sierra de Teruel, 111

Siesta, and lunch, 49

Siles, Jaime, 139

Smoking, 50

Soccer, 73, 76

Society of Jesus, 31–32

Sofía, Queen, 18, 38

Solas (Women Alone), 120

Sotelo, Joaquin Calvo, 147

Spain: birthrate in, 21, 52; bullfighting in, 12–13, 67–70; censorship in, 131; cinema in, 109–22; Civil War, 18, 28–29, 31, 131, 146, 178, 181; climate of, 2–3; currency of, 20; diet in, 49; entertainment in, 49–50; expulsion of Moors and Jews, 17–18; government of, 19; landscape of, 2–9, 21–22; literature of, 125-43; media in, 30–31, 91–106; Muslim legacy of, 16; night life in, 14, 50; past of, 14–18; people of, 9–14, 22–23; performing arts in, 145–65; political parties in, 19; present of, 19–23; "Reconquest," 16–17, 27;

regions of, 1, 3, 9; sense of time in, 48–50; separatism, 20; sex, marriage and family in, 51–56; sports and games in, 70–77; two, 131; visual arts in, 167–83; wines and foods of, 77–87

Spaniards and Sexuality, 55

Spanish-American War, 130

Spanish author-rights society (SGAE), 158

The Spanish Earth, 111

Sports and games, 70–77

Spring celebrations, 58, 62

Storaro, Vittorio, 120

Streep, Meryl, 110

The Sun Also Rises, 62

Superstition and witchcraft, 40

Table wines, 78–79

Tagus River, 6

Tamayo, José, 148

Tàpies, Antoni, 178

Tecglen, Eduardo Haro, 91, 145

Television, 102–6; and cinema, 114; regional, 105

Tennis, 76

Theater, 128–29, 147–52

Theroux, Paul, 52, 68

Time, sense of, 48–50

Todo sobre mi madre, 121

Toledo, 7, 15; Sephardic Museum in, 172–74

Traditional games, 70

Tragedy, 67, 143

Trueba, Fernando, 114, 116

Tu nombre envenena mis sueños (Your Name, My Dreams), 119

Umbral, Francisco, 94

Unamuno, Miguel de, 131

Unemployment, 1, 53

United States, 19

Universities, 31

Urretabizkaia, Arantxa, 142–43

Valencia, 6, 54, 146, 153, 161, 177; cuisine of, 84–85; dance in, 164; religious sects in, 39; visual arts in, 171–73

Valencian Community, 6

Valencian Institute of Modern Art (IVAM), 171–73, 175

Valle-Inclán, Ramón del, 129, 131

Vallejo, Buero, 147

Valls, Joaquín Navarro, 33

Vargas, Rafael, 182

Vázquez Montalbán, Manuel, 91, 99, 102, 132, 158

Velázquez, Diego, 178–79

Vergés, Rosa, 119

Villena, Luis Antonio de, 139

Violence, 119–20

Virginity: cult of, 51; loss of, 53

Viridiana, 111

Visigoths, 15

Visual arts, 167–83; architecture, 175–78; painting, 178–80; photography, 181–83; sculpture, 180–81

Weddings, 53

Wines, 77–79; beer, 79; cider, 79; liqueurs or spirits, 79; *sangría*, 79; sherry, 77–78; table wines, 78–79. *See also* Foods and Cuisine

Women, 22–23; actresses, 118; in architecture, 178; and bullfighting, 68; in cinema, 110; filmmakers, 118–19; and literature, 134–35; 137, 139–43; and marriage, 53–54; and motherhood, 120–21; and painting, 178; and photography, 57, 80, 182; and reading, 93; sculptors, 181

Work ethic, 48, 50

Zambrano, Benito, 120–21

Zaragoza, 5

Zarzuela (light opera), 158–59

Zorrilla, José de, 129

About the Author

EDWARD F. STANTON is the Chair of the Department of Spanish and Italian at the University of Kentucky, where he was the first Bingham Professor of the Humanities. He is the author of several books on Hispanic life and literature, including *Handbook of Spanish Popular Culture* (Greenwood, 1999).

Printed in Great Britain
by Amazon